EUROPE'S NEW NATIONALISM

EUROPE'S NEW NATIONALISM

States and Minorities in Conflict

Edited by

Richard Caplan and John Feffer

New York   Oxford
OXFORD UNIVERSITY PRESS
1996

Oxford University Press

Oxford   New York
Athens   Auckland   Bangkok   Bombay
Calcutta   Cape Town   Dar es Salaam   Delhi
Florence   Hong Kong   Istanbul   Karachi
Kuala Lumpur   Madras   Madrid   Melbourne
Mexico City   Nairobi   Paris   Singapore
Taipei   Tokyo   Toronto

and associated companies in
Berlin   Ibadan

Library of Congress Cataloging-in-Publication Data
Europe's new nationalism : states and minorities in conflict / edited
by Richard Caplan, John Feffer.
p.   cm. Includes index.
ISBN 0-19-509148-5 (cloth : acid-free paper)
ISBN 0-19-509149-3 (pbk. : acid-free paper)
1. Europe--Politics and government--1989-   2. Nationalism--Europe.
3. Europe--Ethnic Relations.   I. Caplan, Richard.   II. Feffer, John.
D2009.E984   1996   320.5'4'094--dc20   95-44607

1 3 5 7 9 8 6 4 2

Printed in the United States of America
on acid-free paper

Acknowledgments

This book began—as many good ideas do—as a conversation with Anthony Borden, director of the Institute for War and Peace Reporting and the editor of *War Report*. Under Tony's direction, the Institute has played a unique and valuable role in response to the crisis in former Yugoslavia, bringing the insights of journalists, scholars, and civic leaders from the region to the attention of the international community. It was Tony who first suggested that we approach the question of contemporary nationalism in Europe in a similar fashion.

A number of people advised and assisted us at various stages of this project, among them Archie Brown, Chris Calhoun, Nanette Funk, Alain Gresh, Paul Hockenos, Joanne Landy, Elzbieta Matynia, Mark Mazower, Susan Mendus, Joyce Neu, André Schiffrin, Michael Shuman, Ronald Grigor Suny, William Ury, Katrina vanden Heuvel, and Judith Vidal-Hall. To all of them we are very grateful.

Throughout the course of this project, Karin Lee consistently offered tremendous patience and support. Eric Wertheimer provided admirable technical and research advice. We thank them both.

We are also deeply grateful to Wade Greene and an anonymous member of the Rockefeller family. Without their aid and encouragement this book could not have been written.

Above all, we are grateful to the contributors to this volume—for their hard work and cooperation, for their vision and imagination, and, especially, for their commitment to achieving a greater understanding of a critical force shaping Europe at this time.

Contents

Contributors

Richard Caplan is a research fellow at the Institute for War and Peace Reporting in London and a MacArthur junior research fellow at the Department of War Studies, King's College, London. He is co-editor (with John Feffer) of *State of the Union: The Clinton Administration and the Nation in Profile* (1994). He was formerly the editor of *World Policy Journal.*

John Feffer is the author of *Beyond Detente: Soviet Foreign Policy and U.S. Options* (1990) and *Shock Waves: Eastern Europe After the Revolutions* (1992). He is co-editor (with Richard Caplan) of *State of the Union: The Clinton Administration and the Nation in Profile* (1994). He was formerly an associate editor of *World Policy Journal.*

Jürgen Fijalkowski held a chair in political science and political sociology at the Political Science Department of the Free University of Berlin from 1975 until 1993, when he became professor emeritus. In 1986 he founded and directed a research unit for the investigation of transnational labor migration, refugee movements, and minority policies. He is the author of several studies on immigration.

Tom Garvin is professor and head of the Department of Politics at University College, Dublin. He is the author of many studies of Irish and comparative politics. His most recent books are *The Evolution of Irish Nationalist Politics* (1981) and *Nationalist Revolutionaries in Ireland* (1987). He has just completed a study on the emergence of Irish democracy.

Alex Grigorievs was a member of the Latvian parliament from 1990 to 1993, serving on the human rights and interethnic relations committee. He is formerly the editor of *Baltic Times* (Riga, Latvia). He currently teaches at New York University.

Michael Ignatieff is a research associate at St. Antony's College, Oxford University. He is the author of *Blood and Belonging: Journeys into the New Nationalism* (1994) and *The Needs of Strangers* (1984). His essay was originally delivered as the J. B. and W. B. Morrell Memorial Address at the University of York on April 22, 1994.

Mary Kaldor is Jean Monnet Reader in contemporary European studies at the University of Sussex and co-chair of the Helsinki Citizens Assembly. She is the author of *The Imaginary War* (1991) and *The Baroque Arsenal* (1982).

Joyce McMillan is an Edinburgh-based freelance journalist and broadcaster specializing in cultural, social, and political commentary. She is currently political columnist and leading theater critic for *Scotland on Sunday*.

Tomaž Mastnak is a scientific counselor at the Institute of Philosophy at the Slovene Academy of Sciences and Arts (Ljubljana, Slovenia).

Adam Michnik is the editor-in-chief of *Gazeta Wyborcza* (Warsaw, Poland). He is the author of several books including *The Church and the Left* (1993).

Andjelka Milić is a professor of philosophy at the University of Belgrade, Serbia. She is the author of several books about women, feminism, and political behavior.

Ghia Nodia is a professor of political philosophy at the Institute of Philosophy in Tbilisi, Georgia.

George Schöpflin teaches politics at the University of London. He is the author of *Politics in Eastern Europe 1945–1992* (1993) and numerous studies of communism, post-communism, and nationalism.

Dan Smith is director of the International Peace Research Institute, Oslo (PRIO). He is co-editor (with Nina Graeger) of *Environment, Poverty, Conflict* (1994), co-author (with Michael Kidron) of *The New State of War and Peace: An International Atlas* (1991), and the author of *Pressure: How America Runs NATO* (1989).

Valery Tishkov is a professor of history and director of the Institute of Ethnology and Anthropology at the Russian Academy of Sciences. He is the author of five books and many articles on indigenous peoples, ethnicity, and nationalism. In 1992, he served as minister of nationalities in the Russian government.

Louis Vos is professor of history at the Katholieke Universiteit Leuven. He is the author of several books and articles on the history of nationalism, student movements, and youth associations in the twentieth century, and co-editor (with Theo Hermans and Lode Wils) of *The Flemish Movement: A Documentary History, 1780–1990* (1992).

EUROPE'S NEW NATIONALISM

Introduction

RICHARD CAPLAN AND JOHN FEFFER

With the end of the Cold War, nationalism has re-emerged as a major force in Europe. From high-level negotiations to street-level demonstrations, nationalism is changing the face of the continent. The dissolution of Yugoslavia, Czechoslovakia, and the Soviet Union; the unification of Germany; the assertion of Flemish, Ossetian, and Lombard identities in Belgium, Georgia, and Italy respectively; and the campaigns—sometimes violent—waged in the name of Armenians in Azerbaijan, Serbs in Bosnia, and Hungarians in Romania are all a testament to the renewed strength of nationalism in Europe today.

The meaning and significance of Europe's "new nationalism," however, are matters of considerable debate. In the former Soviet bloc, nationalism is seen as a liberating force that has enabled once "captive nations" to achieve greater control over their destiny. At the same time it is viewed as a retrogressive force that threatens minority rights and peaceful relations among states. In Western Europe, meanwhile, nationalism has been embraced as a bulwark against the erosion of cultural diversity and popular sovereignty in the face of creeping federalism. Yet it is also seen as a factor contributing to xenophobia and the exacerbation of regional divisions that threaten to undermine the prospects for greater integration.

At first glance it would seem that this new nationalism literally came from nowhere. True, Europe invented nationalism, and the history of modern Europe is the history of nationalism. But in the 1980s, after five decades of relative peace and stability, Europe seemed to many to have transcended the very tradition it had inaugurated.[1] Regional integration

had laid to rest the Franco-German enmity that had long torn the continent apart and was gradually creating a transnational entity of considerable economic and geopolitical substance. In the East, the communist governments were declaring nationalism to be successfully subordinated to the
interests of a transnational working class. For better or worse, the bipo-
larism of the Cold War had created two blocs dependent on ideological
not nationalist allegiances. Where nationalism still generated intense conflict—in Ireland, Corsica, Kosovo—these developments were frequently
understood as archaic, the exceptions to the rule. National differences—
Scottish kilts, Polish hand-kissing, Swiss neutrality—would presumably
continue; nationalist differences, which made the continent a killing
ground for centuries, would gradually fade into the history books.

The collapse of communism in 1989 did not immediately contradict
this vision of a postnationalist age. With a generous flow of resources and
ideas from West to East, it was thought, Europe could come together as a
whole—a "common European home" in Mikhail Gorbachev's words.
What the Berlin Wall had torn asunder, democracy and the market could
repair. True, the postrevolutionary East was still rough around the edges.
But consumerism would tame national passions much as capitalism—*le
doux commerce*—had irrevocably softened the edges of absolutism.[2] And
democracy would fulfill aspirations for popular sovereignty. Indeed, Europe was participating in a much larger march away from communism and
nationalism. It was riding a "third wave" of democratization;[3] it was ush-
ering in an end of ideologies, of history itself.[4]

But this postnationalist era did not dawn—neither in Europe nor any-
where else in the world. The optimism occasioned by the end of the Cold
War quickly soured. The triumph of liberal-democratic values was challenged by economic hardship, environmental degradation, population
growth, and a veritable "clash of civilizations."[5] Chaos had replaced all
naive hopes of a peaceful order.[6] Despite its relative prosperity, Europe
was not immune to these global trends, and the result has been fertile
ground for nationalism. What had once seemed to be "exceptions"—
quirky separatists, fusty old ethnopatriots, marginalized neo-Nazis—rapidly moved to the front and center of the European scene. From East Timor
and Bangladesh to Angola and Quebec, nationalism had been far from dormant during the Cold War. It was the return of nationalism to Europe,
however, that made policymakers, pundits, and journals of opinion prick
up their ears.

Nationalism's most dramatic resurgence has been in the former communist countries of the East. Here entire countries have indeed fallen
apart. Conflicts inspired by nationalism have spread throughout the region, creating a zone of contention stretching from the Balkans to Central Asia. By 1995, the war in former Yugoslavia had claimed as many as
200,000 lives; nations were squaring off in virtually every new state of the
former Soviet Union; and with the Russian invasion of Chechnya, nationalism was threatening the integrity of the Russian federation as well.

Even in countries not overwhelmed by armed conflict, nationalism replaced communism as quickly as one season succeeds another. After years of submitting to Soviet or Russian domination, the countries of the East delighted in their newly reacquired national particularities—a new flag, a new anthem, a new army. During the Cold War, the emphasis was on unity, whether in conformity to Soviet ideology or in dissent to communist rule. With the end of the Cold War, difference was to be celebrated and, in many cases, fought over. Ethnicity became a more emphatic component of identity, making Serbs and Croats out of Yugoslavs, Czechs and Slovaks out of Czechoslovaks, and Abkhazians and Ossetians out of Georgians.

But nationalism has not simply been the offspring of the transition from communist rule in the East. The "postnational" West also witnessed a resurgence of nationalist sentiment. European integration slowed in response to the particular demands of member nations. The hopes for a common foreign policy were frustrated by the collapse of Yugoslavia and the initial lack of coordinated response. Violent incidents of racist intolerance escalated in Germany, Italy, France, and elsewhere. Immigration laws were changed to preserve "cultural integrity." Instead of looking ahead toward a common European home, many nations decided to take another look at their own distinctive identities, whether Polish, Belgian, Catalan, or Ruthenian.

After years of pondering the future—a distant European Union, a distant communist international—the two halves of Europe suddenly seemed much more interested in the past.

It is impossible to think about modern European history without reference to nationalism. Likewise it is difficult to discuss nationalism elsewhere in the world without reference to the European experience, without using the very language developed in Europe to speak of nationalism—nation, self-determination, irredentism, chauvinism.[7] While it is difficult to pinpoint when and where nationalism debuted as an ideology, the French Revolution of 1789 can serve as a useful starting point.[8] The French Revolution, after all, gave shape to many of our current notions of nationalism.

With the French Revolution, nationalism became a complex modern ideology with characteristics so varied that they at times appear mutually exclusive. For instance, from 1789 on, nationalism could be both particular (the "French nation") and universal (appealing to a common urge for popular sovereignty). The French revolutionaries waged a specific struggle in a specific country, but they also encouraged patriots elsewhere to support both *la grande nation* and the national liberation of their own sister republics.[9]

The French Revolution continued a process begun earlier in England of transforming the "nation" from an elite into a popular enterprise. Nationalism, according to the revolutionaries, was a *res publica*, an affair of the people. It could serve as a method by which sovereignty was wrested from the monarch and vested in representative institutions—structures that ideally reflected the popular will and not simply the desires of an intellectual or monied elite.[10] Nationalism transformed the "rabble" into the People.

This "affair of the people" could be understood in either ethnic or political terms: the nation resided either in a shared ethnic heritage or in common citizenship divorced of ethnicity. For their part, the French revolutionaries spoke of general civic principles—liberty, equality, brotherhood—that applied to all within the polity. However, while subjects became citizens by virtue of the Revolution, these citizens were increasingly expected to belong to a dominant ethnic culture of one language and one tradition.

Finally, from the French Revolution on, nationalism could represent very different political motives. It could be radical in its anti-imperialism; liberal in its capacity to build states; or reactionary in its reinforcing of a dominant ethnicity and repression of minority aspirations. Nationalism was thus used by the Serbs against the Ottoman Empire, by the Belgians to build a new liberal state, and by German romantics to imagine an ethnocentric *lebensraum* defined by blood and soil.

This conceptual flexibility served nationalism well. It could attach itself to virtually any political creed and economic program. Flourishing in the nineteenth century, it provided a cohesive identity during a period of mass upheaval, of revolutions both political and industrial. It could also offer a coherent rationale for opposing the existing imperial order. More so than socialism or liberalism, nationalism could mobilize people and give them a compelling reason to sacrifice their wealth or their lives.

In their attempt to stem the flow of these revolutionary ideas, Europe's chief imperial powers entered into a pact in 1815: the Concert of Europe. It was a desperate attempt to forestall the inevitable, for the logic of popular sovereignty—the very allure of nationalism—was irresistible. The Greek Revolution, which claimed Byron's sympathies and eventually his life, broke out in 1821. In 1830, a host of other European countries including Belgium, Poland, and Italy were involved in national uprisings. By 1848—the "springtime of nations"—virtually all of Europe was in upheaval. The Concert of Europe, designed to contain insurgent nationalisms, could barely stave off these challenges. In the second half of the century, Italy and Germany consolidated disparate regions into single countries. The Ottoman Empire withdrew further from the continent, leaving several new Balkan states in its wake.

By the beginning of the twentieth century, the old European order resembled a tottering and highly flammable edifice. While a single spark could set it alight, the old timbers could still burn for a considerable time. The dynamic of nation against empire, so much part of the nineteenth century, carried through to its logical conclusion. Between 1914 and 1918, the absolutist order challenged in 1789 was laid to rest in the bloodiest conflict the world had ever seen.

Two principles—territorial integrity and self-determination—came to define interstate relations in the post-imperial order. Territorial integrity, a legacy of the Peace of Westphalia (1648), locked in the borders of "historically evolved" nations; self-determination wedded the liberal notion of self-rule with nationalism's principle that every ethnically defined nation should have a state. While the established powers preferred to emphasize territorial integrity, geopolitical newcomers such as the Soviet Union and the United States favored self-determination for its capacity to undermine the already weakened European colonial system.[11]

This attempt to wed self-determination to territorial integrity failed. When inspiring secession, self-determination directly challenged the inviolability of borders. A central tension was thus built into the European interstate system. The very term used to define the units of this system—the "nation-state"—underscores this problem. Few states represented a single nation; virtually all countries were ethnically heterogeneous.[12] State and nation, however, became sloppily synonymous, so much so that the League of Nations included only states and excluded many nations.[13] If all nations deserved states, a principle that certainly benefited Poland after World War I, then why didn't Slovakia or Croatia qualify for statehood? Moreover, why were the Germans of the Sudetenland part of Czechoslovakia and not Germany?

In previous ages, monarchs answered these questions with decrees and military action. But the League of Nations had neither force of decree nor arms. At a more prosperous time, the conflicts between the new European "nation-states" perhaps could have been resolved peaceably. Yet nationalism had rich soil in which to grow: the humiliations of the defeated powers, the weak political traditions of Eastern Europe, and the worldwide depression of the 1930s. This last factor encouraged virtually all nations in Europe to pursue "beggar-thy-neighbor" policies that transformed trade into warfare by other means. Communist, fascist, and liberal governments all turned to the state apparatus and the force of nationalism to save their respective economies.[14] The jostling of empires produced World War I; the jostling of nations exploded into World War II.

On the surface, World War II was a conflict between ideologies, not between nations. Beneath the surface, however, nationalism mobilized passions more effectively than either communism, fascism, or liberalism. Few soldiers fought for centralized planning or the welfare state or an abstract disciplined community. They fought and died for Mother Russia, for the German Fatherland, for the "sceptred isle" of Great Britain. The United States entered the war after Pearl Harbor, not Democracy, was attacked. The German campaign to exterminate Jews, Gypsies, and other "undesirables" was ethnonational, not strategic in cause and design. In Yugoslavia, fratricidal hatreds between national groups killed more people than partisan struggles against the Germans and Italians. Once, nations fought primarily against empires. Now they fought almost exclusively against one another.

World War II left a tremendous legacy of national hatred. But it also produced a corresponding desire for a new internationalism, a transideological commitment to conflict prevention.[15] The fruit of this brief global harmony was the United Nations. Subsequently, however, the new internationalism bifurcated into the West's incipient global market and the East's sphere of putative workers' states. Within these two camps, nationalism could only detract from the larger goal of unity in the face of the enemy. So great was this need for unity that a decade after the end of the war, the two Germanies were rearmed and incorporated into their respective alliances, overcoming the two greatest animosities of the twentieth century—Germany and France, Germany and Russia. Nationalism had proven stronger than ideology during World War II; to secure the peace, ideology took precedence over nationalism during the Cold War.

Nationalism did not, however, hibernate during the Cold War. Liberal governments used it selectively to rebuild shattered societies and economies or to forge distinct and independent foreign policies. Just as national priorities were subordinated to larger ideological demands, regional autonomy within countries took a backseat to centralized national control.[16] In the East, communist regimes used nationalism to bolster declining popularity. While "national communists" were purged from the various apparatuses after the Soviet-Yugoslav split, nationalism returned under different guises—employed by the Polish government to discredit dissident students or by the Ceauşescu regime in Romania to give itself some semblance of historical legitimacy. For the oppositions, too, nationalism served to focus wrath on the Soviet Union as an aggressor nation and on communism as an alien ideology. As in earlier times, nationalism was drafted into service against empire, in a manner that resembled the anticolonial struggles then occurring throughout the Third World.

The Cold War, therefore, was not a discontinuity in the history of European nationalism. Rather, it channeled nationalism into different forms and expressions. In the post–Cold War era, nationalism has become more explicit in its manifestations. It has even articulated previously forbidden demands—for state power, cultural autonomy, or territorial control.

In the world of nations and nationalism, history is not simply the stuff of footnotes and monographs. It is a living process, a palpable component of both individual and collective identity. The 1389 war that Serbia lost to the Ottoman Empire, the 1800 Act of Union that incorporated Ireland into a new United Kingdom, the 1920 Trianon Treaty that reduced the size of Hungary by two-thirds—for occupants of these regions today, this history has the impact and currency of the latest World Cup scores. Moreover, the historical ambiguities of nationalism—its civic versus political elements, its anti-imperial or state-building characteristics, its simultaneously universal and particularistic appeal—continue to frame the contemporary European debate, as the essays in this volume amply demonstrate.

One of the principal challenges facing scholars of nationalism has been the subject's conceptual elusiveness. What meaningful generalizations can be made about a label that applies to such disparate phenomena as Marxist rebels in Kurdistan, Serb and Croat paramilitaries, the Russian government's policy toward Chechnya, Helmut Kohl's efforts to unify Germany, and Margaret Thatcher's Europhobia? Nationalism, it seems, can adhere not only to very different philosophies but to very different agents as well—rebels fighting for national liberation, state governments promoting national priorities, reactionaries calling for ethnic cleansing, populists advocating a revival of empire. Inhabiting the vast realm between the concrete individual and abstract humanity, nationalism seemingly defies theoretical precision.

The key to nationalism's elusiveness seems to be its lack of clear objective criteria. All such criteria—race, language, territoriality—can be shown to apply in some particulars, but not in all cases. One method of avoiding this quandary has been to stress the subjective nature of nationalism. Rupert Emerson, for instance, maintained that the "simplest statement that can be made about a nation is that it is a body of people who feel that they are a nation; and it may be that when all the fine-spun analysis is concluded this will be the ultimate statement as well."[17]

Intrepid scholars of nationalism have nevertheless tried to give shape to nationalism's conceptual fluidity. Hans Kohn classified nationalism into "Eastern" and "Western" varieties with a set of corresponding characteristics.[18] Carlton Hayes theorized that nationalism evolves according to a developmental model.[19] Louis Snyder adopted a more horizontal approach that grouped nationalisms by a regional typology.[20]

Rather than treat nationalism like so many rocks to classify, some scholars have instead focused on function, asking the "why" of nationalism and not so much the "what." Karl Deutsch has written on nationalism's role in social communication, its function of transmitting the culture of a people across territory and through history.[21] Benedict Anderson has linked the growth of nationalism to the spread of vernacular print culture—the capacity to publish books in languages that rising nations could understand.[22] Ernest Gellner has argued that nationalism, rooted in the "distinctive structural requirements of industrial society," was the necessary ideological accompaniment to modernization.[23] Nationalism enabled societies to advance economically by providing a common language and a common civic culture, both fostered by a national educational system. With increased standards of living, the further segmentation of society, and the equalization of wealth, this function of nationalism attenuates.

John Breuilly has challenged this link of nationalism and modernization, finding numerous cases of nationalist sentiment around the world that thrive in societies not undergoing modernization. His search for the elusive objective variables that define nationalism leads him to identify a different function. Nationalism, he argues, is simply a form of politics, used most frequently by subordinated elites attempting to seize power (such as Czech nobles within the Habsburg empire or Lithuanian intellectuals within the Soviet system).[24] As such, nationalism functions primarily as an ideology, a way of envisioning power relations in society. Its ethnic character and economic program vary according to context; it cannot be linked to any particular psychological state or social activity. Rather, it absorbs or contests other ideologies in the political marketplace.

A nationalism reduced to its economic and political functions, Walker Connor has argued, is hardly a nationalism at all. The key determinant is ethnicity, and thus nationalism should be understood primarily as a cultural phenomenon. The economic explanation puts too much emphasis on the progressive or divisive effects of modernization; the political explanation gives too much credence to existing states or the desire to create or command states. The true reason for nationalism's appeal, Connor suggests, may lie more in the psychological and cultural domains than in material conditions or political struggles.[25]

Nationalism can thus be poured into various classificatory molds. Its manifestations are so numerous and varied, however, that the number of classifications threatens to equal the number of examples. Nationalism can also be understood as serving a specific function—as consolidating a political ideology, preserving ethnic identity, or aiding economic modernization. These functions in isolation, however, all seem insufficient in explaining nationalism's polymorphousness and perennial appeal. After engaging in a lengthy attempt at definition, Walker Connor concludes: "It may well be . . . that knowledge of the quintessence of nationalism will continue to evade us."[26]

Yet all complex phenomena defy easy categorization. There is no consensus among scholars concerning ideologies such as fascism and liberalism. It would therefore be naive to expect easy answers to the basic questions: what is nationalism and why does it have enduring influence? Not surprisingly, the essays in this volume draw on a number of theoretical traditions when examining nationalism both root and branch.

This collection of essays has two broad aims: first, to provide perspective on the question of nationalism in Europe today from the vantage point of leading scholars and journalists throughout the region; second, to identify and explore some of the more contentious issues that constitute the debate taking place within Europe over the meaning and implications of contemporary nationalism. The range of relevant issues, of course, is vast. And this volume does not presume to address them all. But it can fairly claim to reflect the principal currents of thinking about nationalism in relation to peace and security, democracy, and human rights in Europe. These questions have a critical bearing on the future of Europe in the unchartered waters beyond the Cold War.

This volume is not a consensus document. To the contrary, it seeks to highlight the various intellectual faultlines that cut across Europe's political landscape, along which significant differences of opinion are to be found. Like actual faultlines, these differences will not necessarily be highly visible. The debate surrounding citizenship and constitutional reform in Latvia, for instance, which Alex Grigorievs discusses in his essay, may not be headline news outside the Baltics. Yet the tension between democracy and the preservation of national identity, which this debate represents, arguably has the potential to be every bit as explosive as events elsewhere in Europe that are front-page stories.

As with any major historical development, there is considerable disagreement about the precise nature of nationalism in Europe today. If Eric Hobsbawm is correct, and the various nationalist agitations we are witnessing are largely the "unfinished business of 1918–21,"[27] then what is so "new" about Europe's new nationalism? Or, as Isaiah Berlin has suggested in a similar vein, nationalism in Europe is not "resurgent" for the simple reason that it never died.[28] With respect to Belgium, certainly, as Louis Vos argues in his contribution, the Flemish nationalist struggle today seems to exhibit a virtually uninterrupted continuity with the past, extending back several centuries. In Ireland, too, as Tom Garvin discusses here, the minority tradition of armed violence among Irish nationalists has a long history that predates the country's recent "Troubles."

Yet one can acknowledge continuity while at the same time recognize that there may nonetheless be something distinctive about contemporary European nationalism. This is Mary Kaldor's point in her essay. The new nationalism, she argues, is more particularistic, more fragmenting, than traditional nationalisms, at least in those states that have won, or seek to win, newfound independence. Today's nationalist violence in Europe, moreover, does not simply (or at all) result from age-old nationalist struggles "frozen" by communist domination breaking free again to run their course. The collapse of communism is certainly relevant, but largely insofar as it has generated tremendous uncertainty and dislocation that have encouraged populations to look to their own groups for protection and, in many cases, to scapegoat others. Concepts of ethnic tolerance and compromise have been difficult to implant among sociologically insecure populations seeking instant solutions, George Schöpflin observes here. Whether nationalist leaders have merely exploited these popular attitudes or in fact inculcated them is a subject of some debate in these pages.

Relevant, too, among the former socialist states is the absence of a strong tradition of respect for individual rights and of civil society more generally, the emergence of which has been seriously inhibited by decades of communist rule. "A society anchored in a culture of individual rights and liberties is more easily returned to the practice of toleration than one where social allegiance is invested in ethnicity," Michael Ignatieff writes in his essay. Moreover, because communism was in many cases perceived to be a form of Russian (or Serbian) imperialism, the anti-communist struggle in Eastern Europe often assumed the form of a struggle for national liberation, which only reinforced the central position of ethnicity in politics. The irony, as Valery Tishkov puts it here, is that although nationalist movements contributed to the democratic transformation of the former Soviet Union, many of these movements are now an obstacle to building peaceful democracies in the region.

These observations raise the question of whether it makes sense to talk in roughly the same terms about contemporary nationalism in Eastern and Western Europe. On the one hand, the strong ethnic character of state legitimation in Eastern Europe and the mitigating effects of the political space created for national minorities in Western Europe would support the view of two different types of nationalism today. So, too, do the separate historical trajectories of the two regions—if only because France, Britain, and other West European states achieved relative homogeneity much earlier (and sometimes in no less bloody fashion) than the multinational states of the East now desirous of the same. On the other hand, as Ghia Nodia points out, the mistake we make is to confuse what are in fact ideal types of nationalism—Eastern and Western, ethnic and civic—with actual experience. In reality, all nationalisms are, to varying degrees, mixed. And for all their differences, the heightened national consciousness among Scots today would certainly seem to share much with that of their counterparts in Slovenia, reflecting a common desire to be master of one's own house.

It is this democratic potential inherent in nationalism—the increased freedom of peoples long denied it—that has perhaps represented nationalism's greatest appeal historically. But as Adam Michnik points out in his essay, this freedom conceals a trap. Self-determination can become transformed into the nationalism of domination: "The nations that were oppressed yesterday can easily become the oppressors of tomorrow." The changes wrought by this distortion may be subtle—witness the backlash against feminism in Serbia, discussed by Andjelka Milić in her essay. Here the nationalist obsession with social unity can lead to the denial of women's distinctiveness, except in sexually instrumental terms as procreators of the nation. Less subtle are the attacks on minorities or immigrants, which George Schöpflin and Jürgen Fijalkowski explore respectively. And this distortion can, of course, lead to war on neighboring states.

Some of the sharpest disagreements among European intellectuals arise with respect to this latter question: the relationship between nationalism and conflict. Conventional wisdom holds that nationalism is inherently divisive and therefore inimical to peaceful relations within and between states. Nationalism, by this reasoning, has become the plague of the twentieth century, a view no more clearly articulated than in *The Economist* on the eve of Slovene and Croatian independence in 1991, when it warned that "The virus of tribalism . . . risks becoming the AIDS of international politics—lying dormant for years, then flaring up to destroy countries."[29] In his essay Tomaž Mastnak takes issue with the anti-nationalist agenda that follows from this logic and that, in part, is responsible for the failure of the international community to support the emergence of new states in the former Yugoslavia. Nationalism is a state-building and state-maintaining ideology—a good and necessary function, Mastnak maintains. Yet the West "has sought to prevent the formation of new states on the territory of former Yugoslavia," he argues, "mistaking state-building for the cause, rather than the result, of the breakup of the federal state."

The question of how to respond to nationalism also divides Europe's intellectuals. If for Mastnak support for emerging states is imperative, under certain circumstances at least, for Mary Kaldor it is important to counter the new nationalism with cosmopolitanism: "transnational mechanisms for the control of violence and for the enforcement of certain transnational legal norms." This view is echoed by Joyce McMillan who, with Scotland in mind, attaches considerable importance to the protection of national identity but within the context of a regional and international order that embodies universal values.

Others occupy a middle ground. Thus Dan Smith, in his approach to the resolution of nationalist conflicts, neither endorses nor opposes nationalism. Instead, he provides a framework for constructive engagement that starts from an understanding of the benefits nationalism holds out for a given society—its capacity, in other words, to meet particular human needs. Only on this basis, he argues, will a third party be able to arrive at a meaningful resolution of nationalist conflict. By contrast, any imposition of a settlement (which is how he characterizes Europe's efforts to resolve the Yugoslav conflict) is unlikely to succeed in the long run.

If the debate over nationalism in Europe has bearing on Europe's future, it also has relevance beyond Europe's borders. In North America, the United States is confronting a similar cluster of issues regarding identity, democracy, and national stability as it wrestles with the question of multiculturalism. In South Asia, meanwhile, the secular character of the Indian state is under enormous pressure in the face of the growing appeal of exclusivist, religious identities. And Africa—from Pretoria in the south to Algiers in the north—faces the challenge, many times over, of identities in conflict. Although the historical and cultural contexts of these and other cases are clearly distinct from those of Europe, the latter can nonetheless be instructive.

In his 1979 essay "Nationalism: Past Neglect and Present Power," Isaiah Berlin looked back at nineteenth-century Europe and noted the peculiar fact that the great thinkers of the time failed to anticipate either the persistence or the influence of nationalism.[30] It is our hope that this volume will contribute toward an understanding of this force in Europe—not after the fact, but at the moment when it has achieved renewed importance.

Notes

1. As Ernest Gellner observed in 1965—*Thought and Change* (Chicago: University of Chicago Press, 1965), p.147—both Marxist and liberal thought anticipated the decline of nationalism. Today, these positions are occupied by E. J. Hobsbawm and Francis Fukuyama. Hobsbawm, the Marxist, locates the apogee of nationalism in the period 1918–1950 and considers nationalism "no longer a major vector of historical development." E. J. Hobsbawm, *Nations and Nationalism Since 1780* (Cambridge: Cambridge University Press, 1990), p.163. In terms of classical liberals, Francis Fukuyama also imagines nationalism to be essentially a spent force. Francis Fukuyama, *The End of History and the Last Man* (New York: Avon, 1992). To be fair, neither author denies the current existence or influence of nationalism. They simply suggest, from their different political positions, that in the overall developmental sense, nationalism is past its point of greatest influence.

2. Perry Anderson, *A Zone of Engagement* (London: Verso, 1992), p.337.

3. Samuel P. Huntington, *The Third Wave: Democratization in the Late Twentieth Century* (Norman: University of Oklahoma Press, 1993).

4. Fukuyama, op. cit.

5. Paul Kennedy, *Preparing for the Twenty-first Century* (New York: Random House, 1993); Samuel P. Huntington, "The Clash of Civilizations?," *Foreign Affairs*, Vol. 72, No. 3 (Summer 1993).

6. Robert D. Kaplan, "The Coming Anarchy," *Atlantic Monthly*, February 1994.

7. Hobsbawm discusses the European origins of "nation" in Hobsbawm, op. cit., pp. 16–18; Walker Connor—*Ethnonationalism: The Quest for Understanding* (Princeton: Princeton University Press, 1994), p. 60—notes that "self-determination" was first used in its modern sense in the Proclamation on the Polish Question at the London Conference of the First International; irredentism comes from the name of a nineteenth-century Italian nationalist party; and chauvinism is named after Nicholas Chauvin, a devoted follower of Napoleon.

8. Anthony Smith notes that while some scholars prefer other dates (1642, 1772, 1806), most "opt for 1789—with the proviso that the Revolution served mainly to bring together the elements of the nationalist idea, which were brewing up throughout the previous two centuries." Anthony Smith, *Theories of Nationalism* (London: Duckworth, 1971), p. 27.

9. Yael Tamir, *Liberal Nationalism* (Princeton: Princeton University Press, 1993), p. 91.

10. Liah Greenfeld, *Nationalism: Five Roads to Modernity* (Cambridge, MA: Harvard University Press, 1992), pp. 156ff.

11. Robert Schaeffer, *Warpaths* (New York: Hill & Wang, 1990), pp. 46–59.

12. Walker Connor (op. cit., p. 40) discusses "nation-states" in the post–World War II era. Before the ravages of World War II, European countries were even more diverse, with much larger Jewish and German populations.

13. Ibid.

14. Karl Polanyi, *The Great Transformation* (Boston: Beacon Press, 1957).

15. Consider, for example, Hans Kohn's concluding hopes in 1944 for "higher forms of integration." Hans Kohn, *The Idea of Nationalism* (New York: Macmillan, 1960), p. 576.

16. Regionalism had at this time acquired a Quisling reputation from the Flemish, Slovak, and Croatian collaborations with the Nazis.

17. Quoted in Connor, op. cit., p. 112.

18. Kohn, op. cit.

19. Carlton Hayes, *The Historical Evolution of Modern Nationalism* (New York: R. R. Smith, 1931).

20. Louis Snyder, *The New Nationalism* (Ithaca: Cornell University Press, 1968).

21. Karl Deutsch, *Nationalism and Social Communication* (Cambridge, MA: MIT Press, 1975), pp. 96–104.

22. Benedict Anderson, *Imagined Communities* (London: Verso, 1983), pp. 66–79.

23. Ernest Gellner, *Nations and Nationalism* (Oxford: Basil Blackwell, 1983), p. 35.

24. John Breuilly, *Nationalism and the State* (Chicago: University of Chicago Press, 1994).

25. Connor, op. cit.

26. Ibid., p. 112.

27. Hobsbawm, op. cit., p. 165.

28. Isaiah Berlin, "Two Concepts of Nationalism," *The New York Review of Books*, November 21, 1991.

29. *The Economist*, June 29, 1991.

30. Isaiah Berlin, "Nationalism: Past Neglect and Present Power," *Partisan Review*, Vol. 46, No. 3 (1979), pp. 337–358.

1

Dignity and Fear: A Letter to a Friend

ADAM MICHNIK

The war in former Yugoslavia is a cautionary tale for all post-communist countries. After all, multinational Yugoslavia was once post-communist Europe writ small. And here, in this Europe of ours, there are also no indisputably just borders. The Yugoslav drama could thus repeat itself in a new constellation. Could not the Russians, like the Serbs, fall victim to this syndrome that has unleashed hysteria among the national minorities in other countries? Or the Hungarians, who fall so easily prey to the blackmail of nationalists when the fate of compatriots in Romania and Slovakia is mentioned? And finally what of Poles, who are concerned with the situation of Polish minorities in neighboring countries?

The war in Yugoslavia is Europe's wound and disgrace, a testimony to the helplessness of some and the cynicism of others. It constitutes an insult to common sense and a rejection of a peaceful order. It has become a fuse for the next explosion, perhaps a detonator of the next conflict. No one should remain indifferent toward this war. And no one should feel safe. A sleep of reason has descended on the Balkans and many terrible monsters have been awakened.

At this time, I think of those who are the guardians of hope, those who oppose organized hatred. One of these is my friend, the Belgrade sociologist and philosopher Nebojša Popov.

Nebojša, a year ago in your Belgrade apartment you briefed me on your work in progress. Now I have in front of me the finished product: a wonderfully written, clear, richly documented analysis of the Serbian evolution from Yugoslav totalitarian communism to authoritarian nationalist populism.[1] I attach great weight to your work, a study of the Serbian tragedy by a Serbian intellectual. The message of your work, however, goes beyond Serbia and the problems of the other nations of Yugoslavia. It concerns crucial conflicts to be found in each and every post-communist country, from central and eastern Europe to the former Soviet Union. A debate is taking place in these countries—where do we go from communism? What will be the direction of the changes? Your essay is an important voice in this dispute.

The situation differs in each of our countries but we all share the common challenge of the future. The fall of communism brought freedom, and fear of freedom; it brought changes, and fear of changes. Freedom means democracy and human rights; it also means the right of a nation to self-determination and a national culture, the right to property and a free market economy. Each of these freedoms, however, conceals a trap.

For instance, the right of a people to self-determination and their own culture can easily be transformed into a nationalist striving to revise borders, to the flaring up of ethnic conflicts, to contempt for other peoples and culture. The free market and property rights are not only the key to efficiency and wealth, they also help to break the hold of egalitarian ideology on society. This excites feelings of injustice, frustration, and aggression among the poor, and fear among the wealthy.

A democratic state, a pluralistic and tolerant society, the free market—these do not naturally result from the defeat of a communist dictatorship. The example of Serbia proves this point most emphatically.

Nebojša, you argue that Yugoslavia could have taken different paths of development. One of these was toward the democratization of the state with priority accorded to civil rights and freedoms. The second road was the establishment of collective rights and freedoms.

I am a Pole, therefore I understand very well the value of a nation's collective rights—the right to control one's fate, one's country, one's cultural identity. Such rights acquire particular importance when suspended by alien rule. Poles are perfectly aware of what it means to lose one's state, to be incorporated into other states. Between 1795 and 1918, the Polish nation was deprived of its state. For the five years of Nazi occupation Poland was transformed into a German-occupied territory. Later, in the years of the communist dictatorship, the essential fragments of the Polish inheritance were confiscated or censored.

Such situations encourage both individual apostasy and a nationalism of self-defense. An individual trades sides; the nation closes ranks against the intruder. After its victory, however, the nationalism of self-defense can be easily transformed into the nationalism of domination and aggression. The nations that were oppressed yesterday can easily become the oppressors of tomorrow. Thus, the alien aggressor takes its revenge.

In Poland, populist nationalism never gained the strength it has today in Serbia, because Polish nationalism was never quite so well organized. The program of revising borders and uniting all Poles in one country was never really popular in Poland. Poland is practically a one-nation country. National minorities do not pose a serious political problem. And yet, in recent years, disgraceful actions against Ukrainians, Belarusians, and Germans have taken place, and anti-Semitism has turned up in electoral campaigns. From where did this chauvinism derive?

The xenophobic dislike of strangers, even imagined ones, is always an effective way of consolidating a community around its negative features. Nationalist populism is both a phobia and a political doctrine. Or, rather, it is an anti-democratic doctrine that feeds on the nationalistic phobia and emotions of the crowd and jams its fear with screams.

For Poles, the Russians and Germans traditionally played the role of outside aggressor. For Serbs, meanwhile, it was the Titoist regime that imposed an alien rule. In Yugoslavia, Serbs felt discriminated against, demeaned, deprived of their rights. Croatians, however, considered the power of the Yugoslav regime to be a mask concealing Serbian domination. These two varieties of collective consciousness derive from two different historical memories. Serbian historical consciousness is permeated by the memory of the atrocities of Croatian fascism during World War II and Muslim domination in the time of Turkish rule. The Croatian historical consciousness is formed by the memory of a close union with Europe and the centralization of power in Belgrade during the Yugoslav monarchy. Croatian nationalism produced an enemy image of a primitive and cruel Serbian occupier, an Asiatic barbarian. Serbian nationalism produced an enemy image of Croatians as a fascist and murderous people.

The mechanism is always the same: a focus on the dark pages of another nation's history, an uncritical idealization of one's own country, and a conviction that compromise among different peoples for democratic reform is impossible. This mechanism can be found in all post-communist countries. Everywhere the leaders of nationalist factions popularize images of their own innocence and of alien aggressiveness. Everywhere they reanimate the historical memory in such a way as to expose the guilt of others and bewail their own sufferings. Everywhere they make claims for the rights of their compatriots abroad and demand that the rights of ethnic minorities in their own countries be restricted. Everywhere they invoke the specter of an international plot against a particular nation, namely their own. Everywhere they suspect a conspiracy of foreign capital, which spitefully refuses to invest money in their countries or conversely wants to invest in order to steal all domestic wealth. Everywhere they create an image of the humiliated national dignity, which only they can restore once in power.

These stereotypes have served both former communists and former anti-communists. Slobodan Milošević and Vojislav Šešelj—the Serbian president and his leading oppositionist—are both inspired by the Chetnik tradition and mouth similar nationalist rhetoric. Before our very eyes emerges a new formation: a peculiar merger of the fascist and communist heritage. We do not even have a name for this formation, just as, for a long time, no name could be found to describe the rightist or the leftist totalitarian movements.

But such a formation exists. It speaks the language of aggressive nationalism. It appeals to the masses and is against democratic procedure and compromise, against foreigners and "national traitors." The leaders of nationalist populism willingly seek support from religion and the Church in order to realize their vision of an ethnically pure country that unites all brethren wherever they live. Strong Church support would not only ensure an ethnically pure country (Serbia for the Serbs, Russia for the Russians, Lithuania for the Lithuanians, Poland for the Poles), but would also subordinate the people to a particular, religiously sanctioned idea of the nation. This is the message of the Orthodox Church hierarchy in Serbia concerning the particular religious role of the Serbian people: "The Serbs are the nation that carries God in their hearts. Our fate is to carry the cross at the world's crossroads. Thus, God is in our hearts."[2]

Whoever questions this manner of thinking about the Serbian nation is a traitor. All critics of these nationalist leaders are labeled traitors.

Nebojša, you use "populism" to define this phenomenon of Milošević and the Chetnik Šešelj closing ranks. It appears also in the communist Gennadi Zyuganov and the anti-communist Igor Shafarevich, also in Andrzej Lepper's "Self-Defense" and Stanisław Tyminski's Party X; it appears everywhere as a primitive reaction of self-defense against modernization, against the shock of the new. This is not the ideology of a different modernization, but an instinctive self-defense against a world that poses a threat: it is a reflex rooted in uncertainty and anxiety.

Democracy is particularly difficult to practice in multinational countries that regain freedom after years of dictatorship. Democracy is the art of pluralism and compromise, an art that is difficult to implement in a world accustomed to a monopoly of ideas and a permanent struggle with the enemy. Moreover, as in the epoch of anti-colonial revolutions, national elites eagerly use slogans of independence, for they are the main beneficiaries in the new states. And even if such reasoning leads to bloody war and economic destruction, these slogans usually gain the support of the masses. It requires many years to substitute the process of slow integration for the logic of destruction and war. Only the best quality politicians, courageous and farsighted, can stop this logic of disintegration. It is only they who can choose the way of compromise at the moment when the crowd embraces a philosophy of "all or nothing."

Fear easily stems from the source of threat. Those foreigners: Croatians in Krajina, Albanians in Kosovo, the Vatican and the Cominform, the West and Islam. Each of our nations can compose a list of such threats. But in Serbia the organization of collective emotion around threats of this type allows people to forget the most important threat—the threat of war.

And war did break out. It doesn't make sense to consider today who started what and when. Each—Serb, Croat, Bosnian Muslim—answers that the war was started by the other. And each is to a certain degree right.

You, Nebojša, identified the Serbian sources for nationalist hysteria that led up to the war. This choice of themes does you credit. For it is the responsibility of Serbian intellectuals to search for guilt among their own peo-ple, and give to a Croatian the right to be the first to define Croatian guilt.

Nationalist populism is a tremendous and dangerous narcotic. It be-gins as a marginal stupidity, a bewildering aberration. But in conditions of crisis and frustration, the margins can acquire an ominous dynamic, like a cancerous tissue that infects the entire organism. The hysteria of crowds, assembled in meetings, usually produces fear: fear of the other, but also of one's own community; fear not to be accused of treason, of patriotic disloyalty, of national apostasy. When the People's Leader—and a crowd needs such a leader—says that "no one from now on will degrade you," whether meaning Albanians, Latvians, or Gypsies, it is difficult then for Serbs, Russians, or Poles to protest.

This fear paralyzes the will, mystifies thought. Nobel Prize-winning novelist Ivo Andrić writes:

> It was a time of great fear, invisible, boundless and overwhelming. The kind of fear that sometimes plagues human communities and forces heads to bow or be cut off. Then many were blinded and stunned. They forgot about rea-son and courage, and that all things must pass. Human life, like everything else, has a certain price, but this price is not infinite. And so, dazzled by the transitory magic of fear, they pay for their bare survival more than it is worth. They act in vile and disgraceful ways, and when the fear is over, they discover that they have paid for their lives too dearly or even that there really was no danger—they were under the illusion of fear. . . .[3]

But this realization comes later. In the meantime, fear transforms nation-al pride into the narcotic of chauvinism. The political culture of dialogue withers away. The spirit of democracy is vanquished.

Thus triumphs the logic of war and the desire to destroy the enemy. This is how the last Balkan war broke out. The war with no end in sight. The war that has and will have no victors, only losers.

Against this raging nationalism the spirit of democracy—your spirit, Nebojša—is often helpless. I ask myself: what are the origins of this weakness? Is there some significant flaw in our reasoning? I sympathize with the view, expressed by Jürgen Habermas, that nationalistic doctrines should be challenged in the name of constitutional patriotism. I am in doubt, however, as to whether even Habermas has a sense of the other side of this danger! Imagine satellite television programs that, in the everyday education of German youth, replace the sufferings of young Werther, Hegel's phenomenology of the Spirit, Heine's poetry, and the history of the Buddenbrook family.

True, constitutional patriotism is the only method of creating a com-munity grounded in the common good. Yet there is still something else, namely the common memory, without which it is also difficult to speak of a community. A community of memory constitutes a natural barrier that can prevent the transformation of a nation into a raging mob. Therefore the value of such a community must not be underestimated. Is it possible that the fascination with Western-style democracy and tolerance, coupled with a contempt for national chauvinism, leads us to disregard the natural need to safeguard national identity in the world of mass culture?

I don't have a simple answer to this question. However, I must admit that I feel instinctive anxiety when I see my young son's imagination invaded by American comic-strip heroes rather than the myths and legends of Polish literature. My generation grew up reading the great Polish writers, such as Adam Mickiewicz and Henryk Sienkiewicz, whereas he is fascinated by Donald Duck and the Mutant Ninja Turtles. This seems harmless enough, yet if I feel this anxiety, why should I be surprised by the natural attachment to landscapes, customs, and ways of life in human communities that are afraid to lose a common language of allusion, myth, and symbol? I fear we are losing the capacity to communicate to one another and our close ones with this common language. I see this fear of the invasion of other patterns of culture as an expression of the concern for national identity and dignity. He who feels no need for such dignity is not likely to feel the need for human dignity.

I do not believe that the European people can merge as in the American model. The tragic experience of Yugoslavia is a most instructive lesson. So is the Soviet experience. There never arose either a Yugoslav people or a Soviet people. It seems that only as Serbs and Russians, Croats and Ukrainians can one belong to the wider community: Slavic, Yugoslav, European.

And yet the need to create these broader communities, these more spacious homelands, does exist. This need is not an invention of the Vatican or foreign intelligence agencies. It results from the logic of a world with open borders, common markets, and a free flow of information and ideas. And from this same logic also arises a fear of openness.

This fear, I repeat, easily turns into hysteria and aggression. This fear—which you, Nebojša, have noted—grows out of a conviction that one's country is surrounded by enemies, that there are traitors among one's people that must be rendered harmless. This fear makes people trust in violence and strong-arm leadership.

To face this dictatorship requires courage. To oppose the fear that has terrorized the mob, to face the madness of one's own nation, this demands heroism. The heroism of Thomas Mann who condemned Nazism; the heroism of Andrei Sakharov who condemned communism.

Your heroism, Nebojša.

We are bitterly aware that many of our friends followed a different path. In each of our countries there were intellectuals who used their pens in the service of dictatorial power and totalitarian ideology. The history of intellectuals' romance with fascism and communism is one of the most interesting, most important, and saddest chapters in the history of the European spirit. Consider the case of Martin Heidegger who supported Hitler; of Georgy Lukács who supported Stalin; of the Serbian philosopher Dobrica Čosič who for many years promoted the ideas of freedom and self-government and has now become a defender of greater Serbian chauvinism. Consider also the Russian philosopher Igor Shafarevich who had been a dissident and fought for freedom, but later began to hunt for a conspiracy of Russophobes; and the Polish writer Jarosław Marek Rymkiewicz who defended freedom and later became a spokesman for provincialism and narrow-minded ugliness. These people understand patriotism as the refusal to tell the truth about their nation's past and present. They are ruled by a fascination for strength and a fear of isolation, of being labeled "rootless cosmopolitans."

I know only too well the taste of estrangement, the feeling of isolation that accompanies the decision to tell the truth to the nation. I know that it is a difficult battle. I also know, however, that intellectuals must sometimes take such risks to remain true to their profession. They must say the word, "No!"—even if later they must pay for it with silence. The slain demand that this word be uttered. Raped women and crippled men await this word.

What does it mean, Nebojša, to love one's country? To love Serbia or Poland? I believe it means to give to our homelands the best that we have: a sense of freedom, honest criticism, a willingness to bear witness to bitter truths. Our homelands have always had an excess of flatterers. And always lacked those who demonstrate courage when facing the enemy, and truth when facing their own people.

Intellectuals must never fail to defend their nation when it is threatened by strangers. But, more important, they must defend truth when their people oppress others. Intellectuals must find some point of balance between a sense of the tragedy of their own people and a sense of responsibility for this tragedy. Only a nation that is aware of its own guilt can free itself from such guilt. A consciousness of historical innocence is a "false history that leads to false politics."[4]

Indeed, the first commandment of every patriotic catechism is truth. Patriotism is not solidarity with the screaming crowd. It is not contempt and animosity for other nations and cultures. It is not a truncheon, a gag, or blackmail against those who think differently. Patriotism is a concern for the country and every citizen of that country.

Thus conceived, patriotism demands that we call for the defeat of our soldiers when they rape other peoples. This means—please forgive this banality—that a people are not free when they oppress other peoples.

Did you know, Nebojša, that I called for the defeat of our soldiers when in August 1968 they trampled the freedom of Czechs and Slovaks? I sat then in prison and listened to the investigating officers accuse me of being a Polish traitor. I cited to them the words of the great Russian, Piotr Chaadayev: "I will not learn to love my homeland with closed eyes, with stooped head, with silenced mouth. I believe that I can be useful to my country only as a clear witness; I think that the time of blind silence has passed and now above all we owe our homeland the truth."[5]

I send to you, Nebojša, fraternal greetings.

Notes

1. Nebojša Popov, *Serbski Dramat* (Warszawa: Nowa, 1994).

2. Ibid., p.46.

3. Ivo Andrić, *Konsulowie ich Cesarskich Mości* (Łódź: Wydawnictwo Łódzkie, 1977), pp.513–514.

4. Józef Szujski, *O Fałszywej Historii Jako Mistrzyni Fałszywej Polityki* (Warszawa: Państwowy Instytut Wydawniczy, 1991).

5. Piotr Chaadayev, *Filozofia i myśl społeczna rosyjska 1825–1861* (Warszawa: Państwowe Wydawnistwa Naukowe, 1961), pp.119–120.

2

Post-Soviet Nationalism

VALERY TISHKOV

During this period of deep social transformation in the former Soviet Union, nationalism in its ethnic form (ethnonationalism) has played two very different roles in the political and civic realms. On the one hand, the rise of ethnopolitics was a major factor in tearing apart the unitary Soviet state and undermining its communist ideology. Nationalist movements strengthened concerns for cultural integrity and helped mobilize citizens demanding democratic reform and self-governance. In its cultural and political forms, nationalism has also helped to build the states that have emerged from the wreckage of the Soviet federation.

On the other hand, ethnonationalism has made this area of the globe an arena of destructive war, ethnic cleansing, and uncontrolled violence that have killed thousands of people and displaced millions more, caused enormous material loss, and contributed to growing political instability. The horrors of ex-Yugoslavia, "when under the slogan of democratisation the governments of all the republics have made their lands unmistakably poorer and their people unhappier,"[1] can also be found on the territory of the former Soviet Union where at least a dozen ethnic conflicts and internal wars have been raging. Ethnonationalism has legitimized the activities of ethnic warlords and justified widespread violations of human rights. It has stimulated irresponsible political behavior and increased the spread of xenophobia and intolerance. While helping to build the new post-communist successor states, ethnonationalism also been employed to challenge their sovereignty and call into question their ability to maintain social order and provide an acceptable standard of living. Indeed, ethnic nationalism

and the conflicts it has generated have become one of the major obstacles
to reform and modernization in Russia as well as elsewhere in the former
Soviet Union.

Scholars and journalists have offered many interpretations for the recent "wrath of nations" in the former Soviet Union.[2] At the moment, two
interpretative approaches to ethnonationalism dominate academic and
public discourse. The first, the paradigm of "fallen empire" and "national
revival," ascribes the breakdown of the Soviet Union to its illegitimate imperial character and explains nationalist conflict as an irresistible struggle
for national self-determination within this imperial model. The second
model finds fault in the ethnic principles of Soviet state policy and in the
irresponsible manipulations of ethnicity following the Gorbachev period.
Both models are oversimplifications. The first reflects the narrow-mind-
edness of Cold Warriors celebrating the victory of liberalism; the second
is shaped by the legacies of Marxist determinism and the conservative
rhetoric of Soviet empire-savers.

There are many reasons why ethnicity and nationalism became crucial
factors in burying the Soviet Union and destroying its empire in Eastern
Europe. Rather than an organic phenomenon that can be defined with text-
book formulas, nationalism should be understood as a series of postulates
and actions formulated and initiated by activists within a social space. Ethnonationalism thus becomes a set of simplistic but powerful myths arising
from and reacting to Soviet political practice. Instead of the irreconcilable
enemies depicted in the reference books, nationalism and communism are
revealed to be close political relations.[3] As Zbigniew Brzezinski has noted,
"although communism declared itself to be an international doctrine, in
fact it fostered nationalist sentiments among the people."[4] Another author has gone even further, concluding that "Soviet nationality policy was
devised and carried out by nationalists." Lenin's position on national
rights, this analyst continues, "was one of the most uncompromising positions he ever took."[5]

Before turning to the contemporary post-Soviet experience of nationalism, we should first look more carefully at how Soviet politicians and
theoreticians have traditionally regarded nationalism in the Soviet Union
and how they view it today.

Academic Nationalism

The starting point for the traditional Soviet treatment of nationalism can
be found in the *Soviet Encyclopaedia*'s definition of nation: "an historic
entity of people with its territory, economic ties, literary language, and
specific culture and character comprising the whole of a nation's features."[6] This formula differs little from Stalin's definition of a nation as
"a historically evolved, stable community of language, territory, economic
life and psychological make-up manifested in a community of culture."
Later Soviet scholarship added one more important element: a feeling

of common identity or "national self-consciousness." As such, Soviet scholars defined nations basically in ethnocultural terms, referring to a common history, culture, and language as well as a certain "ethnic territory."

Why the Bolsheviks and Soviet scholarship opted for a federal structure composed of ethnonations instead of territorially based administrative units is not a simple question. Long before their 1917 revolution, the Bolsheviks hotly debated the national question with their closest opponents among the social democrats of Eastern Europe, particularly Austro-Marxists like Karl Renner and Otto Bauer and the German Marxist Karl Kautsky. The national question played an important role in the platforms of many Russian political parties, including leftist radicals. The drive toward centralization within the Russian empire had generated a lively debate about federalism and autonomy. Yet these new notions of governance did not automatically translate into demands for territorial autonomy.

The Bolshevik position on nationalism evolved during the party's search for an appropriate (or opportunist) strategy. After coming to power in October 1917, the Bolsheviks proclaimed Russia a federal republic, but did not define the principles and norms of federalization. Fighting for influence in ethnic regions, the Soviet government supported the idea of buffer republics in the border areas of the country, as well as in the regions of military activity during the Civil War. In the meantime, the government took every opportunity to take back republics and give them the status of administrative autonomies with specific ethnocultural profiles and symbols. Under the pressure of a chaotic situation, the Bolsheviks recognized the independence of what later became union republics and designed ethnoterritorial autonomies in the Russian Federal Republic. Despite political rhetoric, the Soviet government and Lenin himself were not enthusiastic supporters of ethnic federalism. In 1923, however, Soviet nationality policy finally took its ethnonational turn as the Soviets strengthened their power and Stalin became the true "father of nations" (albeit not all nations and not all the time).[7]

Thus, Soviet policy was designed in part to meet the serious political challenges issuing from the ethnic peripheries of the Russian empire and in part to achieve specific political goals. Whatever the precise reasons, however, since the beginning of Soviet rule this ideology of ethnonations required social engineering to put the idea into practice or, more precisely, to construct realities that would correspond to political myths and intellectual exercises.

The first task of this social engineering was an inventory of ethnonations and, where necessary, an invention of nations. After all, in many Soviet regions the cultural mosaic did not conform to strict boundaries, and ethnicity was overshadowed by other forms of identity—religion, clan and dynastic affiliations, and regional and local loyalties. To compile this inventory, the first Soviet census of 1926 asked citizens to indicate their "nationality." The result was about 200 different "national" identities. This list immediately became the subject of scholarly investigation and political manipulation that continues to this day.

Ethnographers, linguists, and historians immediately went to work to redefine the list by declaring some identities dialectal, subethnic, or local variants of larger *ethnie*. Many new names were given; many groups were renamed. In the end, scholars labeled all Soviet nations and *narodnosti* ("peoples") and created a hierarchy of ethnic groups. Thus, Pomors and Cossacks were listed officially as "Russians," Turks and Tatars in Trancaucasus as "Azerbaijanis," Sarts and Bukharzi as "Uzbeks," the Pamirs as "non-Tadjik-speaking Tadjiks," and so on. Ethnic engineers also elaborated ethnic processes such as "consolidation" and "integration" in order to minimize the number of potential claimants for further, more advanced territorial recognition.

The Soviet strategy neatly coincided with nationalism's core rationale. As Ernest Gellner has pointed out, "nationalism is primarily a political principle, which holds that the political and the national unit should be congruent."[8] In the Soviet context, then, ethnographers used ethnic territories as maps for Soviet state-building, and ethnonations only became political facts through territorialization and the assigning of an officially recognized administrative status. The Soviet Union was the only state in the world where the ethnic principle served as such a basis for administrative structure.[9]

Ethnicity also formed the basis for "socialist federalism," which was radically different from "bourgeois" (read territorial) federalism. According to this socialist theory, the federal government of "nation-states" (read ethno-states) granted status to all major Soviet nationalities save the most numerous and dominant—the Russians. Unlike other republics, the Russian Soviet Federal Socialist Republic (RSFSR) did not have any special institutions or policies directly addressing the political and cultural aspirations of ethnic Russians. Roughly 40 percent of its federal territory was assigned to ethnoterritorial autonomies of smaller groups. All of these, with the exception of Chuvashia, Tuva, and the autonomous regions of the Northern Caucasus, contained ethnic Russian majorities.

At the moment of its demise, the Soviet Union included 53 nation-state formations of differing rank, from union republics at the top to autonomous districts at the bottom. Every territorial formation was based on the right to national self-determination for the indigenous nation, and the name of the nation-state reflected the titular nationality: Kazakhstan after the Kazakhs, the Udmurt autonomous republic after the Udmurts (the only exception, Dagestan, was named for a geographical area). The titular nationality could comprise a decisive majority or a striking minority (Mordvinians, for instance, composed only 27.1 percent of the Mordvinian automonous republic in 1989 while Karels constituted only 10 percent of the Karelian republic). Soviet decision-makers often remade this map, abolishing some statuses, reorganizing administrative boundaries, and even reshaping territories. Yet no one could challenge this status from below.

Another important element of Soviet-style ethnonationalism was its image of a nation as homogeneous, as a kind of collective individual with common blood and soul, primordial rights, and a single will. According to Soviet texts, the nation achieved such a level of economic, political, and cultural integration that it could be considered an "ethno-social organism."[10] Over the course of many decades, this organic vision of ethnicity acquired deep emotional and political legitimacy. Only by belonging to a specific nation could an individual acquire proper status and rights, just as only membership in the Party could guarantee power and prestige. The Soviet state registered the ethnic identities of all citizens on internal passports introduced in 1934. Ethnic affiliation thus became subject to mass manipulation, political control, and repression. The notion of nationality as biologically inherited is so strong that the new passport proposed by the Russian government in 1995 still maintains a space for nationality, though there is now an option to leave it blank.

This ideology of ethnic collectivism is the most authoritarian element of nationalism because it presupposes an elite that can interpret the national interest. As Liah Greenfeld writes, "the reification of a community introduces (or preserves) fundamental inequality between those of its few members who are qualified to interpret the collective will and the many who have no such qualifications; the select few dictate to the masses who must obey."[11] Throughout the Soviet Union, elites emerged among most ethnic groups as "national" poets, writers, artists, filmmakers, and academicians all happily engaged in constructing myths of the nation. Among these mobilizing myths, the most popular and universal traced the ethnogenesis of the nation from the late Paleolithic period through its glorious ancient history and to its acceptance into the brotherhood of Soviet nations.

For many decades, the doctrine of ethnonationalism, including the right of nations to self-determination and even secession, was preached in propaganda and incorporated in the various Soviet constitutions. True, a strong unitary political regime strictly controlled this political process and attempted to micromanage interethnic relations. But despite the many crimes committed by the Soviet government toward ethnic groups, enormous resources flowed into comprehensive programs supporting national cultures. No ethnic groups disappeared from the map of the Soviet Union during the twentieth century, and the cultural mosaic was thoroughly documented, academically described, and staged in the repertoires of numerous national theaters, operas, museums, and folk music and dance groups. This policy of nurturing local cultures, facilitated by the professional elite of intellectuals and managers, provided a powerful material and symbolic basis for the local nationalisms that would ultimately challenge the overarching Soviet culture.

These nationalisms, benign in their cultural and anti-hegemonic aspects, soon demonstrated an uglier side. Asbjorn Eide, director of the Norwegian Institute for Human Rights, has written on the many dangers inherent in ethnonationalism: "It can be expansionist, exclusivist, and/or secessionist. In all of these modes it generates conflicts, sometimes with grave consequences for peace and for human rights."[12] Two varieties of conflict-generating nationalism—hegemonic and defensive—flourished before and after the Soviet Union's demise. The interplay between these two phenomena has greatly affected the process of post-Soviet reform and thwarted the development of a less aggressive nationalism based on civic identity.

Hegemonic Nationalism

Hegemonic nationalism often refers to the expansionist or suppressive tendencies of dominant ethnic groups toward other ethnic states or internal ethnic minorities. One obvious example in the ex-communist world is Serbian nationalism, often considered a manifestation of the ambitions and interests of an imperialistic nation to maintain a privileged status at the expense of others. Because hegemonic nationalism is a nationalism of the majority—of titular groups—its elements are also readily found among the dominant groups of the former Soviet republics, now independent states. Of all these hegemonic forces, perhaps the most frequently commented on is Russian nationalism.

The idea of the Russian nation in its ethnic meaning (as people of the same blood, culture, and spirit) was introduced into public discourse rather recently as a logical ingredient of what official propaganda and academic discourse label "the building of Soviet nations." This new nomenclature is not complete without some image of the "great Russian nation." Stalin used similar nationalist rhetoric—the glory of Russia, its deep historical roots, its mystical soul—as part of popular mobilization during World War II. Until the late 1960s, the nationalist paradigm was predominantly patriotic, self-glorifying, and paternalistic. Later the paradigm began to reflect social changes within the Soviet Union, especially in the demographic patterns and growing social mobility of non-Russian nationalities. The new Russian nationalists clothed their hegemonic motives with emotional rhetoric about the extinction of the Russian people and the degradation of their traditions and culture. Writers and social scientists, the true founding fathers of this new Russian ethnonationalism, provided arguments for these emotional appeals, and their texts formed the basis for all later political programs and statements.[13]

As a political movement, contemporary Russian ethnonationalism was born in the 1980s with *Pamyat* (Memory) and its programs for cultural, historic, and ecological preservation. The new organization's ideology was a mixture of Orthodox monarchism, national Bolshevism, and anti-Semitism. *Perestroika* and the crisis of the Soviet state and Communist Party rule politicized *Pamyat*, especially under the charismatic leadership of Dmitrii Vasiliev. In 1989–90, it publicly distributed its "Manifesto," a non-official program of hegemonic nationalism devoted to the Soviet Union's dominant ethnicity—Russians.

According to the *Pamyat* doctrine, the Russian Orthodox religion is the only possible spiritual basis for the Russians and for Russia. The Czarist monarchy, with its sacred base, is the best form of state power. The centralized state should neither disintegrate nor weaken, and the Russian empire must remain intact. As a great nation, Russia must continue as a triangle of Slavic peoples—Russians, Ukrainians, and Belarusians. All negative forces, such as disintegration and conflict, stem from a global Zionist-Masonic conspiracy directed against the Russian people and their state. All power in Russia must reside with Russians, and other groups should be represented proportionally in the institutions of politics, culture, and science.[14]

After a series of internal crises, in part provoked by state interference, *Pamyat* lost its leading place in the Russian nationalist movement. The political project of Russian ethnonationalism was too important and potentially profitable to be undertaken by marginal activists without the proper prestige, abilities, and resources. Since 1991 and the breakup of the Soviet Union, a series of Russian national movements and organizations have emerged with much stronger and more respectfully couched appeals. Responding to new social conditions, these groups have mobilized considerable mass support.

A major reason for the rise in Russia of this newly respectable hegemonic nationalism has been a simple geopolitical fact. With the collapse of the Soviet federation, 25 million ethnic Russians suddenly found themselves part of a new Russian diaspora.[15] These ethnic Russian minorities were excluded from the political process in many new independent states and, in the cases of Latvia and Estonia, were excluded even from membership in the new civic communities. In several regions, such as Central Asia and the Caucasus, ethnic Russians found themselves in a turmoil of ethnic and clan disputes. In this strongly unfavorable psychological climate, many Russians succumbed to fear and joined an exodus back to their "historic homeland." The democratic leaders of Russia—Boris Yeltsin, Yegor Gaidar, Andrei Kozyrev—had believed that their republic allies in the fight against the Party and the Gorbachev center would remain in a common front of 15 independent states. But this was a miscalculation: the ethnonationalism of the titular groups became the only choice for republican leaders and activists who had achieved their independence under a slogan of "national self-determination."

The new Russian diaspora was not the only reason for heightened ethnonationalism. In Russia itself, the collapse of the full-employment economy and the redistributive state—however inefficient and impoverished these institutions were—caused massive social dislocation and growing disparities in individual fortunes. These new challenges affected urban people most of all, especially the predominantly ethnic Russian employees of heavy industry and the military. The demobilization of Russian forces deployed abroad, along with the paring down of the workforce of repres-

sive institutions such as the KGB, produced a pool of ideologically indoctrinated, well-trained, and energetic male officers accustomed to their
privileges and nostalgic for the "good old days." Many citizens, particularly the older generation and war veterans indoctrinated in the verities of
the "great Soviet state" and the "great Russian people," suffered a crisis of
identity and confronted the traumatic loss of their former status.

All these factors pushed nationalism into political debates at the highest levels of Russian society. At the very top, President Yeltsin, Minister
of Foreign Affairs Kozyrev, and Russian parliamentary leaders made the
defense of ethnic Russians in the "near abroad" a political priority after
summer 1992. The most striking example of this new policy, Yeltsin's
speech at the U.N. General Assembly in September 1994, sent a message
not only to neighboring countries and to the West but also to an internal
electorate concerned with the fate of its ethnic compatriots. The same message lay behind Yeltsin's statements on Russia's re-emergence as a great
power in world politics and his support for the resurgent Cossacks, the primarily Russian nationalists active in the southern region of the country.[16]
In this articulation of hegemonic nationalism, Yeltsin found an early ally
in the Russian Orthodox church: the president took his oath of office on
the Bible and, though a professed atheist, soon acknowledged regular visits to church.

Other high-ranking federal officials have articulated more openly extreme ethnonationalism. In Yegor Gaidar's government, for instance, Minister of Information Mikhail Poltoranin was infamous for his nationalism
and anti-Semitism, particularly his notorious remark about the contemporary Russian mass media speaking "a kind of prisoners' Hebrew." His
protégé for the ministerial post in the subsequent government, Boris
Mironov, became known as the "iron nationalist" for statements such as:
"If Russian nationalism is fascism then I am a fascist."[17] Mironov was dismissed from his position in September 1994 following an outcry from liberal journalists.

The December 1993 federal elections ushered into the State Duma a
new phalanx of ultranationalists, the 40 parliamentary members of the Liberal-Democratic Party. The party's leader, Vladimir Zhirinovsky, is one of
the most provocative and charismatic propagandists of Russian nationalism. Leaders of another influential party bloc (the Communists and the
Agrarians) also appeal to the *Russkii narod* (the Russian people). Leader
of the Communist Party of Russia Gennadi Zyuganov, in his recent book
Derzhava (State Power), defines Russia's vital interests as "gathering together under the protection of a unified and powerful state all Russian
people, all who consider Russia as their Motherland, and all those peoples
who agree to share with Russia their historical fate."[18]

Outside the power elite, numerous groups of intellectuals and activists
subscribing to extreme forms of Russian ethnonationalism operate at the
margins. Vasiliev's *Pamyat* continues to organize small-scale meetings and
demonstrations blocking other extremist groups. A similar organization,

Russkaya Partia (Russian Party), places anti-Semitism at the core of its doctrine. Its leader, Nikolai Bondareek, stated the party's main priorities as the following: "In Russia it is the Russians who should govern. . . . Russia must have a Russian government, a Russian parliament of ethnic Russians belonging to the Great Nation by blood and by spirit. . . . Everything is for the Nation and nothing against it—this motto must be in the brain and spirit, in the flesh and blood of every Russian, because we are all only cells of one great organism named the Nation."[19]

On February 1992, a group of Russian nationalist leaders including writer Valentin Rasputin and Communist Party leader Zyuganov established a new organization *Russkii Natsionalnii Sobor* (Russian National Assembly) as an umbrella coalition for the numerous groups operating in Russia, Ukraine, Belarus, the Baltic states, Moldova, and Georgia. Their first congress attracted 1,500 delegates from 117 cities representing over 70 Russian patriotic organizations. RNS calls for unifying Russian and other indigenous peoples of Russia "for the sake of reviving a united Motherland, defending nation-state interests, and preserving the traditional moral and religious values of Russia's citizens." Its Manifesto ends with the words: "We are Russians. God is with us!"[20] In spring 1994, the RNS and the Confederation of Free Labor Unions (now the National Coalition of Russian Trade Unions) signed an agreement, giving the nationalist organization easier access to workers at larger industrial plants.

The relationship between fascism and nationalism in Russia is complex. Russian fascists use Nazi racial doctrine as their theoretical basis, substituting Russians for Germans as the master race. It follows that the Russian ethnonation should enjoy all state privileges and that different forms of racial and ethnic segregation are permissible. The RNS's doctrine, for instance, places strong barriers against mixed marriages, supports an increased fertility rate among Russians, believes in proportional ethnic representation in all state and public institutions, and vows to struggle against all "parasitic" peoples such as Jews and Gypsies. As with all other nationalist formations, the RNS takes a very strong anti-Western stance and dreams of a messianic Russian future.

Aleksandr Barkashov, an alumni of *Pamyat* and the creator of the "Russian National Unity Group," brings together these themes in his 1995 article on the "crisis of world civilization." Russia, he asserts, is the only source of salvation for the dying Western and Eastern civilizations. To safeguard this historic mission, Russians must unite and establish "an organization characterized by rigid discipline and comprised of the strongest and most active."[21]

Some experts are skeptical about the viability of Russian fascism. They argue, first, that because of World War II, Russians are immune to fascism. Second, sociological surveys indicate that no more than 2 percent of the electorate is ready to vote for fascists. These arguments are not very strong, however. The mentality and values of former Soviet citizens are being transformed rapidly. Soviet symbols and history took only a few years to become demythologized, and anti-fascist values are practically absent among the younger generation. The core of fascist groups in Russia is made up of those under the age of 35. Moreover, 2 percent of the electorate comprises over two million people, a large group for any political formation.

Hegemonic nationalism has undergone a serious metamorphosis in Russia since the December 1993 elections, particularly after the war in Chechnya that began in December 1994. Valery Solovei, a leading Russian expert on nationalism, has observed that "since the beginning of 1994, the melody of Russian domestic and foreign policy has been influenced more and more by the nationalistic and 'great power' repertoire. It has reached its crescendo with the start of the Chechen 'expedition.'"[22] Another expert, Andranik Migranian, agrees that the Chechen campaign was designed to overcome the anti-military and pacifist attitudes engendered by the "Afghanistan syndrome." "For the president and the statists," he writes, "there is no other choice but to use all force to overcome the defensive syndrome for the sake of preserving and strengthening the Russian state."[23]

Contrary to these expectations, however, the Chechen war did not cause an immediate upsurge of chauvinist and nationalist feeling. No anti-Chechen sentiment swept Russia and no serious organized right-wing activities took place, including among the Cossacks in regions bordering Chechnya. Unlike in Serbia, no ethnic Russian volunteers came forward to fight for the country's territorial integrity, and many young people avoided the regular military draft. Human rights activists, the liberal mass media, and organizations of soldiers' mothers dominated public discourse. Sergei Kovalev and Yegor Gaidar were the major spokesmen against the "war party" and the danger posed by rising Russian chauvinism. Their political adversary, ultranationalist Aleksandr Nevzorov, could not get air time for his flamboyant patriotic propaganda. Yeltsin even signed a decree against extremists, prescribing criminal prosecution for those who sow ethnic hatred (though this did not prevent his own declarations of Russia's great power status).

Despite popular disaffection for Russian involvement in Chechnya, there are many forces at work strengthening Russian hegemonic nationalism. According to some sociological surveys, the trend toward traditional Russian and imperial values is increasing among the population. As Solovei has suggested, "In a Russian context, there are probably two meta-ideologies— communism and liberalism—that are exhausting their potential and are gradually being replaced by the ideology of Russian nationalism."[24]

Words such as democracy and liberalism now provoke feelings of alienation and hostility among the majority of the country's population. Despite the enormous power granted the president by the constitution, Yeltsin has lost a great deal of popular legitimation. Thus, he and others have appealed to other sources, have chosen their words from a new vocabulary (*derzhava*, national pride), and festoon themselves with the symbols of state nationalism.

There are limits, however, to the degree that Yeltsin and his coterie can transform the Russian state. The Chechen war has marginalized but not destroyed the liberal democrats. The mass media has strongly opposed the nationalist propaganda. Further, the West is monitoring the situation carefully. Thus, Russia's future hangs in the balance and depends a great deal on other factors, including competing nationalisms.

Defensive Nationalism

While Vasiliev and Zhirinovsky brought Russian nationalism to the front pages of Western newspapers, the topic of periphery nationalism became widely known and discussed because of the separatist actions of several autonomous republics within the Russian Federation. These nationalisms sprouting up far from Moscow constitute perhaps the most vital ideological doctrine and political practice of the post-Soviet Union.

Non-Russian nationalisms have long flourished on the political landscape. Some national elites formulated the idea of a nation during the Czarist empire, and several nationalist political movements arose before 1917. But periphery nationalism is really rooted in the Soviet legacy and its emphasis on limited self-determination.[25] The etatization of ethnicity, a key element in constructing Soviet nations, took shape around short-lived independent states such as the Transcaucasus republics in 1918–21 and the Baltic states in 1918–40. Autonomous administrative units mushroomed during the first two decades after the 1917 revolution. The state took charge in building nations. "Though in popular understanding and in nationalists' ideologies the nation is usually thought to exist prior to the state and to be the basis on which the state has been formed, historians have long recognized the importance of states in the creation of nations," writes Ronald Suny in his study of Soviet nationalism.[26]

But relations between the center and the nations that it built were basically imperial. Moscow made all the major decisions, from economic strategy to key political appointments. And the beneficiaries of these decisions were generally ethnic Russians or at least those bureaucratic elites enmeshed in Russian culture. As Suny observes,

> Non-Russian republics were treated as objects of central policy rather than as subjects capable of independent decision-making, and their national destinies were fundamentally altered as a result. . . . A fundamental contradiction between empire and emerging nations grew like a cancer within the Soviet state. Much more than the tsarist empire, the USSR had become a "prisonhouse of nations"—indeed, of nations that had grown up within the Soviet Union.[27]

It is no surprise, then, that the nationalism of titular non-Russian nationalities was essentially defensive: protecting dominant minorities against Russian hegemony but also treating smaller minorities with intolerance. In the former Soviet Union, titular nationalism in the republics created "double minorities"—minorities within minorities—who were frequently deprived of the rights of free expression and decision-making: Tajiks in Uzbekistan or Abkhazians in Georgia. In other words, after acquiring full control of the new independent states, ethnic elites started to behave hegemonically toward their stateless minorities. The goal of radical nationalists became to "normalize" national states that were culturally and even demographically more homogeneous and that excluded "non-natives" from access to resources, power, and even citizenship. Armenians expelled Azeris and Azeris expelled Armenians from their republics. Uzbeks expelled Meskhetian Turks. Georgia, where former President Zviad Gamsakhurdia formulated the policy "Georgia for Georgians," has been a particular locus of conflict. The Georgian nationalist government abolished Southern Ossetian autonomy in 1989 causing a three-year open conflict that has yet to be resolved. Georgia still refuses to accept back Turks who were deported during Stalin's repression.

Trapped by the legacies of Soviet nationalism, the new leaders of the successor states found themselves unprepared to transform ethnonationalism into civic nation-building. The enforcement of citizenship and official language laws based on ethnic exclusivity in societies with sizeable, culturally distinct, and historically autochthonous communities has caused massive discontent and interethnic tensions in Estonia, Latvia, Moldova, Georgia, Ukraine, and elsewhere. Former "double minorities," together with "new minorities," have called for their own national states or started irredentist movements, preferring to exit political systems where they have neither proper voice nor representation. The Armenian enclave in Nagorno-Karabakh has fought to reunite with its "historic motherland" of Armenia. Abkhazian leaders have responded to Georgian hegemony with a ferocious struggle for secession that resulted in the expulsion of ethnic Georgians from Abkhazia. In Moldova, the Russian-Ukrainian minority has proclaimed its own state in the Transdniester region while the Gagauz minority has demanded greater territorial autonomy. In Crimea, the Russian majority wants to be a part of Russia, not Ukraine, while the Tatar minority dreams of making Crimea a Tatar national state. The list of mutual dissatisfactions can go on and on, and there are many more potential candidates for future confrontations.

Conflict has exploded in these cases primarily because ethnonationalists have tried to realize the principle of "one ethnic group—one state" cherished for decades by Soviet academic theory and propaganda. True, nationalist movements contributed to crushing the Communist Party's rule and thus paved the way for democratic transformation. But today, titular ethnonationalism has become a major obstacle in building peaceful civic societies on the territory of the former Soviet Union.

The Russian Federation inherited a more complicated ethnic politics than any other successor state. A large multiethnic entity very much like the Soviet Union, Russia is still a country where periphery nationalism has not exhausted its potential for dismantling a highly centralized state structure and pluralizing a political and cultural realm dominated by one ethnic group. In virtually every ethnic enclave of this vast country, micronationalisms are incubating. Consider, for instance, the nationalist manifesto of an author representing the stateless minority of Shors (an Altaic group of 16,000 people in southern Siberia): "The time has come for Great Russians to concentrate themselves in their historical motherland. . . . Conquered lands should be returned to their original owners, with whom they can establish equal relations. . . . We must make all efforts to form a united state in Altai and Sayani under one name, a project that our predecessors unfortunately could not realize."[28]

In recent years, defensive nationalism at the peripheries has moved from cultural revival to well-organized political movements that have vaulted their advocates into power positions in practically all autonomous ethnic regions of the Russian Federation. Ironically, radical nationalists have managed to bring to or to keep in power former Party officials who have skillfully exchanged their communist ideologies for nationalist doctrines and used such nationalism as a counterbalance in negotiations with the center for control of local resources.

The most striking example is the Republic of Tatarstan. Here, the ruling elite used Tatar ethnonationalism, radically expressed by ultranationalist organizations and local intellectuals, to establish a firm and indisputable political order based on titular representation. About 85 percent of all key appointments at republican and local levels have gone to ethnic Tatars, who constitute no more than half the population. Using the powerful slogans of national sovereignty and self-determination, the Tatarstan authorities defined their republic as a fully independent state and "a subject of international law." This provocative assertion was used effectively with other popular slogans ("democratic and sovereign state," "equal partnership with Russia") to defy both the federal constitution and the Russian authorities.

In March 1992, the Tatar authorities organized a referendum that asked the question, "Do you want the Tatarstan republic to be a democratic and sovereign state building its relations with Russia on a partnership basis?" Documents accompanying the referendum clearly stated that voting yes would not mean secession from Russia. Manipulated by local administrators and by the mass media, the public passed the referendum by a slim margin—1 percent. Yet the results were immediately proclaimed as an expression of the people's will to an independent state. As a realization of this "will," the Tatarstan Supreme Soviet passed a new constitution in November 1992; Article 61 defines the republic as a sovereign state associated with the Russian Federation.

It seemed as though a standoff was imminent. But after two years of intensive negotiations, Tatarstan and the federal authorities signed a treaty in February 1994. It grants more responsibilities and rights to the republic

and also demonstrates symbolically the possibility of peacefully accommo-
dating even the most radical nationalist scenarios. By concluding this
treaty with Moscow authorities, the Tatarstan government has achieved at
least three goals: strengthening the republic's position and legitimacy, eas-
ing potentially dangerous tensions betweeen the two major local ethnic
groups, and minimizing the political role of Tatar extremists.

Other republics carefully watched the dispute between Kazan and
Moscow. Regional leaders soon learned that challenging the center was
much more impressive and legitimate when framed in the language of
ethnonational demands. In confronting this challenge of political nationalism, the federal authorities had to negotiate more responsibly than in
cases of mere regional separatism (as when Yeltsin simply dismissed the
local governor of the self-proclaimed Urals Republic in the Sverdlovsk administrative region).

Thus, moderate official ethnonationalism became an appealing model
for other ethnoterritorial elites of how to behave in the federal political
arena. That is why republican leaders in Russia still strongly oppose any
attempts to grant equal status to all units ("subjects") of the federation or
to deprive the republics of their constitutional definition as "national
states." They see in these moves a danger of losing a special status based
not on economic or demographic resources but on ethnicity, a factor
viewed in post-Soviet societies as indispensable for claiming political power.

Not all ethnonationalists on Russia's periphery are choosing negotiations over military confrontation. Separatist leaders in the Chechen republic
of the Northern Caucasus opted for a coup-d'état style of political behavior since fall 1991 when the former Soviet general Dzhokar Dudayev
proclaimed an independent Chechnya. Here, nationalism has proven quite
literally to be "ethnicity plus an army."

Seizing army arsenals throughout the republic and supplying arms to
the local population, Chechen leaders created internal disorder and a situation ripe for outside interference. Over 100,000 ethnic Russians left the
republic, causing great damage to the local economy. Oil production fell
under the control of criminal structures, and local clans started to compete
for dividends and prestigious positions. Armed groups refused to obey decrees and orders issued by Dudayev. As a result, civic life in this republic
disintegrated, bringing great economic and social sufferings. In September 1994, the opposition forces declared war on Dudayev's regime and the
federal authorities provided support for this opposition. After the failure
of the November assault on Grozny, Dudayev started to regain his popularity and the federal center found itself in an awkward position. Encouraged by incompetent generals, Yeltsin decided to suppress Chechnya by
massive military force. These ambitions led to the escalation of the conflict
into a large-scale war.

Chechen militant nationalism has sent a strong message to its potential proponents. Its irresponsible strategy has had a sobering effect on
other regions of the country where ethnonationalism is still strong. Eth-

nic leaders in Russia are becoming more interested in avoiding conflict-generating confrontations, thus following the Tatar and not the Chechen lead. For instance, at a meeting in January 1995 in the Hague, top leaders of breakaway regions met with senior officials of Russia, Ukraine, Georgia, and Moldova to discuss conflict avoidance and resolution. All agreed that the case of Tatarstan, not Chechnya, should be presented as a model. Russia was not above criticism, however. As the president of Tatarstan noted,

> In an effort to find nonviolent ways to resolve the status of Tatarstan, we conducted negotiations for three years with President Yeltsin. We managed to arrive at a compromise and we signed the Treaty on the Mutual Delimitation and Delegation of Authority. . . . The Treaty is a safeguard against the possible unitary development of Russia. The imperial mentality, unfortunately, is still prevalent in Russia today. The main point now is to focus on building a democratic federation.[29]

Compared with the failure of compromise in Chechnya, this kind of persistent nonviolent nationalism has become an encouraging model for many secessionist leaders. Even the most aggressive Abkhazian separatist leader, Vladislav Ardzinba, has changed his uncompromising position. According to *The Economist*, "rebels in Abkhazia said they would give up their struggle for independence from Georgia, citing Chechnya as evidence that the West would do nothing to help separatist states."[30]

In contrast to the conservative status-quo quality of hegemonic nationalism, periphery nationalism usually challenges the order of things and prefers an "exit" from the system. This "revolutionary" stance makes periphery nationalism no less conflict-generating than hegemonic nationalism. The violent ethnic protests in Transdniester (Moldova), Abkhazia (Georgia), Karabakh (Azerbaijan), and Chechnya (Russia) have all failed to achieve their stated goals and have led to huge destruction and loss of life. The main reason for this lack of success has generally been the disparity in resources between the minority combatants and the dominant state.

Despite and often because of this disparity in resources, periphery nationalism continues to erupt. Certain factors are critical for determining this transformation of ethnonationalism from "mild to wild." First, a particular historical and socioeconomic background—for instance, the real or imagined "historic injustices" and the suffering of previous generations, transmitted through literary texts or oral tradition—is needed to mobilize the emotions of rank-and-file fighters to support the elite's programs. Second, charismatic leaders are needed, recruited from the intelligentsia willing to sacrifice relative comfort for the sake of social transformation; these leaders must be capable of formulating irrational appeals to rally people to the "interests of the nation." Third, the leaders require access to military arsenals or money for arms to build up paramilitary groups. Finally, the minority rebels require both internal allies and outside support such as local nontitular or military garrisons of the Russian army, as happened in Abkhazia and Transdniester. Outside support may also range from the insti-

tutions of the international community to mercenaries who travel from
one hot spot to the next. The most powerful outside resource is an ethnic
diaspora that can provide decisive support for secessionists.

Some separatist projects are lucky in one respect and unsuccessful in
others. The Chechens benefited from having a charismatic and militant
leader imposed by the center to carry out local "de-communization" after
the failed 1991 putsch in Moscow. The Chechens also received a great
deal of military ammunition from the corrupt Russian military. However,
the Chechens made a fatal mistake by expelling ethnic Russians from the
republic, causing in-group rivalries as well as provoking Russians elsewhere
in the federation. Because of its weak diaspora and reputation for organized crime, the Chechens received only belated and formal international
support. Finally, the Chechens did not challenge a weak and disoriented
new government, as in Georgia or Moldova, but the authoritarian rule of
the Kremlin and its massive military machine.

To date, separatist projects on the territory of the former Soviet Union
have neither fully failed nor been completely successful. Clearly, however,
the prize cherished by periphery ethnonationalists is inadequate; instead
of acquiring a proper voice and thus improving governance, they aspire to
exit the system and build their own states.

Civic Nationalism

Russia has another tradition of nationalism to draw on that is more benign than either the hegemonic or periphery varieties. The roots of this
civic nationalism can be found in earlier Russian history and the attempts
of intellectual and political figures to construct the idea of a Russian (*Rossi-
iskaya*) nation.[31] This Russian nationalism was collectivist and authoritarian by character but not purely ethnic in appeal. First of all, several early
advocates of the Russian nation—Aleksandr Pushkin, Nikolai Karamzin,
Konstantin Aksakov—were of mixed ethnicity. More important, however,
the very notions of the people (*narod*) and nation were used with the ad-
jectives *rossiskii* and *russkii*, both synonyms at that time for the Russian
state, not the Russian ethnic group. Before the Bolsheviks came to power,
Russian hegemonic nationalism carried strong elements of this civic nationalism and its emphases on nation-building and policies of integration.
The new regime interrupted the process of civic nation-building and substituted instead an ethnic formula for nation-building. Soviet citizens
embarked on a journey of hardships and moments of glory that stretched
across seven decades. This experience of a unitary Soviet state produced
a real commonality, which communist ideologists and social scientists
awkwardly propagated as the "new historical entity of a unified Soviet
people" and Western writers ironically labeled Homo Sovieticus. This
overarching Soviet identity reflected in a common language, historical experience, cultural values, patterns of behavior, and interpersonal ties still
remains after the breakup of the Soviet Union. It could not be abolished

overnight by state decrees and political appeals. Rather, this identity is transforming itself into new post-Soviet patriotisms linking new state polities.

In calling for cultural pluralism and the equality of all citizens, this civic nationalism/patriotism in its mild and nondiscriminatory forms is a more promising project for the demographically, culturally, and politically complex societies of all the successor states. If Russian ethnonationalism connotes the exclusivism and intolerance of the majority toward the minority, civic nationalism or "Rossian" patriotism asserts its legitimacy on *étatist* principles and feelings. Unfortunately, in the turmoil of the Chechen war, this patriotism is more about the integrity of the country than about consolidating multiethnic people with equality and respect. Non-Russians are therefore skeptical of civic nationalism, which they see simply as a camouflage for Russian chauvinism or a modern version of the "Soviet peoples" doctrine. At the same time, because the majority of non-Russians live outside their own autonomous regions, they are more inclined to accept non-exclusive civic (Rossian) and ethnic identities. Many of them feel more comfortable with a doctrine of nation based on the idea of co-citizenship

In today's Russia, despite vocal hegemonic and periphery ethnonationalists, civic nationalism remains a viable policy choice, and this is not only because of the liberal orientation of the Russian government. Put bluntly, ethnonationalism would be an extremely harmful and unrealistic political line for the country's leaders to take. Although comprising one of the most homogeneous successor states with 80 percent of the population, Russians live side by side with 27 million non-Russians, many of whom enjoy territorial autonomy and are politically well organized. Any strong linkage of the state and its doctrines with ethnic exclusivism would immediately strengthen centrifugal aspirations among these non-Russians. Moreover, the top Russian leaders come from varied ethnic backgrounds: Ukrainians, Jews, Armenians, Chechens, Avars, Tuvans, as well as people of mixed ethnic heritage who are strongly tied to Russian culture but meanwhile keep their distinct or multiple ethnic identities.

At the level of federal authority, therefore, Russian ethnonationalism unavoidably transforms itself into a variant of civic nationalism or patriotism. When Yeltsin speaks of himself or is called by others the leader of the "nation," the nation here refers to all the multiethnic people of Russia, not just ethnic Russians.

It is possible that, with some prodding, nationalism can turn in this more positive direction. It can expand the realm of protection in which individuals and groups are shielded from the brutalities and oppression of others, and it can expand individual autonomy. Nonexclusivist nationalists are capable of recognizing the value of not only their own cultures, but also those of others, and of supporting political regimes that safeguard such pluralism. There are still good prospects for this kind of nationalism to emerge in a future Russia.

Notes

1. Dubravka Ugresić, "Parrots and Priests: 'Before' and 'After' in Yugoslavia," *Times Literary Supplement*, May 15, 1992, p.12.

2. William Pfaff, *The Wrath of Nations: Civilization and the Furies of Nationalism* (New York: Simon and Schuster, 1993).

3. Roman Szporluk, *Communism and Nationalism: Karl Marx Versus Friederich List* (New York: Oxford University Press, 1988); Walker Connor, *The National Question in Marxist-Leninist Theory and Strategy* (Princeton: Princeton University Press, 1984).

4. Zbigniew Brzezinski, "Post-Communist Nationalism," *Foreign Affairs*, Vol. 68, No. 1 (Winter 1989–90), p.2.

5. Yuri Slezkine, "The USSR as a Communal Apartment, or How a Socialist State Promoted Ethnic Particularism," *Slavic Review*, Vol. 53, No. 2 (Summer 1994), p.414.

6. *Bol'shaya Sovetskaya Entsiklopedia*, Vol. 17 (Moscow: Soviet Encyclopaedia Publishing House, 1974), p.375.

7. Slezkine, op. cit., p.414. Also see Albert Nenarokov, *K edinstvu ravnykh: kulturnye faktory ob'edinitel'nogo dvizhenia sovetskikh narodov, 1917–1924* (Moscow: Nauka, 1991), pp.91–93.

8. Ernest Gellner, *Nations and Nationalism* (Oxford: Basil Blackwell, 1983), p.1.

9. Ronald Suny, "Nationalism and Ethnic Unrest in the Soviet Union," *World Policy Journal*, Vol. VI, No. 3 (Summer 1989), p.528.

10. See Yulian Bromley, *Ocherki teorii etnosa* (Moscow: Nauka, 1983).

11. Liah Greenfeld, *Nationalism: Five Roads to Modernity* (Cambridge, MA: Harvard University Press, 1992), p.11.

12. Asbjorn Eide, "In Search of Constructive Alternatives to Secession," paper prepared for the United Nations Sub-Commission on Prevention of Discrimination and Protection of Minorities, 1993, p.5.

13. For more on the history of Russian nationalism, see John Dunlop, *The Faces of Contemporary Russian Nationalism* (Princeton: Princeton University Press, 1993) and *The New Russian Nationalism* (New York: Praeger, 1985).

14. "Pamyat" in *Russkoie delo segodnya*, Vol. 1, ed. I. Erunov and V. Solovei (Moscow: Institute of Ethnology and Anthropology, 1991).

15. See Valery Tishkov, "Russians as a Minority: The Estonian Case," Working Papers in Urgent and Applied Ethnology, No. 52 (Moscow: Institute of Ethnology and Anthropology, 1993); Valery Tishkov, "Russians in Central Asia and Kazakhstan," Working Papers in Urgent and Applied Ethnology, No. 51 (Moscow: Institute of Ethnology and Anthropology, 1993); Pål Kolstø, "The New Russian Diaspora," *Journal of Peace Research*, March 1994.

16. In June 1992, Yeltsin issued a decree legitimizing the movement and its claim to the exclusive defense of ethnic Russians residing in autonomous republics.

17. *Moskovskie Novosti*, August 28–September 4, 1994, p.11.

18. Gennadi Zyuganov, *Derzhava*, second enlarged edition (Moscow: Informpechat, 1994), p.77.

19. *Rech*, No. 1 (1993), p.4.

20. RNS leader Aleksandr Sterligov, a former KGB general and associate of former vice president Aleksandr Rutskoi, has fulminated in print against Zionist conspirators and internationalism with an anti-Russian face. *Russkii Sobor*, No. 10 (1994), p.2.

21. Aleksandr Barkashov, "Krisis mirovoi tsivilizatsii, rol' Rossii i zadachi russkogo natsionalnogo dvizhenia," *Russkii Poryadok*, No. 1–2 (1995), p.2.

22. Valery Solovei, "Natsionalizatsiya rezhima budet prodolzhatsya," *Nezavisimaya Gazeta*, March 15, 1995, p.3.

23. Andranik Migranian, "1995—god velikogo pereloma ili okonchatel'nogo krakha rossiiskoi gosudarstvennosti," *Nezavisimaya Gazeta*, January 17, 1995, pp.1–2.

24. Solovei, op. cit.

25. See, e.g., Ronald Grigor Suny, *The Making of the Georgian Nation* (Bloomington: Indiana University Press, 1991); Azade-Ayse Rorlich, *The Volga Tatars: A Profile in National Resistance* (Stanford: Hoover Institution Press, 1986).

26. Ronald Grigor Suny, *The Revenge of the Past: Nationalism, Revolution, and the Collapse of the Soviet Union* (Stanford: Stanford University Press, 1993), p.97.

27. Ibid., pp.112–113.

28. A. P. Kashkachakov, *Shoriyu–Shortzam!* (Zemlya Sibirskaya: Dal'nevostochnaya, 1992), No. 11–12, p.14.

29. *Bulletin of the Network of Ethnological Monitoring and Early Warning of Conflict* (Cambridge, MA: Conflict Management Group, 1995), p.11.

30. *The Economist*, February 18, 1995.

31. See Valery Tishkov, "What is Rossia? Prospects for Nation-Building," *Journal of Peace Research*, March 1995.

3

Cosmopolitanism Versus Nationalism: The New Divide?

MARY KALDOR

In a celebrated article in *Foreign Affairs*, Samuel Huntington envisages that the post–Cold War world order will be defined by the "clash of civilizations"—Western, Confucian, Japanese, Islamic, Hindu, Slavo-Orthodox, Latin American, and possibly African.[1] The problem with his paradigm, as he calls it, is that it is still based on territorial assumptions: civilizations supplant ideological blocs and/or nation-states as a way of classifying human beings into vertically organized categories associated with chunks of territory.

Consider Sarajevo. As of this writing, the city is divided territorially between a Bosnian Serb-controlled part and a Bosnian (mainly Muslim) part. Huntington would argue that Bosnia represents the borders of three civilizations—Slavo-Orthodox, Islamic, and Western. But Sarajevo can also be defined in terms of a non-territorial divide. There is a group of people who can be described as cosmopolitans—U.N. peace-keepers, humanitarian aid workers, journalists, and Sarajevans who speak English and are employed as assistants, interpreters, and drivers. Protected by armored cars, flak jackets, and blue cards, these cosmopolitans move more or less freely in and out of the city and across the territorial divide. They are distinguished from the non-cosmopolitan inhabitants of the city: those in the besieged section are prey to sniper fire and occasional shelling, and live off humanitarian aid or the black market (if they are lucky enough to have Deutschmarks); for those on the other side, material conditions are somewhat better, although the climate of fear is worse. On both sides they are vulnerable to the press gang and the various militias and mafia-types that roam the streets and claim a particularistic legitimacy.

Sarajevo is emblematic of a historical transformation currently underway in the world, akin perhaps to that which produced nation-states. As a consequence of this transformation, the fundamental ways in which we classify human beings will no longer be identified with territory. There will, of course, be particularistic clashes about claims to territory, but the defining classification will be non-territorial. It will be the product of a growing cultural dissonance between those who see themselves as part of an international network, whose identity is shaped within a globally linked and oriented community of people who communicate by e-mail, faxes, telephone, and air travel, and those who still cling to or who have found new types of territorially based identities even though they may not actually live in the territory. Both are contemporary forms of identity that emerge from the conditions of the modern world. While the latter may take the guise of traditional nationalism, it is actually a new phenomenon. It is much more particularistic and fragmenting than earlier forms of nationalism and, at the same time, it is often transnational in character since it is much more prone to reach beyond territory through new networks in the diaspora.

This new divide is associated with a process variously described as globalization, post-Fordism, or post-industrialism. The new nationalism can be understood as a reaction to that process, although its specific characteristics are shaped by evolving political and social circumstances. It is a process that began to intensify during the past two decades but became much more transparent in the aftermath of the events of 1989.

In what follows, I will describe some of the key features of the process of globalization and the factors that shape the new nationalism. I will then put forward some suggestions for a cosmopolitan agenda to overcome or manage the new divide.

One preliminary qualification: the new nationalism is primarily a European phenomenon, especially East European. While the new divide between non-territorial cosmopolitan communities and various territorial and non-territorial types of particularistic and parochial communities is global, the forms of particularism vary. In other parts of the world, they may take the form of religious communalism, tribalism, clanism, and so forth. Although in this essay I focus on European nationalism, the analysis is relevant to other forms of particularism.

The Characteristics of Globalization

In his book *Nations and Nationalism*, Ernest Gellner analyzes the association between nationalism and industrialization.[2] He describes the emergence of secular, locality-tied national cultures based on vernacular languages that enabled people to cope with the demands of modernity—everyday encounters with industry and government. As varied rural oc-

cupations were replaced with factory production and as the state intrud-
ed into more and more aspects of daily life, people needed to be able to
communicate both verbally and in writing in a common administrative
language, and they had to acquire certain standardized skills. Earlier societies were characterized by pan-regional "high" cultures, such as Latin,
Persian, and Sanskrit, which were based on religion and not necessarily
linked to the state. These were combined with a great variety of vertical
"low" folk cultures.

The process of globalization, it can be argued, has begun to break up
these vertically organized cultures. Emerging instead are new, secular, horizontal cultures arising from the expansion of transnational networks alongside a medley of local, national, and regional cultures resulting from a new
assertion of particularisms.

The term globalization conceals a complex, contradictory process that
actually involves both globalization and localization, integration and fragmentation, homogenization and differentiation. On the one hand, the
process creates inclusive transnational networks of people. On the other
hand, it excludes and atomizes large numbers of people, indeed the vast
majority. On the one hand, people's lives are profoundly shaped by events
taking place far away from where they live and over which they have no
control. On the other hand, there are new possibilities for enhancing the
role of local and regional politics through linkages to global processes.

In the economic sphere, globalization is associated with a set of
changes variously described as post-Fordism, flexible specialization, and
fujitsuism. These changes refer generally to a shift in what is known as the
techno-economic paradigm—the prevailing way in which the supply of
products and services is organized to meet the patterns of demand. The
relevant features of these changes are the dramatic decline in the importance of territorially based mass production, the globalization of finance
and technology, and the increased specialization and diversity of markets.
Improved information means that physical production is less important as
a share of the overall economy both because of the increased importance
of services and because a larger proportion of the value of individual products consists of know-how—design, marketing, legal and financial advice.
Likewise, the standardization of products, which is linked to territorially
based economies of scale, can be supplanted by greater differentiation according to local or specialist demand. The implication is that global and
local levels of economic organization have grown in importance while national levels of organization, associated with an emphasis on production,
have correspondingly declined.

Globalization also involves the transnationalization and regionaliza-
tion of governance. There has been, since World War II, an explosive
growth in international organizations, regimes, and regulatory agencies.
More and more activities of government are regulated by international
agreement or integrated into transnational institutions; more and more
departments and ministries are engaged in formal and informal forms of

cooperation with their equivalents in other countries; more and more policy decisions are delegated upward to often unaccountable international
forums. At the same time, the past two decades have witnessed a reassertion of local and regional politics especially but not solely for development purposes. This reassertion has taken a variety of forms ranging
from science- and business-led initiatives as in the case of "technopoles"
like Silicon Valley or Cambridge; a rediscovery of municipal socialist traditions as in Sheffield, England, or Northern Italy; peace- or Green-led
initiatives such as nuclear-free zones or waste-recycling projects; as well
as new or renewed forms of local clientelism and patronage.[3]

Parallel to the changing nature of governance has been a striking
growth in nongovernmental organizations (NGOs), both those that un-
dertake functions formerly assumed by government, such as humanitarian
assistance, and those that campaign for global issues, such as human rights,
ecology, and peace.[4] These NGOs are most active at the local and transnational levels partly because these are the sites of the problems they are concerned with and partly because the formulation of national policy remains
the closely guarded province of nationally organized political parties.
Thus, organizations like Greenpeace or Amnesty International, though
known all over the world, nonetheless have relatively limited influence on
national governments.

These economic and political changes also involve far-reaching changes
in organizational forms. Most societies are characterized by structural uniformity or what Bukharin called a "monism of architecture."[5] In the modern era, nation-states, enterprises, and military organizations have had very
similar vertical forms of hierarchical organization, reflecting the pervasive
and persistent effects of war-time economies, particularly that of World
War II, on organizational forms. Robert Reich, in his book *The Work of
Nations,* describes how enterprises have been transformed from national
vertical organizations, where power is concentrated in the hands of owners at the top of a pyramid-shaped chain of command, into global phenomena whose organizations most resemble a spider's web, with power in
the hands of those who possess technical or financial know-how and who
are spread around the points of the web:

> Their dignified headquarters, expansive factories, warehouses, laboratories,
> and fleets of trucks and corporate jets are leased. Their production workers,
> janitors, and bookkeepers are under temporary contract; their key researchers,
> design engineers, and marketeers are sharing in the profits. And their distin-
> guished executives, rather than possessing great power and authority over this
> domain, have little direct control over much of anything. Instead of impos-
> ing their will over a corporate empire, they guide ideas through the new webs
> of enterprise.[6]

Something similar is happening to governmental and nongovernmental organizations. Government departments, at all levels, are developing
transnational links; government activity is increasingly contracted out

through various forms of privatization and semi-privatization. The decentralized and horizontal forms of organization typical of NGOs or new social movements are often contrasted with the traditional, vertical forms of organization typical of political parties.[7] Political leaders, like corporate executives, are, at most, facilitators and opinion shapers; at the least they are images or symbols—public representations of interconnected webs of activity over which they have little control.

Globalization has profoundly affected social structures as well. The traditional working classes have declined or are declining in tandem with territorially based mass production. Because of improvements in productivity and because production work is less skilled, manufacturing production employs fewer and lower-paid workers, especially women and immigrants, or has relocated to low-wage countries.

What has increased is the number of people Alain Touraine calls information workers[8] and Reich terms symbolic analysts—those people who possess and use know-how; who solve, identify, and broker problems through "manipulations of symbols—data, words, oral and visual representations."[9] These are the people who work in technology or finance or in the growing myriad of transnational organizations. The majority of people fit neither of these two categories, however. They either work in services, as waiters and waitresses, salespersons, taxi drivers, cashiers, and so on. Or they join the growing ranks of unemployed made redundant by the productivity increases associated with globalization. This emerging social structure is reflected in growing income disparities both between those working and those not working and among workers on the basis of skill level.

Income disparities are also associated with geographical disparities, both within and across continents, countries, and regions. Within the advanced industrialized world, comparative advantage has shifted from the United States to Japan and to some parts of Europe because of their technological edge in the new paradigm, and this is expressed in international disequilibrium. More important than this imbalance is the growing disparity between these advanced industrial regions that capitalize on their technological capabilities and the rest of the world. Some areas may thrive, at least temporarily, by attracting volume production—for instance, Southeast Asia, Southern Europe, and potentially Central Europe. The remainder are drawn into the global economy as traditional sources of livelihood disappear, but they do not participate very much in either production or consumption. Maps drawn by global enterprises of the segmentation of their markets generally leave out this larger part of the world. Finally, within countries and even within cities—and this is true of both the advanced industrial world and the rest—physical boundaries are being drawn between protected and prosperous cosmopolitan enclaves (what Reich calls "symbolic analytical zones") and the anarchic poverty-stricken areas beyond.

The trends outlined above are simultaneously haphazard and constructed. There is no inevitability, for example, about the growth of social, economic, and geographical disparities; in part, they are the consequence of disorganization or of organization evolving out of past inertia. What can, however, be accepted as a given is the historic shift away from vertical cultures, characteristic of the era of the nation-state, which gave rise to a sense of national identity and of security. Abstract symbols like money and law, which form the basis of social relations in societies no longer dominated by face-to-face interactions, were a constitutive part of these national cultures.[10] It is now commonplace to talk about a postmodern "crisis of identity"—a sense of alienation and disorientation that accompanies the decomposition of cultural communities.

It is also possible, however, to point to certain emerging forms of cultural classification. On the one hand, there are those who see themselves as part of a cosmopolitan community of like-minded people, mainly well-educated information workers or symbolic analysts, who spend a lot of time on airplanes, in teleconferences, and so on, and who may work for a global corporation, an NGO, or some other international organization, or who may be part of a network of scholars or athletes or musicians. On the other hand, those who are excluded may or may not see themselves as part of a local or particularistic (religious or ethnic) community.

As yet, these emerging cultural groupings are not politicized or at least are hardly politicized. That is, they do not form the basis of political identities—identities that could define political communities on which new forms of power could be based. One reason is the individualism and anomie that characterize the current period: the sense that political action is futile given the enormity of current problems, the difficulty of controlling or influencing the web-like structure of power, the cultural fragmentation of horizontal networks and particularistic loyalties. Both what Reich calls the laissez-faire cosmopolitan, who has "seceded" from the nation-state and who pursues his or her individualistic consumerist interests, and the restless young criminals, the new adventurers, to be found in all the excluded zones reflect this new identity-less tendency.

Nevertheless, there are seeds of politicization in each grouping. Cosmopolitan politicization can be located both within the new transnational social movements and at certain levels of international organization around a commitment to human values (universal social and political rights, ecological responsibility, peace and democracy, etc.) and to the notion of transnational civil society—the idea that self-organized groups, operating across borders, can solve problems and lobby political institutions. Meanwhile, the new nationalist ideologies can be viewed as a form of particularistic politicization—as an attempt to construct or recreate an identity that is capable of mobilizing the excluded. Thus, the emergence of the new nationalism can be interpreted as a response to these global processes, but its specific form has to be explained in terms of an immediate concatenation of circumstances that expresses the growing impotence of nation-states.

The New Nationalism

Gellner defines nationalism as "a political principle, which holds that the political and the national unit should be congruent."[11] Definitions of nation are notoriously elusive—language, culture, race, and religion are all criteria but never apply universally. What all communities that define themselves as a nation share, however, is the exclusive claim to territorial sovereignty. As Elie Kedourie has written,

> The theory of nationalism admits of no great precision, and it is misplaced ingenuity to try and classify nationalisms according to the particular aspect they choose to emphasise. What is beyond doubt is that the doctrine divides humanity into separate and distinct nations, claims that such nations must constitute sovereign states, and asserts that the members of the nation reach freedom and fulfilment by cultivating the peculiar identity of their own nation and by sinking their own persons in the greater whole of the nation.[12]

The new nationalism that has emerged during the past two decades has involved both a renewed commitment to existing nation-states and a rediscovery or reinvention of past greatness and past injustices. Thus, secessionist claims to new states are often based on the more or less artificial construction of some ancient lineage. Nationalism tends to involve either irredentist claims—claims to Greater Serbia, Greater Russia, and more recently, Greater Italy—or secessionist claims. This is because the territory is rarely coterminous with the nation as defined.

All nationalisms are based on a "we–them" distinction in which the "them" are enemies who generally pose potential military threats and have to be excluded from the claimed territory. Ethnic nationalism, which characterizes much of Eastern Europe, is a particularly virulent form of exclusivism, in which the "we" is defined as an *ethnie*, a common culture that can only be acquired through birthright and not assimilation. Ethnic cleansing, which has been the goal of wars in the former Yugoslavia or the Caucasus, involves the expulsion of all members of different ethnic groups—hence the huge numbers of refugees. In Western Europe, movements like the National Front in France, the neo-fascists in Italy, or the neo-Nazis in Germany are characterized by their hostility to foreigners. Although there are more benign forms of nationalism in both halves of Europe, in every case in this globalized world, the claim to a state, traditionally understood, necessarily involves a measure of exclusivism.

Nationalism should be distinguished from progressive demands for greater regional or local autonomy. Globalization does involve decentralization of decision-making and a reassertion of politics at the local and regional levels. The extent to which this can enhance democracy depends on whether these demands are part of a cosmopolitan project and whether local institutions, groups, and individuals have access to and, indeed, influence on global centers of decision-making. In other words, local autonomy can only be enhanced through increased global or regional integration. The claim to a state implies a much more absolutist form of political sovereignty where borders are clearly defined and "we" are distinguished from "them."

This definition of nationalism in terms of the claim to territorial sovereignty also applies to other forms of particularisms in other parts of the world, especially religious fundamentalism. In Northern Ireland or in South Asia, communalism has more to do with exclusive political claims than with the content of religion. What is important is religious identity, not religious beliefs. And in many cases—Northern Ireland, for instance—religious identity is a birthright; it cannot be acquired, at least for the purposes of communalism, through conversion. In the historical context of the division of human beings into nations, many religious groupings were transformed into nations. The transformation of the Jews in Europe into a race or a nation is brilliantly described by Hannah Arendt in *The Origins of Totalitarianism*.[13] The Catholics in Ireland and the Bosnian Muslims have undergone a similar transformation.[14]

The new nationalism has two main sources, both linked to globalization. First, it can be viewed as a reaction to the growing impotence and declining legitimacy of the established political classes. From this perspective, it is a nationalism fostered from above that plays to and inculcates popular prejudices. It is a form of political mobilization, a survival tactic, for politicians active in national politics either at the level of the state or at the level of nationally defined regions, as in the case of the republics of the former Yugoslavia or the former Soviet Union or in Wales, Bretagne, or the Basque provinces. At the same time it emerges out of what can be described as the parallel economy—new legal and illegal ways of making a living that have sprung up among the excluded parts of society—and constitutes a way of legitimizing these new shadowy forms of activity. Particularly in Eastern Europe, the events of 1989 compressed the impact of globalization both in undermining the nation-state and releasing new forms of economic activity into a short "transitional" space of time so that this nationalism from below joined with nationalism from above in an explosive combination.[15]

The use of nationalism as a form of political mobilization predates 1989. In the former communist multinational states in particular, national consciousness was deliberately cultivated in a context in which ideological differences had been disallowed and when societies had, in theory, been socially homogenized and "socially cleansed."[16] Nationality, or certain officially recognized nationalities, became the main legitimate label for pursuing various forms of political, economic, and cultural interests. This was especially important in the former Yugoslavia and Soviet Union, where national difference was "constitutionally enshrined."[17]

Particularly important in this respect was the functioning of economies of shortage. In theory, planned economies are supposed to eliminate competition. They do, of course, eliminate competition for markets. But this gives rise to another form of competition—competition for resources. In theory, the plan is drawn up by rational planners and transmitted downward through a vertical chain of command. In practice, the plan is "built up" through a myriad of bureaucratic pressures and subsequently "broken down." In effect, the plan operates as an expression of bureaucratic compromise and, because of the "soft budget" constraint, individual enterprises always spend more than is planned. The consequence is a vicious circle in which shortage intensifies the competition for resources and the tendency among ministries and enterprises for hoarding and autarchy, which further intensifies shortage. In this context, nationality becomes a tool that can be used to further the competition for resources.[18]

Already in the early 1970s, a number of writers were warning of a nationalist explosion in the former Soviet Union as a result of the way in which nationality policy was used to prop up the decaying socialist project.[19] In a classic article, published in 1974, Teresa Rakowska-Harmstone used the phrase "the new nationalism" to describe "a new phenomenon which is present even among people who, at the time of the revolution, had only an inchoate sense of a common culture."[20] Soviet policy created a hierarchy of nationalities based on an elaborate administrative hierarchy in which the status of nationalities was linked to the status of territorially based administrative units—republics, autonomous regions, and autonomous areas. Within these administrative arrangements, the indigenous language and culture of the so-called "titular" nationality were promoted and members of the titular nationality given priority in local administration and education.[21] The system gave rise to what Victor Zaslavsky has described as an "explosive division of labour"[22] in which an indigenous administrative and intellectual elite presided over an imported Russian urban working class and an indigenous rural population. The local elite used the development of national consciousness to promote administrative autonomy, especially in the economic sphere.

Something similar took place in the former Yugoslavia, especially after the 1974 constitution entrenched the nations and republics that made up the federation and restricted the powers of the federal government. Moreover, the former Yugoslavia was exposed to the global economy much earlier than elsewhere in Eastern Europe. The reaction to structural adjustment and deregulation was simultaneously an increased tendency toward autarchy and restrictive practices within the different republics and autonomous provinces, and a nationalistic appeal by local elites (or opposition intelligentsia) to the increasing numbers of unemployed and rural poor. In economic terms, the new statelets made their appearance during the 1980s before the formal disintegration of the Yugoslav state.[23]

What held these states together was the monopoly of the Communist Party. In the aftermath of 1989, when the socialist project was totally discredited, the monopoly of the party was finally broken, and democratic elections were held for the first time, nationalism erupted into the open. In a situation where there is little to distinguish parties, where there has been no history of political debate, where the new politicians are hardly known, nationalism becomes a mechanism for political differentiation. In societies where people assume that they are expected to vote in certain ways, where they are not habituated to political choice and may be wary of taking it for granted, voting along national lines becomes the most obvious option.

Nationalism represents both a continuity with the past and a way of denying or "forgetting" a complicity with the past. It represents a continuity partly because of the ways in which it was nurtured in the preceding era (not only in multinational states) and partly because its form is very similar to the preceding Cold War ideologies. Communism, in particular, thrived on a we–them, good–bad, war mentality and elevated the notion of a homogeneous collective community. At the same time, it is a way of denying the past because communist regimes overtly condemned nationalism. As in the case of rabid attachment to the market, nationalism is a form of negation of what went before. Communism can be treated as an "outside" or "foreign" ideology particularly in countries occupied by Soviet troops, thus exculpating those who accepted, tolerated, or collaborated with the regime. National identity is somehow pure and untainted in comparison with other professional or ideological identities that were determined by the previous context.

Some similar, although much less pronounced, tendencies can be observed in the rest of Europe. The erosion of legitimacy associated with the growing impotence of the nation-state and the corrosion of autonomous sources of social cohesion became much more transparent in the aftermath of 1989. It was no longer possible to defend democracy with reference to its absence elsewhere. A specifically Western identity defined in relation to the Soviet threat was undermined. And the distinctive character of national identity lost its substance in relation to the Cold War; for example, Gaullism in France, the British special relationship with the United States, or the Greek role as East–West broker in the Balkans. Germany is, of course, a special case, gaining a new national identity in the ruins of the Berlin Wall and making possible the rediscovery of buried history.

Of equal significance is the political vacuum, the decline of the left, and the narrowing space for substantive political difference. Nationalism, or seeds of nationalism like asylum laws, are exploited by political parties across the spectrum. The left offers no clear opposition, if any, particularly those parts of the left discredited by the fall of communism. Le Pen and his National Front draw support from former communist voters, while PASOK, the Greek socialist party, plays the nationalist card.[24]

Western countries do not, of course, share the mentality of collectivism. Democratic culture is established; the experience of political choice is genuine. Nevertheless, the distrust of politicians, the alienation from political institutions, the sense of apathy and futility that provides fertile grounds for populist tendencies is growing. Among the reasons are the "secession" of the new cosmopolitan classes and the fragmentation and dependence of those excluded from the benefits of globalization.

The other main source of the new nationalism is the parallel economy. This is, to a large extent, the product of neo-liberal policies pursued in the 1980s—macroeconomic stabilization, deregulation, and privatization— which effectively represented a speeding up of the process of globalization. By increasing unemployment, resource depletion, and disparities in income, these policies provided an environment for growing criminalization and the creation of networks of corruption, black marketeers, arms and drug traffickers, and so on. Often these networks are linked to wars—for instance, in Afghanistan, Pakistan, and large parts of Africa—and to the disintegration of the military-industrial complex in the aftermath of the Cold War. Often they are transnational, linking up to international circuits of illegal goods sometimes through diaspora connections.

A typical phenomenon is the new bands of young men—the new adventurers—who make a living through violence or threats of violence, who obtain surplus weapons through the black market or looting military stores, and who either base their power on particularistic networks or seek respectability through particularistic claims. Hostage-takers in the Caucasus capture people to exchange them for food, weapons, money, other hostages, and even dead bodies; mafia-rings in Russia demand protection; the new Cossacks put on their traditional uniforms to "protect" Russian diaspora groups in the "near abroad"; nationalist militia groups of unemployed youths in Western Ukraine or Western Herzegovina all feed, like vultures, on the remnants of the disintegrating state and the frustrations and resentments of the poor and unemployed. A similar breed of restless political adventurers is to be found in conflict areas in Africa and South Asia.[25]

The new nationalism combines these two sources of particularism in varying degrees. Former administrative or intellectual elites ally with a motley collection of adventurers on the margins of society to mobilize the excluded and abandoned, the alienated and insecure, for the purposes of capturing and sustaining power. In conditions of war, such alliances are cemented by shared complicity in war crimes and a mutual dependence on the continued functioning of the war economy. One explanation for the ferocity of nationalist sentiment in the former Yugoslavia, apart from the vicious experiences within living memory, is that all the various sources of the new nationalism are concentrated there: the former Yugoslavia had the most Westernized, indeed cosmopolitan, elite of any East European country, thus exacerbating the resentments of those excluded; it experienced nationalistic bureaucratic competition typical of economies of shortage; and since it was exposed to the transition to the market earlier than other East European countries, its parallel economy was more developed.

The new nationalism may appear on the outside to be a throwback to the past. But while memory and history are certainly important elements, it has entirely new contemporary attributes. First of all, it is non-territorial as well as territorial, transnational as well as national. In nearly all the new nationalisms, the diaspora plays a much more important role than formerly because of the speed of communications. There are two types of diaspora: the first consists of minorities living in the "near abroad"; they are fearful of their vulnerability to local nationalisms and are often more extreme than those living on home territory. They include Serbians living in Croatia and Bosnia-Herzegovina, Russian minorities in all the ex-Soviet republics, and the Hungarian minority in Vojvodina, Romania, Ukraine, and Slovakia. The second type consists of disaffected groups living far away, often in the new melting-pot nations. They find solace in fantasies about their origins that are often far removed from reality. The idea of a Sikh homeland, Khalistan; the notion of uniting Macedonia and Bulgaria; and the call for an independent Ruthenia all originated from diaspora communities in Canada. Irish-American support for the Irish Republican Army (IRA), violent conflict between the Greek and Macedonian communities in Australia, the pressure from Croatian groups in Germany for recognition of Croatia are further examples. These groups provide ideas, money, arms, and know-how often with disproportionate effects. Among the individuals who make up the new nationalist compact are romantic expatriates, foreign mercenaries, dealers and investors, and Canadian pizza-parlor owners.

There is another reason why the new nationalism cannot be said to be a simple throwback to the past. The new nationalism is much more particularistic and fragmenting than earlier nationalisms. It is about labels much more than substance; national identity is no more than a label, not a prerequisite for democratic participation or cultural regeneration. Labels can be divided and subdivided as individual adventurers seize their own independent routes to power.

Finally, the new nationalism has its own evolving organizational forms. It makes use of new technology, especially the electronic media—television and videos—to disseminate its message. It is brutal and authoritarian, although it does not necessarily depend on vertical hierarchies of command since control can be exercised through communicative networks and the manipulation of images. The Serbian war machine is an example of the deceptive nature of appearances. It has at its disposal the stores of mass-produced weapons that formerly belonged to the Yugoslav National Army (JNA). Many of its officers and soldiers were formerly part of the JNA, yet the war machine operates more like a coalition of independent warlords connected to each other and Belgrade through efficient means of communication and mutual dependence.[26]

Toward a Cosmopolitan Agenda

The new nationalism is a counterproductive project. The main implication of globalization is that territorial sovereignty is no longer viable. The effort to reclaim power within a particular spatial domain will merely further undermine a group's ability to influence events. This does not mean that the new nationalism will go away. Rather, it is a recipe for new closed-in chaotic statelets with permanently contested borders dependent on continuing violence for survival.

Nor is it possible to envisage, in the long run, protected fortresses of cosmopolitan communities busily identifying, solving, and brokering the problems of how to increase their own enjoyment. Globalization, as the term states, is global. Everywhere, in varying proportions, those who benefit from globalization—the new cosmopolitans—have to share territory with those excluded from its benefits who are nevertheless deeply affected by it. Both losers and gainers need each other. No patch of territory, however small or large, can any longer insulate itself from the surrounding chaos.

A cosmopolitan political project has to be able to cross the divide between these two groupings. It must be able to offer an appealing and convincing alternative around which people can be mobilized, which can overcome apathy, resignation, and fear, and can compete with particularisms. Such a project would have to be elaborated through the demand for or access to new types of political institutions that would be able to:

1. Direct transnational problem identifying, solving, and brokering activities away from the current preoccupation with electronic gimmickry, financial speculation, health fads, and similar concerns and toward the problems of poverty, resource depletion, pollution, and the control of violence.
2. Intervene in nation-states to protect local communities and provide space in which local problems can be identified, solved, and brokered.

In effect, such political institutions would have to establish a transnational rule of law. In other words, there would have to be certain transnational mechanisms for controling violence and enforcing certain transnational legal norms, which could, if necessary, override national sovereignty. These institutions would also have to have regulatory powers and budgetary resources that would enable them to redistribute and restructure economic activities. Nevertheless, they would differ from states in that they could not command exclusive or absolute sovereignty and they would operate horizontally within diverse fields of activity, such as the environment or security, rather than vertically within clearly defined territories. The European Union (EU) at present comes closest to being a model of such an institution in that it operates horizontally in the economic and social fields and can, on certain issues, override national sovereignty. One can imagine other institutions—say, U.N. agencies—developing these characteristics.

In effect, such institutions would constitute a new transnational layer of governance that would co-exist with other layers—national, local, and regional. This new diversity of political institutions might resemble the premodern period in Europe, which was characterized by multiple, overlapping sources of political power, including city-states, principalities, kingdoms, and the Holy Roman Empire. The crisscrossing of horizontal issue-based political institutions and vertical overlapping territorially based political institutions could be described as the "new medievalism."[27]

This layering of governance would differ from the present situation in that the national level would simply become one layer, not the exclusive site or ultimate arbiter of political sovereignty. Entities known as nation-states would still exist, but they would share power with other layers of governance. They would not enjoy absolute control over territory or over a range of issues or fields of activity that might be managed at global, local, or regional levels. They would be subject to more and more transnational laws, they would not be able to use violence unilaterally, and they would not unilaterally control the supply of money.

Precisely because of the complexity and web-like structure of modern global society, such transnational political units would have to exercise power primarily on the basis of consent; traditional vertical forms of coercive power are increasingly ineffective. They might use force in their role as transnational law enforcers, but the legitimacy of this use of force would depend on consent and some form of accountability through democratic institutions. And this consent would in turn depend on the emergence of a cosmopolitan political consciousness in the Kantian sense, in which "a right violated in one part of the world is felt everywhere."[28] There has to be a sense of belonging to a political community with a shared commitment to uphold human values.

Two possible sources of a cosmopolitan political consciousness can be identified. One, which could be described as cosmopolitanism from above, is to be found in the growing myriad of international organizations, a few of which, most notably the EU, are developing supranational powers. These institutions develop their own logic and internal structures. They enable activities to be carried out rather than undertaking them through their own resources. They function through complex partnerships, cooperation agreements, negotiation, and mediation with other organizations, states, and private or semi-private groups. They are restricted both by lack of resources and, relatedly, by the intergovernmental arrangements that make it extremely difficult to act, except on the basis of time-consuming and often unsatisfactory compromises. In many of these institutions, there are committed idealistic officials. They have an interest in seeking alternative sources of legitimacy to their frustrating national masters.

The other source is what could be described as cosmopolitanism from below, the new social movements and NGOs that have developed over the past two decades primarily in response to new global problems. These movements differ from earlier social movements. They tend to be horizontal rather than vertical in organization, operating most effectively at local and transnational levels. Their form of activism tends to be individualistic. They are usually skeptical about politics. They express their individual commitments through vegetarianism or driving convoys of aid to war zones. Although they have in the past organized mass demonstrations, their actions tend to be symbolic or spectacular, in the manner of the Greenpeace vessel, *Rainbow Warrior*. Terms like "anti-politics," "self-organization," and "civil society" express their disaffection with conventional political forms.

Yet such movements cannot entirely dispense with power. As with international organizations, they too are blocked by the dominance of nation-states and nationally organized politics. Access to national politics is denied by the continued sway of political parties while transnational and local political units, to which the new movements increasingly have access, are weak and vulnerable to the pressures of nation-states. Essentially, a cosmopolitan project would involve a reconceptualization of democracy not in terms of the formal procedures that currently characterize national politics, although formal procedures are necessary, but in terms of a redistribution of power. Political power is currently concentrated at the level of nation-states despite the fact that nation-states have become ever more impotent. If democracy is understood as empowerment, then new forms of effective and accountable political units must be constructed that can provide a framework in which individuals and groups, if they choose, can have space to act and participate in decision-making that affects their lives. In other words, the divide between cosmopolitanism and nationalism can be interpreted as a contest for the post-nation-state political order—between those who favor a new diversity of transnational, national, and local forms of sovereignty and those who want to build fractional territorial fiefdoms.

At present, cosmopolitanism and nationalism coexist side by side in the same geographical space. Cosmopolitanism tends to be more widespread in the West and less widespread in the East and South. Nevertheless, throughout the world, in remote villages and towns, both sorts of people are to be found. The new particularistic conflicts throw up courageous groups of people who try to oppose war and exclusivism—both local people and those who volunteer to come from abroad to provide humanitarian assistance, to help mediate, and so forth. Local groups gather strength insofar as they can gain access to or support and protection from transnational networks. Perhaps the biggest failure in the former Yugoslavia was the failure of the international organizations involved—primarily the U.N. and the EU—to recognize that their natural partners were local peace and human rights groups, however small; that their role was not to mediate and find compromises between particularistic groups; and that no solution based on borders in a globalized world has any long-term future. Rather, the role of international organizations should have been to support, listen to, and offer proposals that could foster local sources of cosmopolitanism.

As chaos spreads, the space for cosmopolitanism is narrowed. More and more no-go areas come into being like Rwanda or Afghanistan, where isolated humanitarian agencies gingerly negotiate and bribe their way through to help those in need. Some argue that such situations are the harbingers of the future for much of the world.[29] Nothing is more polarizing and more likely to induce a retreat from utopian inclusive projects than violence. "Sarajevo is Europe's future. This is the end of history," the city's disenchanted cosmopolitans will tell you. But politics is never predetermined. Whether another future can be envisaged is, in the end, a matter of choice.

Notes

1. Samuel P. Huntington, "The Clash of Civilizations?," *Foreign Affairs*, Vol. 72, No. 3 (Summer 1993).

2. Ernest Gellner, *Nations and Nationalism* (Oxford: Basil Blackwell, 1983).

3. See Margit Mayer, "The Shifting Local Political System in European Cities," in *The Global-Local Interplay and Spatial Development Strategies*, eds. Mick Dunford and Grigoris Kafkalas (London: Belhaven Press, 1992); also Manuel Castells and Peter Hall, *Technopoles of the World: The Making of 21st Century Industrial Complexes* (London: Routledge, 1994).

4. Figures on the upsurge of private, nonprofit activities in various parts of the world, sometimes known as the "associational" revolution, are provided in Lester M. Salamon, "The Rise of the Non-profit Sector," *Foreign Affairs*, Vol. 73, No. 4 (July/August 1994).

5. Nikolai Bukharin, *Economics of the Transformation Period* (New York: Bergman, 1971).

6. Robert Reich, *The Work of Nations: Preparing Ourselves for 21st Century Capitalism* (London: Simon and Schuster, 1993), p. 97.

7. Alberto Melucci, *Nomads of the Present: Social Movements and Individual Needs in Contemporary Society* (London: Hutchinson Radius, 1989).

8. Alain Touraine, *The Post-Industrial Society* (New York: Random House, 1971).

9. Reich, op. cit., p. 178.

10. Anthony Giddens calls these symbols "embedding mechanisms." The key characteristic of modernity was what he calls "time-space distanciations," in which social relations can be constructed with "absent" others. He defines globalization as a stretching of time-space distanciation. See Anthony Giddens, *The Conditions of Modernity* (Cambridge: Polity Press, 1990).

11. Gellner, op. cit., p. 1.

12. Elie Kedourie, *Nationalism*, 4th ed. (London: Basil Blackwell, 1993), p. 67.

13. Hannah Arendt, *The Origins of Totalitarianism* (London: Allen and Unwin, 1958).

14. Dzikover Rebbe wrote in 1900: "For our many sins, strangers have risen to pasture the holy flock, men who say that the people of Israel should be clothed in secular nationalism, a nation like other nations, that Judaism rests on three things, national feeling, the land, and the language, and that national feeling is the most praiseworthy element in the brew and the most effective in preserving Judaism, while the observance of the Torah and the commandments is a private matter depending on the inclination of each individual. May the Lord rebuke these evil men and may he who chooseth Judaism seal their mouths." Quoted in Kedourie, op. cit., p. 70.

15. I am indebted to Ivan Vejvoda for this point.

16. The term is used by Katherine Verdery in "Nationalism and National Sentiment in Post-Socialist Romania," *Slavic Review*, Vol. 52, No. 2 (Summer 1993), pp. 179–203.

17. Ibid.

18. This argument is also used by Katherine Verdery. See, in particular, "Ethnic Relations, Economies of Shortage and the Transition in Eastern Europe," in *Socialism: Ideals, Ideology and Local Practice*, ed. C. M. Hann (London: Routledge, 1993).

19. See, for example, Andrei Amalrik, *Will the Soviet Union Survive Until 1984?* (London: Penguin Books, 1970); and Hélène Carrère d'Encausse, *Decline of an Empire: The Soviet Socialist Republics in Revolt* (New York: Newsweek Books, 1979).

20. Teresa Rakowska-Harmstone, "The Dialectics of Nationalism in the USSR," *Problems of Communism*, Vol. XXIII, (1974), pp. 1–22.

21. In many cases these titular nationalities were artificial. Tajikistan, for example, is an invented territorial unit. The Tajik language is a Persian dialect spoken in parts of Iran and Afghanistan that was given a Cyrillic alphabet. The main Tajik centers of civilization, Samarkand and Bukhara, ended up in Uzbekistan.

22. Victor Zaslavsky, "Success and Collapse: Traditional Soviet Nationality Policy," in *Nations and Politics in Soviet Successor States*, eds. Ian Bremmer and Ray Taras (Cambridge: Cambridge University Press, 1993).

23. Susan Woodward locates the new nationalism in the growing divide between the rural poor and urban employed. See her *Socialist Unemployment: The Political Economy of Yugoslavia, 1945–1990* (Princeton: Princeton University Press, 1995) and *Balkan Tragedy* (Washington, D.C.: The Brookings Institution, 1995).

24. Particularly fascinating in Greece is the way in which the civil war has been reinterpreted in recent years. Earlier it was interpreted as an ideological conflict. Had it not been for the Anglo-American intervention and the pressure on Stalin and Tito to withdraw, it was argued, Greece would have been a socialist country. Now it is argued that the main aim of the communists was to create a united Macedonia, including the Greek and Bulgarian parts. Hence anti-Macedonian attitudes represent a way of distancing oneself from a past sympathy with communism.

25. For a description of the phenomenon, see the Médecins sans Frontières report on world crisis intervention, *Life, Death and Aid* (London: Routledge, 1993).

26. At the same time that these warlords are dependent on one another they are also relatively autonomous, as became apparent when the so-called Bosnian Serb Assembly at Pale rejected the Vance-Owen plan in May 1993 despite the cajoling of Bosnian Serb leader Radovan Karadžić and Serbian President Slobodan Milošević.

27. The term was used by Hedley Bull. See *The Anarchical Society: A Study of World Order in World Politics* (London: Macmillan, 1977).

28. From Immanuel Kant, "Perpetual Peace: A Philosophical Essay," in *Kant's Political Writings*, ed. H. S. Reiss (Cambridge: Cambridge University Press, 1970).

29. See Robert D. Kaplan, "The Coming Anarchy," *Atlantic Monthly*, February 1994.

4

Fascists, Liberals, and Anti-Nationalism

TOMAŽ MASTNAK

Diese sogenannte unparteiische Geschichtsschreibung glaubt ihren Stand-
punkt in der Mitte zu haben, wenn sie gar keinen hat: sie will die Person des
Schreibenden nicht hervortreten lassen und zeigt uns daher nichts weiter als
diese blöde, urteilsscheue Ängstlichkeit: sie gibt uns nicht einmal die Fakten
rein und klar, weil sie immer nur mit Abwägen und Beschneiden beschäftigt
ist: sie will alles, auch das Nichtsnutzige, zu seinem Rechte kommen lassen
und ist daher die Ungerechtigkeit selber.[1]

"This is a great victory for democracy," one of the leaders of the self-styled
Republika Srpska, the Serbian chiefdom in Bosnia, said immediately after
negotiations with former U.S. President Jimmy Carter in December 1994.
Bosnian Serbs had successfully staged yet another peace-making diplomatic
performance, strengthening their position and adding legitimacy to their
chimerical "republic" founded on war crimes. The average Western reader (assuming that such exists) would intuitively dismiss such a statement:
"How could those Serbian nationalists possibly speak of democracy?" I
would like, however, to offer a counter-intuitive interpretation: that Bosnian Serbs are serious when they speak of democracy and that Western
spectators are wrong to dismiss these statements as so much nationalist
rhetoric. What if Bosnian Serbs are really democrats, not nationalists?

This question brings us into the middle of today's most heated political discussions. To consider this question responsibly, we must not swim in
the mainstream of contemporary political debate, for this stream contains
quite a few dead fish. Instead, I would like tentatively to explore alternative possibilities of looking at some of the key problems of the post-Cold

War world—not because I take pride or pleasure in running counter to mainstream discourse, but because I find much of this common talk intellectually unsatisfactory and politically dangerous.

It has become almost a cliché to consider nationalism the "plague" of the late twentieth century. As such, nationalism has been associated with ethnocentrism, chauvinism, xenophobia, racism, and fascism. In my view, these associations are a substitute for conceptual clarity and are bound to produce a simplistic politics of anti-nationalism, designed to avoid tackling the very phenomenon commonly linked to nationalism. One kernel of truth in the politics of anti-nationalism, however, is its aversion to the formation of new states on the ruins of the communist empires, that is, an identification of nationalism with state-building. I call this a kernel of truth because the question of state lies at the core of the problem commonly glossed over as nationalism. This question is not addressed openly. Rather, it is suppressed by talk of ethnocentrism, chauvinism, xenophobia, racism, and fascism. The real if unrecognized targets of anti-nationalism are those new, potential, or already existing states. Thus, the question needs to be raised whether the target of anti-nationalism is the state itself.

To shed light on some of these issues, I suggest beginning with a strong juridico-political notion of the nation. The concept I will use, drawing on strands of political thought often overlooked in today's debate, defines the nation as a civic territorial unit sovereignly governing itself. I understand nation neither in terms of cultural and ethnic genealogies, nor as a community—be it imagined, political, cultural, ethnic, religious, racial, historical, or other.[2] As a civic territorial unit that is not subjected to an outside supreme authority, the nation conceptually overlaps with the state. Such an identification of the nation with the state may seem a simplification. Accepting for the moment that it might be, I would still like to explore the implications of such a concept of nation for our understanding of "nationalism" and "anti-nationalism." If nothing else, such an approach can potentially challenge other simplifications more prevalent in current political discussions.

Much of the nationalism debate is less academic than politically interested. This essay may therefore also be read as a political intervention. The starting point for the politics of my argument is nationalist, that is pro-statist. I understand nationalism as state-centered. As an ideology, nationalism is a state-building and state-maintaining ideology; as politics, nationalism is the politics of the state, by the state, and for the state. As I will argue, the state was invented to establish and maintain civil order, and as long as there is no institutional alternative to perform this function, the withering away of the state can only lead to anarchy, chaos, violence, and destruction. My politics is anti-communitarian because the nation that conceptually overlaps with the state is by its nature anti-communitarian. As one of its key defining features, the state is a form of public power based on the depersonalization of power and, as such, on the separation of public authority not only from the person of the ruler but also from the body of the ruled.[3] My argument is also anti-liberal, because the liberal politics that today sways the world is anti-nationalist and anti-statist. And for the same reason, my position is also anti-fascist.

My discussion of nationalism and anti-nationalism focuses on the war in Bosnia. I will argue that this war should be understood as a war against the Bosnian state waged by Serbian anti-nationalists. I understand this war as a war of totalitarian civil society against the state. But I will also argue that in this war—on the basis of shared anti-nationalism and, consequently, common opposition to the Bosnian state—an unholy international alliance of liberals and fascists came into being.

It is difficult to determine if, and how much, the Bosnian war is paradigmatic for post-Cold War developments, a prefiguration of the world to come. Suffice it to say, the involvement of the Western powers, Russia, supranational organizations such as the United Nations, and international nongovernmental organizations (NGOs) has been too prominent to allow one to brush the Bosnian war aside as a case of Balkan exceptionalism.

"The Nation Is a Sovereign State"

A classical formulation of the statist understanding of the nation is found in Emmerich de Vattel, whose *Le Droit des Gens ou principes de la Loi Naturelle* (1758) has been characterized as "the first recognizably modern book on international law."[4] Its influence has been considerable, but not in France as one might expect. Vattel's work became the handbook of European and American statesmen, and it was used and praised by such nationalists as Benjamin Franklin and Immanuel Kant. "It came to us in good season, when the circumstances of a rising State made it necessary frequently to consult the Law of Nations," Franklin wrote to Charles Dumas, who had sent him three copies of Vattel's book.[5] And Kant advised his students that the best they could read on *jus gentium* was Vattel.[6]

Vattel summed up the tradition of thought that some 50 years later Jeremy Bentham christened "international law." At the same time Vattel's work represented a break within the tradition of the law of nations. The aspect of this break of special interest to my argument is Vattel's rejection of the idea of one great republic, of a universal state or world community. Vattel formulated his position in polemics with Christian Wolff's *Jus Gentium*, arguing that Wolff fallaciously deduced the voluntary law of nations from the "idea of a sort of great republic (*civitas maxima*), set up by nature herself, of which all the nations of the world are members." Consequently, the law of nations would be the civil law of the universal republic, which Vattel considered a groundless assumption, a useless fiction.[7]

The contractual theory of the formation of the state, shared by both Wolff and Vattel, could not be, in the latter's view, applied to the relations between nations. "I know no other natural society between nations except that one only that nature established between all men," Vattel argued. "It is in the essence of every *civitatis* that each member should yield part of his rights to the body of society, and that there should be an authority capable of giving commands to all its members, giving laws to them, and constraining those who would refuse to obey. It is impossible to conceive of, or suppose, anything like that between nations."[8] Nations are to be considered "free individuals," the state a "nation apart."[9] "The Nation is here a Sovereign State, an independent Political Society," and as such subject to international law that "reigns between nations or sovereign states."[10]

This is a brief (and unavoidably simplifying) summary of the modern understanding of nation. I accept it as the departure point for my argument, even though it is easy to anticipate objections. As an abstract formulation, this conceptual coincidence of nation and state cannot do justice to all possible "real-life situations." However, as a formulation of theoretical principles, it provides normative standards for understanding (and judging) historical realities. One consequence of the conceptual overlapping of nation and state is that one cannot think of the two engaging in conflict. What is often seen as states lining up against nations and nations against states must be conceptualized differently. If, on the one hand, we take France versus Provence as an example of "states opposing nations," Provence is not a nation but an ethnic community. The concept of nation I have proposed dissociates the nation from ethnicity, shared culture, and historical destiny.

On the other hand, let's take as examples of nations opposing states the developments in ex-Yugoslavia and ex-Soviet Union. First, especially in the Yugoslav case (with the exception of Serbia that I will discuss later), the entities that have constituted themselves as nations—that is, the constituent states of Croatia, Slovenia, Bosnia, and Macedonia—were initially conceived not as ethnic communities but as political and administrative units; under the old regime, they had existed as semi-nations/states. Second, it is open to discussion whether ex-Yugoslavia or the ex-Soviet Union conformed to the modern notion of state. Even assuming they were states in the modern sense of the word, they had ceased to function as such prior to the formation of these new nations.

If the nation, in modern international law, equals the state, and the state is subject to this law and can only exist in systemic relations to other states, we still need to consider, however briefly, the state "in itself." The state, as I understand it, is the most distinctive political invention of modernity. The invention of the state—as is well known but often not well comprehended—was a response to social violence ravaging late medieval and early modern Europe. The state was conceived and instituted in order to put an end to that violence by disarming society, and monopolizing and legalizing the means and the use of violence. The creation of a sovereign public authority—that is, supreme, indivisible, absolute power—over a clearly delineated territory made it possible to establish and maintain civil order and guarantee basic security to those living under its jurisdiction.

As an "abstract entity above and distinct from both the government and the governed," the state can be seen not only as "impersonal in character,"[11] but also as non-social, stripped of social determinants that had informed the social warfare against which it had been raised (and that could at any time generate the violence of all against all). Abstract in this sense, the state could, for example, prevent religion from authorizing violence. The complement of this freedom of the public authority from social determinants was that residence in the territory ruled by a state, not social qualities or virtues, qualified a person for citizenship. Moreover, the concept of law implied in the state's monopoly on legalized violence was abstract and equal for all the citizens.

This is a rudimentary—and if one wants to see it this way, undemocratic—notion of the state. The state here is an institutional setting concerned not with the common good (or happiness) but rather with civil order. Or, to put it less drastically, the state is concerned with the common good only insofar as *status civilis* is a common good. As Kant commented, "What constitutes the principle of state establishment and the idea of the state is not the principle of general happiness but freedom according to general law."[12] As the modern public authority maintaining civil order, the state is a peace-enforcing and peace-keeping institution. Indeed, the peace of modernity was a state-made peace, and the security of modern Europe was conceptually and practically built around the state.

Although quite elementary, this view is not universally shared. And disagreements about elementals tend to be radical. Those concerned with peace both in the past and today commonly blame the state for war and believe that there will be no peace until states cease to exist.[13] What these pacifists happily overlook is that the invention of the state succeeded in ending indiscriminate social warfare. And while war cannot realistically be done away with by irenic decrees, wars between states are limitable and controllable in principle. Charging the state with "structural violence," pacifists refuse to see that the alternative is structureless violence, a scenario presently unfolding in former Yugoslavia. The war in Bosnia has been represented as one large peace-keeping operation, and Western politicians seem to be determined to build peace on the ruins of the state.

"Civil Society Against the State" Revisited

The war in Bosnia has been conceived, started, and directed by anti-nationalists, unveiling the true face of anti-nationalism. It is the latest—but not necessarily the last—of the wars that have followed the dissolution of Yugoslavia, and it is in Bosnia that the nature of this warfare is most fully expressed. Post-Yugoslav wars have not been wars between states, but against states. The aim of the first military campaign was to prevent Slovenia from constituting itself as a state. In the next move, military force was used to destroy the new Croatian state. And the war in Bosnia is a war against the Bosnian state.

The aggressor in all these wars has been Serbia, and Serbia, as I see it, is not a state, properly speaking. Like a medieval ruler possessed of a bundle of rights that some historians mistake for sovereignty, the Serbian regime contains an assortment of apparatuses that states normally need to perform their functions and that therefore has led many an observer to believe that Serbia is a state. But Serbia has no internationally recognized borders.[14] The regime in Belgrade has territorial claims on neighboring states and has so far refused to recognize the internationally recognized borders of Bosnia and Croatia. That Belgrade has usurped the name of Yugoslavia and claims to be the inheritor of Yugoslav statehood is not a juridical fact. It is true that Western and Russian diplomats flock to Belgrade to persuade Serbian president Slobodan Milošević to exercise his power on Serbian racial formations in territories not under his jurisdiction. But this diplomatic activity does not constitute international recognition of the Belgrade regime. It simply makes these diplomats accomplices in that regime's criminal policy.

The idea of the Serbian "state"—that is, the Serbian *Reich*—is based on blood and soil (*Blut und Boden*), and this racial construct contradicts the essence of citizenship. In Serbia today, there is no equality of law, which is one of the defining characteristics of the state. Different laws apply—and the same laws apply differently—to those who are considered subhuman, like Kosovo Albanians. There is no monopoly on the means and use of violence. The regime's (or the ruling party's) repressive apparatuses are thus only the largest among many armed gangs.

What is mistakenly taken to be the Serbian state is a fascist regime of a new type, and fascism (as I will argue below) is a non-state, if not an anti-state. Those who describe Milošević's rule as communist and neo-Bolshevik, as a relic of the now old world order, are wrong. This is a new type of power and domination: a *sui generis* fascism that is shaping the new world order to a greater degree than anyone would comfortably like to believe. No less wrong than those still haunted by the specter of communism are those who see the Serbian regime as a materialization of nationalism. Serbia is, in fact, the bastion of anti-nationalism in ex-Yugoslavia. With Milošević's ascent to power the Serbian nation has dissolved into "the people." Like Nazism in Germany, the new Serbian fascism is based on the *Volkwerdung der Nation*—the nation becoming the people.[15] The Serbian regime, in contrast to the surface image of dictatorial presidential rule, can be understood as a direct democracy founded on *Blut und Boden*. Serbia is a totalitarian community, an unbounded civil society lacking its counterpart, the state.

It is this entity—or rather, from the statist point of view, non-entity—that has attacked the Bosnian state. Because of its unexpected cruelty, which resembles what in the Middle Ages was called *bellum mortale* or war to the death, the Bosnian conflict has been often interpreted as an atavism, a simple case of Balkan tribalism. But the war in Bosnia is neither social atavism nor a return to the Middle Ages. It is a postmodern war of civil society against the state, a war of Serbian (and, for a period, Croatian) civil society against the Bosnian state.

This characterization of the Serbian regime as a totalitarian civil society, and of the Bosnian war as a war of civil society against the state, requires a brief explanation of what is meant by "civil society." The use of this concept here is both dependent on and at odds with the recent civil society discourse. While possessing a long tradition in Western political thought, civil society was also reinvented in the 1970s in Eastern Europe, from where it migrated to the West.[16] It is this reinvention that has shaped our current understanding of the concept of civil society.

In the Eastern Europe of the 1970s and 1980s, the concept of civil society framed and directed the democratic opposition to the communist *ancien régime*. In that context, civil society was conceived of as a sphere different from, independent of, and opposed to the state. The basic viewpoint was that of "civil society against the state."[17] Because it was the leading idea of those who professed to struggle for democracy, civil society began to represent the morally good pole against the evil (corrupt, repressive, totalitarian) state. This moralization of the concept, resulting in civil society becoming a value, has overshadowed the analytical potential of the concept.

Already in the 1970s and 1980s, the majority of those speaking the language of civil society had been turning a blind eye to the undemocratic and anti-democratic elements and potential of civil society. Civil society came to stand for democracy, and democracy was accepted as the unquestionable good. The strengthening of civil society was seen as proportional to the growth of democracy: more civil society, more democracy.

But the concept of civil society only makes sense in relation to the state. If we look at the concept in a longer historical perspective, the decisive shift in the meaning of civil society occurred in the late eighteenth century in classical German philosophy, the Scottish Enlightenment, and—to a lesser degree—in the writings of French liberals and some English radicals. This new conceptualization defined civil society as the counterpart to the state, a sphere distinct from state action (*Staatswirksamkeit*). This modern meaning of the concept lay at the basis of the reinvention of civil society in Eastern Europe of the 1970s and 1980s. And in this perspective, civil society, as distinct from and opposed to the state, is a necessary condition of democracy—but not necessarily democratic itself. It is the tension between the independent society and the state that is a condition of democracy. As soon as one of the two spheres prevails, eliminating the other, democracy is threatened or lost. In late communist Eastern Europe, the state was seen as all pervasive and the democratic struggle focused on the construction of social spaces independent of the state. But equally ruinous for democracy would be if civil society ousted the state.

Unfortunately, those involved in civil society discourse and struggles, having indulged in the idea of "anti-politics," failed to seriously address the question of the state. While in their democratic imagination they tried to limit state action by reconstructing civil society, they neglected the question of limits on civil society itself. Undermining the totalitarian power of the communist state, they left the gate open for a new type of totalitarianism—that of an unlimited civil society. This unlimited civil society, though a contradiction in terms, nonetheless helps us better understand the current situation in Bosnia.

Perhaps the most significant political development of the war was when the Bosnian political leadership refused to be the model civil society championed in the West. This refusal came after the possibilities for the existence of such a civil society had been bombed to the ground, with Western consent. "One thing is certain," said Enes Duraković, the former Bosnian Minister of Education, "Sarajevo is not going to be the zoo of multiculturalism to which Europeans come to admire what they have helped to destroy."[18] With this shift of perspective, the Bosnian leadership adopted as the aim of their struggle the development and defense of the state. Because European politicians have made them "Muslims," the state the Bosnians envisage is a Muslim (but not Islamic) state.[19] "The creation of this state is *jihad par excellence*," the new Minister of Education has stated.[20] With the awakened consciousness of the importance of the state among Bosnians, it has become even clearer that what is at stake in this war is the state.

Bosnia has been emphatically called "the last Balkan state" and "the only true state in the Balkans,"[21] and in their war against it Serbian fascists have not been alone.

The West's Bosnia Policy

Western policy has not been a failure. The destruction of the Bosnian state has also been the aim of Western policy, led by England and France, and skillfully manipulated by Russia. The West has been assisted by several NGOs and by supranational organizations led by the United Nations. A prevailing feature of this policy has been anti-nationalism.

The West consistently opposed the dissolution of the unitary Yugoslavia, especially after that state had already ceased to exist. Subsequently, it has supported and lent legitimacy to the anti-state in Belgrade. And it has sought to prevent the formation of new states on the territory of former Yugoslavia, mistaking the state-building for the cause, rather than the result, of the breakup of the federal state. When the politics of prevention turned out to be ineffective, the West denied existence to these new states for a considerable period by refusing to recognize them diplomatically (as in the cases of Slovenia and Croatia). While Western anti-nationalists encouraged war against nationalists, Serbian anti-nationalists were eager and creative projectors and executioners of such a policy.

The expeditious recognition of Bosnia-Herzegovina might have, for a moment, looked like a turn in Western policy. The most unfortunate victims of this illusion, however, have been the Bosnians and their government. It is not only that the recognition was inconsequential. Even before it happened, Western politicians, along with their Serbian counterparts, had already elaborated the ethnic division of the country (the cantonization plan of March 1992) that effectively undermined the possibility of a Bosnian state. With much map drawing, this policy was followed throughout the war, recognition of Bosnia notwithstanding, only to be solemnly reconfirmed in July 1994 by a Euro-American-Russian consortium's "international plan" for the ethnic partition of Bosnia-Herzegovina.

The European political elite, animated by French *esprit* and solidly based on English custom, has been consistently imposing as a peaceful solution the very same idea that the Serbian—and for a time Croatian—military and paramilitary forces have been putting into practice with their genocidal war. Serbian war and European peace have been two faces of one and the same policy. This partition is now being hailed as the *Endlösung*, the final solution, of the Bosnian crisis. As envisaged from the start, the final solution was the wholesale destruction of the Bosnian state. And this holocaust is not a simple remake of what we have sworn would never happen again. Half a century ago, the people almost exterminated by fascists with Western consent were given a state; now another people is being exterminated by fascists with the consent of the heirs of Chamberlain and Pétain in order to deprive them of their state.

This ethno-policy, then, is anti-statist and anti-nationalist in principle and in practice because it contradicts the defining abstractness of the state and the socially indifferent equality of its laws. Moreover, Western powers, lately joined by the Russians, have been systematically dismantling the very structures of public authority in Bosnia, thus not only undermining the government but also making any kind of civil order impossible. The deconstruction of the Bosnian government by Western politicians is a Herostratian masterpiece of our times.[22] Here, postmodernism has been much more than vacuous jargon. Western diplomats seem to have felt no discomfort in promoting Serbian war criminals from Bosnia as "statesmen," as their equals. They have also chosen to treat Bosnian Croats, who were represented in, and by, the Bosnian government, as a separate entity. Finally, the government was declared representative only of Bosnian Muslims (thus invoking the primordial European fear and hatred of the Muslim) and put on an equal footing with self-styled Croatian leaders and Serbian terrorists. Instead of treating the latter as outlaws, the West has outlawed, as it were, the elected Bosnian government,[23] making it a problematic "warring faction." While the state has been reduced to an ethnic group, the enclaves of ethnic banditry have been treated as "states."

The United Nations entered Bosnia not to stop the war but to manage it. In full agreement with the U.N.'s mission of global dispensation of injustice, and loyally following the objectives set by the leading Western powers, this international management of the war in Bosnia has effectively ruled out the existence of a Muslim state in Europe. A key aspect of U.N. policy has been to create a language with which to understand the war in Bosnia, a language as clean as American "surgical strikes" in the Persian Gulf war, and to apply enforced conformity (*Gleichschaltung*) to coverage of the war to ensure that world media serve and promote U.N. objectives. But the central piece of U.N. policy in Bosnia has been the arms embargo: the denial of the right of self-defense to the Bosnian state. Practically, this measure ensured the initial military successes of the Serbian aggressors and terrorists, and made possible the genocide that has prepared the way for the country's ethnic division. Normatively, it deprived the Bosnian government of a state's basic prerogative: the sovereign right to make war (without which the right to make peace has no meaning).

This unmaking of the Bosnian state through the arms embargo has profound implications for international law. It destroys the one certainty on which the security of the modern European order has been based.[24] If Bosnians have been slaughtered like sheep, one should see both the hand that slaughters them and the hand that ties them to be slaughtered.[25] If those who kill *violate* the law, those who deny the right of self-defense sanction the killing and *annihilate* international law. Justice, inherent in the idea of law, is thus being expurgated from international relations, and the international community is turning into brigandage, a global *latrocinium*.[26] International law, at its outset, maintained that "brigands do not make war" (*latrones bellum non gerunt*)[27] because only legitimate authorities could wage war. Today, Western leaders who accept that Serbian brigands make war should themselves be considered *latrones* because they both refuse the right to make war to the legitimate government and do not themselves make war on those who are violating the international law. Together, Serbian brigands and Western leaders promote global lawlessness.

The policy of humanitarian aid has often been described as a smoke screen to hide Western political failure in Bosnia. Actually, the antipolitics of humanitarian interventionism[28] has been consistent with the overall policy of the so-called international community. If humanitarianism has saved lives, it has nevertheless contributed prominently to creating a situation in which lives are threatened and therefore need to be saved. Fundamentally, humanitarian intervention has negated civic existence. This policy has addressed Bosnians not as citizens but as "human beings," thus helping to destroy the Bosnian state and the very possibility of civic existence. Indeed, the denial of civic existence comes close to the denial of any existence. As an American historian wrote in dramatic tones before the Thatcherite and Reaganite revolutions, "In the world today, the worst fate that can befall a human being is to be stateless . . . if he is stateless he is nothing. He has no rights, no security, and little opportunity for a useful career. There is no salvation on earth outside the framework of an organized state."[29] And if one recalls the old humanist adage that if one is not a citizen, one is not a "man" (*si non est civis, non est homo*), the Western policy of humanitarian aid is dehumanizing for Bosnia and ultimately for the West as well.

NGOs are by definition not only non-statist but—if not always, then often—anti-statist. Their mandate to contract with people, not states, worships the mysticism of the "people" and practically interferes with (and potentially negates) the jurisdiction of the state whose "people" they decide to "contract." National sovereignty is an impediment to their political or anti-political free-marketeering. In Bosnia, these impediments have, to a degree, been removed. Consequently, NGOs rushed in—not to counter evil but, in the best of cases, to make it bearable, most often bearable for themselves. Some organizations have certainly done a measure of good. But the very logic of their action, and the trading of their ideas and ideologies, play into the hands of those who aim to destroy the Bosnian state. NGOs are agents of civil society; they want to strengthen civil society; and the war in Bosnia is a war of civil society against the state.

The Unholy Alliance

Anti-nationalism is a consistent political ideology, and because of this consistency it brings together seemingly incompatible political forces. The correspondence between the political language and practical policies of Serbian fascism and the predominantly liberal-democratic West is not accidental. The alliance between liberals and fascists that has come into existence with the Bosnian war is held together by their shared anti-statism.

Liberalism's main concern has always been the limitation of state power (and in this context liberals have often been willing to endorse violence). Consequently, liberalism has not developed a positive theory of state. Practical liberal statecraft aside, the liberal theory of state is negative; only its theory of non-state is positive.[30] Today, with the historic triumph of liberal democracy, liberal anti-statism has become more than ever before a global policy. It would be instructive to analyze how this anti-statism shapes the development aid policies for the "Third World." But in Europe itself, anti-nationalism is not only fashionable political jargon: considerable anti-statist tendencies are at work in the policy of "European integration." I do not think it an exaggeration to argue that this policy is deconstructing national sovereignty and thus the state, and that what is taking shape in the space rendered free of state is a universal (European) civil society. Hegel has acquired considerable ill repute for ascribing ethical qualities to the (Prussian) state. But in our own time, like in a Hegelian farce, civil society is becoming the "embodiment of the ethical idea."

The other eminently anti-statist policy gaining prominence is fascist. That the fascist state is a non-state was argued in one of the best analyses of the fascist system of power, Franz Neumann's *Behemoth*. In his view, Nazism was a social formation in which the ruling groups controlled the rest of the population directly, without the mediating role of the coercive apparatus that could be, if nothing else, considered rational and had been known as the state.[31]

Traditionally, a faith in the West as the repository of democracy has been coupled with a belief that democracy is irreconcilable with fascism. Difficult somehow to accommodate to this political religion has been the fact that democratic politics—as politics—has never defeated fascism; that fascism has never been effectively or symbolically destroyed and overcome; that democratic politicians, instead of fighting fascism, have sought appeasement. In our own times as well, Western policy toward Serbian fascism has resembled political appeasement. New developments have made such a policy easier and more credible, for one of the outcomes of the end of the Cold War is a democratic transformation of fascism.

This new fascism has adopted democratic language and, where it has established itself as the ruling system, functions within liberal democratic structures. This fascism has, in both theory and practice, accepted a multiparty system, free elections, parliamentarianism, freedom of the press, and a market economy. This fascism can therefore satisfy international conditions for economic aid tied to the establishment of liberal democracy. But these new fascists have not been motivated by the economy to make their democratic transformation. In fact, they are not primarily concerned with the economy. They have made this democratic transformation as pragmatic politicians: it makes them stronger, lets them function better.

Democratic, for example, is fascism in Serbia; democratic are Serbian chiefdoms in Bosnia and Croatia. Serbs ostensibly went to war against Croatia and Bosnia over a concern for human rights and the rights of minorities. What Serbian leaders have been saying throughout this time, and what Western ears have wanted to hear, are neither lies nor cynical manipulation (for one simply cannot manipulate political language to such an extent). It is something much more worrying. Serbian warmongers can indeed justify their actions in the language of Locke's *Second Treatise*. And the path from a Lockean "appeal to heaven" to the holy war that Serbs— the "heavenly people" as they see themselves—believe to be fighting is not a long one.

Fascism today is less a non-state than an anti-state ideology. What distinguishes this new democratic fascism from the Nazism described by Neumann is not that the ruling groups control the population without the mediation of the state, but that distinct and fixed ruling groups are disappearing. It seems that ruling, as we used to understand it, can no longer be taken for granted. The reality has become very fluid, and it is possible to imagine a state of affairs where all rule all, so that whoever happens to gain some power will use it until met by a greater force that can in turn maltreat others and engage in plunder. Situations in which everyone may rule, if only for a moment, and no one is safe, have ceased to be just fantastic images. Hobbes's famous words—about "continuall feare, and danger of violent death; And the life of man, solitary, poore, nasty, brutish, and short"—seem to be becoming a description of real life, of situations where might has been freed from the law to become the only right, where the state has ceased to exist and still existing states are being unmade. This is what I call the coming of the anti-state: civil society rising as a natural and absolute force against the state.

The war in Bosnia may be seen as a brutal expression of this tendency, stripped bare of anaesthetic political aesthetics—as a warning of a possible future, as a prefiguration of a global *ordine nuovo*. The West has watched voyeuristically as this stateless world emerges. But not only does the free market accept Serbian videotapes of ritual rape and murder, the West has been politically involved in creating this new world. This is the fruit of anti-nationalism.

What does not come as a surprise is that Italian fascists, immediately after having gained power in their own country, started to forge official ties with their Serbian brothers. If Italy is being "Serbianized," as a Bosnian newspaper commented,[32] an Italian visit to the vanguard of European fascism was indeed a political priority. Meanwhile, Serbian connections with Russian liberal-democratic fascists[33] are more longstanding. If, however, some might find the appearance of a fascist international alarming, what seems more threatening still is that such a development is neither antagonistic to nor antagonized by democratic forces. Partly, this is a result of the democratic transformation of fascism that has widened and strengthened the basis for European unity. But more important, fascists and democrats share a fundamental political interest: anti-statism. The fascist international is an element of international anti-nationalism.

Franz Neumann pictured the Nazi power as Behemoth. He was referring to the Jewish eschatology (of Babylonian origin) in which Behemoth, a male monster, ruled the land and his female counterpart Leviathan ruled the sea. Both were monsters of the Chaos. The apocalyptic writings of the Old Testament predicted that Behemoth and Leviathan would reappear shortly before the end of the world and establish a rule of terror—but would ultimately be destroyed by God. In other versions, Behemoth and Leviathan fight each other incessantly and to their mutual destruction, after which comes the day of the righteous and just who eat the meat of both monsters in a feast announcing the advent of the realm of God.[34]

Neumann's other reference was to Hobbes, to "the foundational philosopher of our political institutions."[35] It was through Hobbes that Leviathan and Behemoth entered the modern mind. Hobbes employed Leviathan as a symbol for the peace-keeping state and Behemoth as a symbol for disorder, rebellion, and civil war.[36] Or, as Neumann put it, Hobbes's Leviathan is the analysis of a state, the political system of coercion in which vestiges of law and individual rights are still preserved, while his Behemoth, discussing the English civil war of the seventeenth century, depicts a non-state, a chaos, a situation of lawlessness, disorder, and anarchy.[37]

Today, we seem to be much closer to the reign of Behemoth than 50 years ago. And it also appears that the "day of the just" is unlikely to come. For the two monsters are not destroying each other. One is winning, and with it monstrosity is winning. Liberals and fascists, joined in an anti-nationalist international, appear to be successfully destroying Leviathan all around the globe. With triumphant anti-nationalism, we are passing from order into chaos. We are entering the age of Behemoth.[38]

Notes

1. "This so-called non-partisan historiography believes its position is in the middle, yet it has no position at all; it does not want to allow the person of the writer to show, and, thus, all it shows to us is this stupid anxiety that shies away from making judgments; it does not even convey the facts neatly and clearly, because it is always busy only with weighing out and trimming; it wishes that everything, even that which is good for nothing, would be given its justice, and is consequently the injustice itself." Edgar Bauer, "Geschichte Europas seit der ersten französischen Revolution," *Die Hegelische Linke* (Leipzig: Philipp Reclam, jun., 1985), p.522.

2. On these notions, see Benedict Anderson, *Imagined Communities: Reflections on the Origins and Spread of Nationalism*, 2nd ed. (London: Verso, 1991); Anthony Smith, *National Identity* (Harmondsworth: Penguin, 1991).

3. See J. H. Shennan, *The Origins of the Modern European State 1450–1725* (London: Hutchinson, 1974), p.114; Quentin Skinner, "The State," in *Political Innovation and Conceptual Change*, eds. T. Ball, J. Farr, and R. Hanson (Cambridge: Cambridge University Press, 1989).

4. Emmerich de Vattel, *Le Droit des Gens ou principes de la Loi Naturelle, appliqués à la conduite & aux affaires des Nations & des Souverains* (Washington, D.C.: The Carnegie Institution of Washington, 1916); F. H. Hinsley, *Sovereignty*, 2nd ed. (Cambridge: Cambridge University Press, 1986), p.194.

5. Benjamin Franklin to Charles Dumas, December 1775. Cited by Albert de Lapradelle, "Introduction," in Vattel, op. cit., Vol. I, p.xxx. Cf. ibid., p.xxxv: "plus les Etats-Unis progressent, plus Vattel prend d'autorité."

6. *Kant's gesammelte Schriften (Akademieausgabe)* (Berlin: Preussische Akademie der Wissenschaften and [from Vol. XXIV on] Akademie der Wissenschaften der DDR/Akademie der Wissenschaften zu Göttingen, 1900–), Vol. XXVII/2.2, p.1392: "das beste Buch hier von nachzulesen ist Vattels."

7. Vattel, op. cit., Vol. I, "Préface," p.xvii. Cf. Christian Wolff, *Jus gentium methodo scientifica pertractatum* (London: The Clarendon Press/Humphrey Milford, 1934), Prolegomena, §§ 9–10. Cf. F. H. Hinseley, *Power and the Pursuit of Peace: Theory and Practice in the History of Relations between States* (Cambridge: Cambridge University Press, 1963), p.187.

8. Vattel, op. cit., Vol. 1, "Préface," p.xvii.

9. Ibid., pp.xvii, xviii, "Préliminaires," § 11.

10. Ibid., "Préface," pp.xiii, viii.

11. Shennan, op. cit., p.114; Skinner, op. cit., p.112; Cf. Skinner, *The Foundations of Modern Political Thought*, Vol. 2 (Cambridge: Cambridge University Press, 1978), pp.353, 358.

12. "Nicht das princip der allgemeinen Glückseeligkeit sondern Freyheit nach allgemeinen Gesetzen macht das princip der Staatserrichtung und die Idee davon aus." Kant, *Akademieausgabe*, Vol. XIX, R 7955. Cf. "Naturrecht Feyerabend": "Der Zweck der Republique ist die Administration des Rechts. Nicht einzelner Glückseeligkeit, sondern der Zustand der öffentlichen Gerechtigkeit ist die Hauptsache dabei," ibid., Vol. XXVII/2.2, p.1328.

13. "There is only one way in which war between independent nations can be prevented; and that is by nations ceasing to be independent." David G. Ritchie, *Studies in Political and Social Ethics* (London/New York: Swan Sonnenschein & Co., Ltd., 1902), p.169.

14. This—and not only this—is also characteristic of Israel, a case I cannot discuss here. But one might be tempted to see Serbian designs as an attempt to build yet another "New Israel."

15. For this concept, see A. R[osenberg], "Europa in Rom," *National-sozialistische Monatshefte*, No. 3 (1932), p. 532. In the Serbian newspeak this phenomenon was called, less *begrifflich* and more sentimentally, *dogodio se narod* (the people has happened).

16. See Manfred Riedel, "Gesellschaft, bürgerliche," in *Geschichtliche Grundbegriffe: Historisches Lexikon zur politisch-sozialen Sprache in Deutschland*, eds. O. Brunner, W. Conze, R. Koselleck, Vol. 2 (Stuttgart: Ernst Klett Verlag, 1975); Riedel, *Bürgerliche Gesellschaft und Staat: Grundprobleme und Struktur der Hegelschen Rechtsphilosophie* (Neuwied-Berlin: Luchterhand, 1970); François Rangeon, "Société civile: histoire d'un mot," C.U.R.A.P.P., *La société civile* (Paris: Presses universitaires de France, 1986); John Keane, *Civil Society and Democracy* (London-New York: Verso, 1988); Z. A. Pelczynski, ed., *The State and Civil Society: Studies in Hegel's Political Philosophy* (Cambridge: Cambridge University Press, 1984); Pelczynski, "Solidarity and the 'Rebirth of Civil Society' in Poland, 1976–81," in *Civil Society and the State: New European Perspectives*, ed. John Keane (London-New York: Verso, 1988); I discuss the reinvention of the concept in Eastern Europe and Yugoslavia in *Vzhodno od raja: Civilna druzba pod komunizmom in po njem* (Ljubljana: DZS, 1992).

17. Andrew Arato, "Civil Society Against the State: Poland 1980–81," *Telos*, No. 47 (Spring 1981), p. 24.

18. Quoted in Ervin Hladnik-Milharčič, "Zadnja balkanska država," *Mladina*, No. 51, December 28, 1993.

19. Josip Engel, a judge of the Supreme Court in Sarajevo, in an interview "Ja sam za muslimansku državu" ("I personally am for a Muslim state"), *Ljiljan*, April 6, 1994. Engel, it might be pointed out for those who care to know, is not a Muslim, but a Jew.

20. Enes Karić, "Džihad je ime naše borbe," *Ljiljan*, February 23, 1994.

21. Hladnik-Milharčič, op. cit.; and the heading of an interview with Ivo Banac, *Ljiljan*, April 6, 1994.

22. Herostratus burned down the temple of Ephesus in 356 B.C. in order to make his name immortal. [*Editors*]

23. The British Foreign Minister Douglas Hurd, a leading figure in the war against Bosnia, was happy to endorse the fascist turn in Italian politics in 1994 by saying that the Italian government was democratically elected. It appears that it never crossed his mind to apply the same standards to the Bosnian government. Cf. Hasan Rončevič, "Saveznici proizvode dugotrajni rat na Balkanu," *Ljiljan*, July 6, 1994.

24. See Richard Tuck, *Philosophy and Government 1572–1651* (Cambridge: Cambridge University Press, 1993), p. xvi, Ch. 5.

25. On New Year's Eve in 1992, crowds in Sarajevo greeted the U.N. Secretary General Boutros-Ghali with chants of "Assassin! Assassin!"

26. "Justice being taken away, then, what are kingdoms but great robberies?" St. Augustine, *De Civitate Dei*, Book 4, Ch. 4.

27. Alberico Gentili. *De iure belli libri tres* in "The Classics of International Law" (London: Clarendon Press, 1933), Book 1, Ch. 4.

28. Generally on this problem, see the thematic issue of *Middle East Report*, Vol. 24, Nos. 187–188 (1994). But Russians, too, at one point in their military

campaign against Chechnya, presented the capture of Grozny as a humanitarian necessity: they wished to cleanse the streets of corpses on which cats, dogs, and rats feed, thus to prevent the spread of infectious diseases.

29. Joseph R. Strayer, *On the Medieval Origins of the Modern State* (Princeton: Princeton University Press, 1970), p. 3.

30. This claim is to be understood against the background of the discriminative state concept to which I subscribe. If the state is modern, premodern political traditions can hardly be seen as an inspiration for the theory of state. If the origins of liberal democracy are to be found in medieval constitutionalism, this is likely to feed into what I see as a theory of non-state: as would as well a desire to revive the ideals of Italian city republics. See, for example, Brian M. Downing, *The Military Revolution and Political Change: Origins of Democracy and Autocracy in Early Modern Europe* (Princeton: Princeton University Press, 1992); and Maurizio Viroli, *From Politics to Reason of State: The Acquisition and Transformation of the Language of Politics 1250–1600* (Cambridge: Cambridge University Press, 1992), Epilogue.

31. Franz Neumann, *Behemoth: Struktur und Praxis des Nationalsozialismus 1933–1944* (Frankfurt: Fischer Taschenbuch, 1984), p. 543. See also Wolfgang Benz, "Partei und Staat im Dritten Reich," in *Das Dritte Reich: Herrschaftsstruktur und Geschichte*, ed. M. Broszat and H. Möller (München: Beck, 1983).

32. Nusret Čančar, "Zloslutna budućnost Evrope," *Ljiljan*, June 15, 1994.

33. Their leader Vladimir Zhirinovsky is of course a declared anti-nationalist (despite the misleading image Western media create of him). See the interview in which he singled out the dangers of nationalism. "Čistili boste škornje nemškim in britanskim oficirjem!" *Mladina*, No. 5. February 2, 1994. Cf. Enes Duraković, "Krvavo praskozorje panslavizma," *Ljiljan*, February 16, 1994.

34. Neumann, op. cit., p. 16; cf. Stephen Holmes, "Introduction" to Thomas Hobbes, *Behemoth or the Long Parliament* (Chicago: The University of Chicago Press, 1990), p. ix.

35. Tuck, op. cit., p. xvii.

36. Holmes, op. cit., pp. ix, xlix.

37. Neumann, op. cit., p. 16.

38. This essay was completed in December 1994.

5

Scotland's Quiet Nationalism

JOYCE McMILLAN

Successful cultural hegemony works in ways that are sometimes more mysterious and embarrassing than brutal. In the 1950s and 1960s, when I was growing up in Scotland, the idea of "Britishness" was probably stronger than at any time since the high Victorian age. The experience of World War II had created a powerful sense of solidarity among all the peoples of Britain—of England, Scotland, Northern Ireland, and Wales. The moral and actual victory of 1945 had left behind a strong and proud conviction, even among those who considered themselves patriotic Scots or Welshmen or Ulstermen, that Britain as a whole was an exceptionally "good" nation, a place of special destiny and virtue, which had led the fight against the manifest evil of Nazism. In the postwar period, the powerful structures of the war-time state and the psychological legacy of solidarity generated by the war were used to create a new "welfare state"—free health service, enlightened pension and benefit systems, good public housing, free education to university level—which gave most ordinary Britons powerful reasons to be satisfied with a polity that provided for its people on relatively generous terms. At the same time, the growth of the new broadcast media was helping to create a situation in which the whole of Britain was drawn together around a common stream of news, information, and culture produced mainly in London.

The effect on me, as a little girl of 10 or so in the early 1960s, was that although I knew I was Scottish, and was in some way proud to be Scottish, I had no idea of Scotland as an arena in which anyone could expect to lead a complete or fulfilled life. My ambition was to be a glamorous career girl, and to have a modern flat with a pink telephone. In this imaginary life, I would have a new English name (Claire Braithwaite was the one I fancied) and a boyfriend who looked like a BBC newsreader. It never occurred to me that I could do any of these things without going to London, the center of the psychological universe. I certainly knew that nothing sexy, exciting, grown-up, or modern could happen in Scotland, a place by definition bereft of glamor and power, whose culture was popularly represented, at the time, by infantilized boy-men in kilts singing ingratiating comic songs on television. In my own interest, too, parents and teachers constantly badgered me to "talk properly," that is in a more standard-English way, not to use Scottish words or grammar or too strong a Scottish accent. And like children of the British Empire everywhere, from Barbados to Benares, I was taught to regard the work of Chaucer and Shakespeare, Keats and Shelley, as the pinnacle of literary achievement in English or any other language. "Dialect" writing, we knew, was fit only for comedy.

I can remember, too, the process of education and revelation through which, as Scotland began to stir and change in the 1970s, those ingrained assumptions of mine about the status of Scottish culture began to crumble and shift. There was the moment, at university, when I first read the great, glittering Scottish poetry of the late medieval period—Henryson, Dunbar, Sir David Lyndsay's magnificent *Satire of the Thrie Estaites*— and realized, with an almost physical pain of recognition, that the Scots speech I had been taught to avoid as a slovenly and incorrect form of English was actually the surviving remnant of what had once been the court language of a powerful European state, a language fit for everything from philosophical and theological debate to rich erotic verse. There was the opening night, one evening in Edinburgh in the late 1970s, of a play (John Byrne's *Slab Boys*) that seemed to prove once and for all that Scottish culture was not a fading nostalgic phenomenon, a thing of the past, but an aspect of modernity—tough, complex, fast-moving, but still alive and present in the world of sex, drugs, and rock'n'roll.

On these occasions, I could almost hear barriers in my mind crashing down, parts of myself that had been painfully disconnected from one another by the cultural assumptions of my childhood reconnecting in great surges of energy and recognition. And this sense of escape from a cultural hegemony that devalues, stunts, or marginalizes a vital part of one's own identity is the key to the intense sense of liberation and exhilaration that people often find in the early stages of a struggle for national self-determination.

Yet for myself, I was always conscious that nationality was only one element—and probably not the most important—of the mechanism of power and powerlessness that I was coming to understand. The cultural hegemony against which I was rebelling, for instance, had as much to do with class and wealth—and with the general aspiration throughout the British Empire to the language and manners of the southern English upper middle class—as with nationality. If Scottish children were nagged to "talk properly" inside that cultural system, so were most British children not born into that narrow social stratum whose ways had been accepted as the cultural standard.

Yet it is also clear that the idea of national identity, while it provides no complete explanation of the politics of power, is a real factor in that power equation. People genuinely identify with national groupings, feel better or worse about themselves according to whether that group is powerful and respected, or weak and marginalized. Moreover, national identity is an exceptionally sharp and powerful key in unlocking existing power structures and in dreaming of alternatives. Despite the unified and essentially English face it presents to the wider world—where most people seem convinced that the terms "Great Britain" and "United Kingdom" are simply fancy synonyms for "England"—Britain has always been what its flag of three superimposed crosses shows it to be: an explicitly multinational state, formed when the Scots' Parliament reluctantly voted itself into Union with England in 1707 and when the Irish Parliament did the same in 1800. That quasi-federal structure has been masked by the unitary political system centered at Westminster and by the sheer numerical dominance of the English, who form more than 80 percent of the whole population of the British and Irish islands. But there has never been any systematic attempt to obliterate the idea of Scottish, Irish, or even Welsh identity, to make the non-English peoples of Britain describe or think of themselves as "English." On the contrary, and within limits, the British state has actually prided itself—through the names of its military regiments, and so on—on the fact of its size and diversity, and its ability to command loyalty from people of different cultural nations.

It therefore follows that whenever the British state begins to fail, whenever a large proportion of its citizens feel dissatisfied with it or rebellious against it, these strong, surviving national identities begin to re-emerge as strong psychological presences, as mini-utopias or alternative polities in which things might be managed better. Of course, the nagging unease and mild humiliation of living in a stateless nation dominated by a much larger neighbor is always present for most Scots, and expresses itself in the pain we feel when foreigners call us "English," when London commentators treat our culture as a kitsch tartan joke on the edge of serious affairs, or—most notoriously—when we see the "auld enemy" enjoying a sporting victory against anyone at all.

But throughout much of the Union's history, since 1707, most lowland Scots—a predominantly Protestant people with an Anglo-Saxon language, far more at ease in union with the English than the Irish could be—were prepared to accept that discomfort as the price of belonging to one of the most powerful and successful nations on earth, a nation whose grand imperial adventure, throughout the eighteenth and nineteenth centuries, provided ambitious Scots with unparalleled opportunities to trade and manufacture, to travel the world and help shape its modern infrastructure, to make fortunes and exercise talents on the widest possible stage. Even when the imperial dream began to fade, the British state gained a new lease on life from its victories in two world wars and from the relatively enlightened welfare-state society of the years following 1945. It was only in the 1970s—with Empire finally gone, the memories of war fading into history, the social-democratic consensus crumbling, problems of economic stagnation and mismanagement beginning to force Britain into ever-steeper decline vis-à-vis its European neighbors, and the discovery of oil in the North Sea holding forth a sudden vision of Scotland as one of the richest small nations in Europe—that the idea of a self-governing Scotland began to take root in the public imagination as a genuine and realistic alternative to the decaying British state.

But even in the mid-1970s, the most optimistic of Scottish nationalists could hardly have predicted the catastrophic failure of the politics of Union that was about to engulf the country with the election of Margaret Thatcher as prime minister in 1979. For it was not simply that the post-1979 Conservative governments—elected, as usual under the British system, on a minority of the popular vote—set about implementing a contentious free-market vision of society that was largely supported only in the populous southeast of England and was overwhelmingly rejected by voters in Scotland, Wales, and the north of England as economically foolish and morally repugnant. It was, much more seriously, that instead of reacting to this growing regional discrepancy in the mood of British politics by allowing greater local and regional autonomy, the new-model Conservative governments did the reverse: they began to centralize power, to discredit and emasculate local government, and to abolish dissident layers of municipal and regional elected authority at a rate unprecedented in British peacetime politics. Confronted by a Scottish electorate rejecting Conservative policies and politicians by a ratio of three to one, they actually stepped up their opposition to Scottish home rule and began to use the country as a testing ground for some of their most unpopular free-market policies. As a result, the Conservative share of the vote in Scotland declined, between 1955 and 1995, from over 50 percent to 20 percent or less.

Worse, this growing Conservative hostility to the idea of democratic home rule for Scotland began to be accompanied by a radical growth in the strain of reactionary Anglo-British nationalism in Conservative politics— strident, inward-looking, anti-European, and overwhelmingly southern English in accent. Like many of the reactionary new nationalisms in Europe, this surge of national chauvinism in mainstream British politics is probably best understood as a reaction to the growing powerlessness of nation-states in the face of global markets and currency speculation, a kind of knee-jerk effort by national politicians to re-assert the significance of the polities in which they work by whipping up a national pseudo-politics built around fears of immigration, hatred of the European Union and other international institutions, and increasing paranoia about dissident "enemies within." But Scots, by definition able to identify with

British nationalism only in its most liberal and culturally inclusive form, looked on at this shrill post-imperial *folie de grandeur* with increasing incredulity and a growing sense that the old liberal settlement of the British state, which had made life as a subject nation relatively congenial and tolerable, could no longer be relied on. In the early 1990s, a *Glasgow Herald* poll found 90 percent of young Scots disinclined to describe themselves as "British" at all, and a large majority ranking "Britishness" as less important to them than their identity as "Europeans."

Once again, Scots were not the only people in Britain disgusted and alienated by this new tone in British politics, by the dogma of Thatcherism, and by the coarseness and rigidity of Britain's winner-takes-all political system that took place in the 1980s. At the London launch, in January 1995, of a new campaign by Britain's growing constitutional reform movement Charter 88, there were representatives not only of reform movements in Scotland, Wales, and Northern Ireland, but of black Britons, homeless people, disabled people, public-service media workers, the unemployed, health service workers, liberal police officers, trade unionists, electoral reformers, and environmental activists, all complaining of similar feelings of marginalization and exclusion after 16 years of one-party Conservative rule.

But once again, the idea of Scotland as a viable alternative community provided a focus for criticism of the current British order and an arena in which to develop positive visions for the future that constitutional reformers in England often lacked. "Work as if you were living in the early days of a better nation," wrote the great Scottish novelist Alasdair Gray on the flyleaf of his postmodern epic *Lanark*, first published in 1981. And during the 1980s, many thinking Scots—artists and politicians, journalists, trade unionists, and church leaders—began to take him at his word.

But beyond the recognition that the old British state is facing some kind of crisis of legitimacy and identity, and must reform itself or risk disintegration, the consensus on political change in Scotland begins to fall apart. No doubt, if the British state had reached its present low ebb in the early years of the twentieth century—that period of romantic nationalism, eugenics, and loose talk about inherited national and racial characteristics—the configuration of opinion in Scotland would have been more straightforwardly nationalistic. Even now, it is difficult for a Scot to visit small European nations that gained their independence at that time—nations like the Irish Republic or Norway—without feeling a strange yearning for a Scotland that might have been, kicking the English ascendancy out of the castle like the bold boys of the Irish revolution, or like the Norwegians, rescuing a fragile northern European landscape of lochs, seacoasts, and mountains from the holocaust of population clearance and crude exploitation by absentee landlords that reduced the Scottish Highlands to their present barren, melancholy, and depopulated state.

But in the conditions of the 1990s, in Scotland as in the emergent "historic nations" of post-Franco Spain, those interested in a fuller politi-

cal expression of national identity tend to divide sharply between ideological "nationalists"—those who believe, in Gellner's terms, that the primary and sovereign political unit should always match the unit of national
identity—and those who recognize Scottish national identity as one
of many strands of culture and politics inadequately respected in the present British state but are willing to seek constitutional remedies that fall
short of full independent statehood. The full independence option, within the European Union, is gradually gaining ground and appears, in the
mid–1990s, to have the support of about a third of the Scottish electorate.
But the option of home rule within the United Kingdom is favored by
about 40 percent. And on neither side of the debate is there much nationalist fervor of the kind that makes people take to the streets, turn to
violence, or indulge in public demonstrations of discontent.

Certainly, after almost 300 years of Union, sheer lack of confidence—
alternating with brief bursts of fragile bravado—plays its part in maintaining this quiet and moderate climate of opinion. Despite Scotland's
obvious attributes as a fairly well-educated north European nation, un-
usually rich in natural resources, with a similar population to that of Denmark and a much larger land mass, the debate on Scottish independence
still has a tendency to circle round the oddly phrased question of whether
Scotland "could survive" without England. But other factors are at work,
notably the fact that despite the tensions associated with the ten-to-one
disparity in population size and influence between the two nations, the
Union has never failed Scotland, as a whole, in any catastrophic or decisive
sense. There has been no incident remotely comparable, for instance, to
the great Irish famine of 1845–50, in which the British government allowed
half the population of Ireland either to starve to death in conditions of the
most abject horror or to be driven into exile to North America, and which
played such a vital role in radicalizing and hardening the Irish nationalist
movement that won independence for the 26 southern counties two generations later. On the contrary, most Scots have tended to prosper within
the Union, and despite some appalling pockets of deprivation and demor-
alization—Glasgow, for instance, has one of the worst urban health records
in Western Europe—Scotland remains, on average, one of the richer regions
of the United Kingdom. Nations tend to turn to militant nationalism at
the moment when they feel, or are persuaded, that they must fight or die,
that the alternative to full national sovereignty is cultural or actual extinction. Scots within the United Kingdom have never, yet, been near
that position.

Then there is, understandably, an increasing skepticism about whether
"national sovereignty," in modern global conditions, represents any kind of
answer to basic social problems. Most Scots are socialists or social democrats by political persuasion. And while that fact increases their alienation
from the British state in its dogmatic free-market mode, it also increases
their skepticism about the idea of a sovereign Scottish government as a
panacea for problems like unemployment, which they can see affecting peo-

ple across Europe almost regardless of the constitutional conditions under which they live. The presence of the European Union, as an increasingly significant supranational source of authority and legislation, also tends to blunt the edge of arguments about self-determination. And a certain consciousness of the miserable track record of European nationalism in the twentieth century, reinforced by the tragic aftermath of the breakup of former Yugoslavia, probably also plays a part in cooling nationalistic fervor.

This moderate ethos is helped, too, by the fact that there is no strong tradition of official ethnic nationalism in Britain. Ever since Shakespeare penned his famous lines describing England as "this sceptred isle. . . . This precious stone set in a silver sea / Which serves it in the office of a wall," it has been traditional in Britain to regard national identity as something defined by geography instead of blood, language, or religion. That is why the British tend to become hysterical on the issue of passport controls at ports of entry, while their citizenship laws, in point of offering full civil rights to legal residents of other races and cultures once they are established in the country, are among the most liberal in Europe. The idea of "British" nationhood itself reflects a certain acceptance of cultural diversity, so that black Britons living in England often find it easier to describe themselves as "British" than "English." Mainstream Scottish nationalism follows this tradition in simply according Scottish nationality to everyone living in Scotland. Only a tiny fanatical fringe movement in Scotland—vigorously repudiated by the mainstream Scottish National Party—talks the language of blood and ethnicity in relation to Scottish nationhood. And although the egalitarian and inclusive tradition of "civic nationalism" lacks the blood-and-guts passion of ethnic nationalist politics, it also lacks its immediate connection with racism and intolerance.

But even in such a moderate, civic, and pragmatic context, something about the quest for outright national sovereignty seems to lead to a dangerous inflation of the importance of national self-determination and identity, both as an aspect of individual personality and as a guiding principle in politics. In making the case for independence as the best policy for the Scottish people, for example, the Scottish National Party must constantly imply that Scotland is suffering from a whole range of economic and practical problems, from unemployment to poor housing, precisely because it has no Scottish government looking after its specific interests, as if northern England, ruled by an English-dominated government, must somehow be in a better position, which it patently is not. Likewise, although Scottish nationalists—like their Catalan counterparts—are very keen on solidarity within the European Union, their policy of national separation requires an assumption that problems cannot be tackled by working with like-minded people in our nearest neighbor nation.

The politics of independentist nationalism, in other words, compels its advocates to exaggerate the differences of experience between Scotland and England, and to "talk down" the possibilities of human understanding and cooperation between, say, Scottish and English social democrats within the United Kingdom. Nothing upsets a Scottish nationalist ideologue more than to be reminded of the simple fact that England is not some kind of reactionary monolith but a hugely diverse nation full of people and interest groups who object to the politics of the present British state on grounds very similar to those of Scots.

The difficulty is, though, that those who try for these reasons to resist the politics of independentist nationalism, and to advocate an approach that seeks to deal with tensions by cooperation rather than separation, are continuously undermined by the behavior of existing nation-states. Suppose, for example, that what Scots want is a broadly social-democratic domestic politics, an enlightened and cooperative international politics based on strong support for the European Union, and the chance to elect a Scottish legislature that, in or out of the United Kingdom, will control those aspects of Scottish domestic policy currently administered by the Scottish Office (the U.K. government department in charge of Scottish affairs), and will represent Scottish opinions, interests, and culture on the wider European stage. How, pragmatically speaking, are they to reach that point?

Ideally, they ought to be able to do so by a process of campaigning and discussion within the British state. But despite the formation of campaign after campaign and the existence since 1988 of the Scottish Constitutional Convention—a huge forum for home rule and constitutional reform within the United Kingdom that brings together an overwhelming majority of elected representatives from Scottish local authorities and the Westminster and European parliaments, as well as churches, trade unions, women's organizations, and other civic bodies—Scotland's aspirations in this direction have been dismissed by the British government with contempt and abuse. The national politicians who still dominate political affairs do, of course, pay lip service to the principles of pluralism, civility, minority rights, the rule of law, and the resolution of disputes by debate and consensus. But in practice, they seem dedicated only to an ugly realpolitik dominated by two guiding principles: the preservation of the prerogatives of sovereign national governments and the maintenance of order within their own borders. Under this system, Boris Yeltsin can get away with describing the vicious war in Chechnya as "an internal matter." Under this system, European nations are allowed to exercise their "right" to turn the Roma people of Europe into a caste of stateless non-citizens. And under this system, Scots plodding their way wearily through correct political procedures in an attempt to achieve a modest measure of home rule are dismissed as "teenage madmen," while the British government suddenly discovers, in the wake of two huge Irish Republican Army bomb explosions in London's financial district, that the views of armed Irish nationalists in Northern Ireland must be discussed with sensitivity and respect.

What we are looking at, in other words, is a climate of international politics, based on power rather than principle and brute force rather than law, which perfectly mirrors, in its ethical emptiness and bankruptcy, the amoral economic and social climate unleashed in Britain during the 1980s.

And just as that ethos encouraged cynical, callous, and self-serving behavior on the part of individuals, so the current ethos in international affairs encourages the same kind of behavior from nations seeking survival and respect. So long, for example, as the European Union project remained in the dynamic phase of the late 1980s, it was possible, at least in a West European country like Scotland, to argue that full sovereign nation-statehood was not necessary for national minorities seeking respect, security, and a place on the European stage. If the European project succeeded, sovereignty would no longer be vested in a single layer of government but would be shared among nations, regions, local authorities, and European institutions. And all those levels of government would have their own rights and standing within a pluralistic and federal European framework.

But now that the European Union seems to be retreating to a more traditional intergovernmental mode of operation, characterized by vigorous defense of national interests and growing popular skepticism about projects like European monetary union, that argument is increasingly difficult to make. Likewise, in wider security issues, the failure of the United Nations in Bosnia and elsewhere makes it progressively more difficult to suggest, to small nations seeking to secure their existence, that they need not arm themselves to the teeth, "cleanse" themselves of potentially disloyal national minorities, and generally take up an aggressive and threatening posture toward their neighbors. And it is impossible, in this climate, to persuade national minorities interested in physical and cultural survival that they need not launch a struggle for nation-statehood.

The truth is that just as the rule of law in society creates space for civil and civilized interaction between individuals, so the rule of international law is necessary to sustain a civil and mutualistic culture in the matter of national identity and self-expression. And so long, therefore, as the great nations of the world continue to act, on the international stage, in a primitive and anarchic way, breaking international law and agreements at will, fomenting xenophobic attitudes at home in order to buttress their own power, abusing minorities, blatantly valuing the lives of their own nationals far more highly than those of "foreigners," and cynically undermining the strength, credibility, and finances of international institutions, they can expect exactly the same type of primitive and egoistic behavior from small emergent nations, and from national minorities seeking the security of sovereign statehood.

The conclusion one can draw from these experiences is that national identity is a real and compelling factor in human affairs, and one that has to be recognized and accommodated in any stable political system, but it does not matter as much, or in as simplistic a way, as the present Wilsonian construction of international politics, based almost entirely on the rights and prerogatives of nation-states, would suggest. There is no doubt that a shared national or communal identity—passed on in songs and stories and language, from generation to generation, in rich and poor families alike—is a profoundly human and enriching phenomenon, and a vital source of human resistance to the reductive brutality of crude economic and material power. And we have, in the nation-state, a political structure capable of capturing and expressing that reality. But there is no doubt, too, that most people experience within themselves complex overlapping circles of identity and belonging that—in the absence of sophisticated systems of federal and pluralistic government—are often misrepresented or suppressed by the simplistic call to a single national loyalty.

More important, there is no doubt that human beings share basic values, aspirations, and needs across national boundaries to an extent that is dangerously obscured by the present political structure, as well as by the post-1960s orthodoxy of moral and cultural relativism that leads, at both individual and national levels, to a reactionary rejection of any possibility of common perception, common understanding, and common action. The truth is that humanity, in the nineteenth and twentieth centuries, has superbly succeeded in creating a political structure that continuously embodies, emphasizes, reifies, and exaggerates our national differences but has so far failed—despite the brave attempts of 1918 and 1945—to produce powerful and credible international institutions capable of embodying the much more important and enduring values we hold in common.

The new states that crawled blinking into the light of European day, after the revolutions of 1989 and the collapse of the Soviet Union and the Yugoslav federation, were essentially embryonic, half-formed things, waiting to take on the stamp of the "world community" in which they found themselves. We should look at them, five or ten years on, and see in their new shapes—in their militarism or chauvinism, paranoia, or ethnic intolerance—not evidence of their own failures but the harsh reflection of the world we all inhabit, the world we have made for ourselves.

6

Nationalism, Democracy, and the Belgian State

LOUIS VOS

"The crisis of the Belgian state, that model of nineteenth century modernisation, may well be terminal."[1] Whether this grim prognosis by a British political scientist is accurate or not remains to be seen. But there can be no doubt that in Belgium, as elsewhere in Europe, the forces of nationalism are effecting social and political change so far-reaching as to threaten the cohesion of the nation-state. The Flemish and Walloon communities—Belgium's constituent nations—are increasingly polarized. Extreme nationalism is gaining popular support. And the delicate political compromise that has contributed to the formation of a tolerant, democratic culture is yielding under the pressures of competing subnationalisms.

It is this relationship between nationalism and democracy that concerns us here. And in this regard the Belgian experience is particularly instructive. Nationalism, it is often assumed, fosters intolerance and is inimical to democracy. While there is certainly evidence to support such a view in the Belgian case, it is no less true that there are nationalist traditions in Belgium compatible with democracy. This essay will examine Belgium's various nationalist traditions and explore their impact on the country's current crisis. The ultimate challenge, I will argue, is not to contain nationalism but to strengthen its democratic content.

Characteristics of Nationalism

The current theoretical discourse about nationalism provides a useful framework with which to appreciate the distinction between Belgium's two dominant traditions of nationalism. As Ernest Gellner has defined it, "nationalism is primarily a political principle, which holds that the political and the national unit should be congruent."[2] The political unit (the state) is predicated on universal principles deriving from notions of the common good: protection of the rights of citizens and the promotion of their welfare. The national unit refers to the shared identity and culture of particular communities. Nationalism strives to combine the universal principles of statehood with the particular identity of a national community in a single nation-state.

For Gellner, nationalism as an ideology and a political movement is a by-product of modernization—a social force that serves to satisfy the requirements of modern nation-building. Every nationalism, moreover, has ethnic features, as Anthony D. Smith has shown.[3] These ethnic elements by themselves, however, are insufficient to serve as determinants of national identity. They must be transformed in the minds of a people into symbols of a community. Nationalists thus plunge deep into the reservoir of shared characteristics (real or imagined) and come up with particular elements that they raise to the status of national symbols: a common history, an ancestral territory, ancient institutions (some of which may even have disappeared), language, race, religion, or specific traditions and rituals. This is the "invention of tradition" about which Eric Hobsbawm and Terence Ranger have written.[4]

Because nationalism results from the modernization of society and also makes use of "primordial" ethnic elements to promote its own identity, we can trace two routes to the creation of the nation-state throughout history. The first and oldest route is "state-to-nation," whereby an existing dynastic or feudal state develops within its own territory into a nation-state. This path emerged alongside and was legitimated by the notion that the sovereignty of the state does not derive from the emperor or the king, or from the privileged classes of nobility and clergy, but from the people. Examples of this road to nationhood are England, France, and the United States.

The second route, the journey from an ethnic group to a nation and finally to the nation-state, we call the "nation-to-state" route. Its starting point is not that of an existing state but rather an ethnocultural community that initially has no political structure but succeeds in building up its own state. The state boundaries are made to coincide with those of the area where people of the same community live. This can take the form of unification-nationalism, which unites in one nation-state a people hitherto politically divided. It can also take the form of secession-nationalism, by which a nation separates itself from an existing state.

Belgium's history of nation formation contains elements of both the state-to-nation route and the nation-to-state route. An example of the first is the Brabant revolution of 1789, which brought into existence a short-lived sovereign nation-state in the Austrian Netherlands. Within the boundaries of an existing state and in reaction to the enlightened despotism of the emperor, the revolutionaries favored restoration of the *ancien régime* and developed a national ideology with Catholic overtones and legitimized by "Belgian" history. National symbols were invented and some new national political bodies were created—albeit with more than a nod toward pre-Enlightenment traditions—thereby giving birth to a new cultural and political national identity.

An example of the second route is the Belgian revolution of 1830, when the Belgian revolutionaries, acting in the name of the Belgian "nation," reclaimed liberty and sovereignty from the Dutch. In this case the emergence of a national community preceded the establishment of a state, whose boundaries were to coincide with the territory of the Belgian nation.

The two routes of development, state-to-nation and nation-to-state, have been linked in the literature with two types of nationalism: "Western" and "Eastern" nationalism (Hans Kohn) or "territorial" and "ethnic" nationalism (Anthony D. Smith).[5] James G. Kellas makes a further distinction between "social" nationalism based on a shared national culture and "ethnic" nationalism founded on common ancestry.[6] This typology is useful for purposes of classification, but to understand better the historical process I propose to use the binary distinction of "civic" and "ethnic," which allows us to describe nationalism in a more dynamic way.

Nationalism contains in most cases both civic and ethnic components. The civic component refers to the institutions of the modern state, which, we have noted, is itself grounded in the sovereignty of the people. These legal institutions form a democratic and typically inclusive civic framework for its citizens. (We can call the predominantly civic nationalism inclusive because it does not concern itself with ethnic descent and allows outsiders, under certain conditions, the possibility of entry into the nation.) The ethnic component, which is often exclusive, refers to the content of the national identity developed by means of shared values, institutions, symbols, traditions, culture, language, or religion.

An analysis of the historic process of nation formation makes clear that this dual character—civic versus ethnic—is a part of every national experience irrespective of the route followed. In the nation-states that have traveled the route from state to nation, the starting point has indeed been voluntary and civic—"*le plebiscite de tous les jours*" (Renan)—but very quickly those states have also singled out certain ethnic characteristics as features of their nationhood. On the other hand, those nation-states that have grown from an ethnic group via a nation to a state have sought to consolidate their independence through laws and legal institutions, including universal human rights guarantees. A state founded purely on universal principles and where abstract individual citizens go about their daily business does not exist.

As an ideology, nationalism is very versatile. The exclusive province of neither the left nor the right, nationalism refers only to a community that is "ours." This has led some postmodern philosophers to the conclusion that, at a time when ideology presumably is dead, nationalism is the appropriate belief system to fill the void because it encourages us to replace our blueprints for society with the simple—but tautological—re-iteration that "we are who we are."[7] Although perhaps one explanation for the success of nationalism today, it is not the only or even the most obvious one. In most cases, historically speaking, nationalism has attached itself to an ideological movement. It becomes a regulatory principle that helps to introduce another ideology to the community. It has been used in the service of both dominant (hegemonic) political classes and opposition (counter-hegemonic) groups. Fascist, liberal, anti-colonial, and even communist movements have in the past embedded their ideology in a nationalist discourse.[8]

The growth of nationalism throughout Europe and the success of the extreme right identified with nationalism have opened up a new debate about the viability of democratic nationalism. In Belgium the debate has been prompted by the official policy that extends to migrant workers, under certain conditions, the possibility of full citizenship and facilitates their cultural integration in the Flemish community. But some left-of-center Flemish intellectuals reject both the notion of integration and a national culture, seeking to distance themselves from any form of nationalism.[9] Their position is that the state must guarantee equal rights to all citizens and must protect their material and spiritual interests, including the right to speak one's own language and maintain one's own cultural traditions, irrespective of ethnic background. The state must not, according to this view, identify with a particular language or culture, not even that of the majority of the people. Otherwise a state may be guilty of forced assimilation and undemocratic treatment of its minority population.

Because nationhood entails a congruence of culture and power, the argument goes, a nation by its very nature will oppress cultural minorities. To avoid this, a state must strive, as best it can, to rest on universal principles. The state must not become involved with culture or ethnic issues; this is the role of civil society, not the state. Anti-nationalists invoke the vision of a democratic and multicultural South Africa as a model for Belgium.[10]

My position is different. Notwithstanding the validity of certain criticisms of nationalism, my view is that democracy and nationalism need not necessarily exclude one another. As long as the national community accepts the entry of others, one can call it democratic, even if these newcomers are asked to respect the dominant culture and traditions of public life. For they should, nonetheless, enjoy the freedom to preserve and cherish their own ethnic traditions. On the other hand, wherever biological descent or the cultural background of ancestors (the genealogical principle) is used as the criteria for deciding who may and who may not belong to the national community, the civic component of the nation is weakened. Such an exclusive nationalism is by definition undemocratic. The extension of this logic leads ultimately to deportations and ethnic cleansing.

Those concerned with the growing intolerance in society must not turn a blind eye to nationalism. Nor should they be misled by the illusion that simply to reject nationalism will somehow make for a better world. For more than two centuries, nationalism has retained its appeal. Rather than deny this reality it is better to accept it and try to strengthen the civic component of nationalism.

The Roots of the Current Crisis

Popular though it is to talk about nationalism in Europe as if it has erupted on the scene with the end of the Cold War, today's nationalist contest in Belgium is not of recent origin. Indeed in certain respects it exhibits uninterrupted continuity with the past, extending back several centuries. A proper understanding of the current Belgian situation, therefore, requires some appreciation of the historical antecedents of the present moment.

Although Belgium as a nation-state did not come into existence until 1830, its establishment was not the beginning but rather the culmination of a process of nation-building. The Netherlands split up in the sixteenth century as a result of the Dutch revolt against Spanish rule and a distinct Southern Netherlandic identity developed as a consequence of this struggle.[11] This identity grew into modern nationalism during the so-called Brabant revolution in 1789. The revolution was directed against the enlightened but authoritarian rule of the Habsburg Emperor Joseph II. It resulted in the establishment of an independent Belgian state. However, this state was only to survive one year before falling first to Austrian troops and then to Napoleon.

The Congress of Vienna in 1815 created the United Kingdom of the Netherlands, an artificial conglomeration of the present-day Benelux states under the rule of the Dutch King William I. William attempted to weld North and South together but his new state lasted only 15 years; it never became a nation. The Belgians increasingly came to see this new dispensation as domination by Holland. Catholics and liberals thus united under the banner of freedom. This dissatisfaction led to a rebellion in the summer of 1830 that developed into a national revolution. Out of this revolution came the modern nation-state—constitutional, liberal, democratic, and centralized. Its sovereignty was vested in the Belgian people and its national identity was legitimized by a historically formed common culture and tradition within which freedom—understood to mean a ruling system based on consent "from below"—was seen as the most important national value. This is a typical example of the development of a nation following the "nation-to-state" route.

After the establishment of Belgian independence and the strengthening of the Belgian institutions that formed the civic component of the new nationalism, some patriots—cultural nationalists—felt called on to build up a national Belgian culture. They wanted to bring about the moral renaissance of the Belgian people, to give them their own national history, their own art, and their own literature. To this end, some of them used the French language, either because it was their mother tongue or because it had been declared the official language shortly after independence.

Others saw this process as flawed. If all that was Flemish was to disappear or even to be reduced to a second-class culture, Belgium would be all the poorer. They wanted not one, but two national languages. They believed that the resulting interaction of the Germanic and Romanic traditions within Belgium would lead to a new cultural synthesis.

Already one can see the roots of the present nationalist tension in Belgium, at least concerning questions of language. In the 10 years following Belgian independence, the public and cultural life of the entire country, including those areas where Dutch was the main language, was largely dominated by French. By resort to petitions and the establishment of Flemish organizations and societies, and later through legislation, the Flemish movement tried to create breathing space for Dutch. Both support for and the success of the Flemish movement remained rather limited until 1890. Its active membership comprised students, priests, and intellectuals from the Flemish middle classes.[12] These Flemish language activists did not initially intend to divide the country into distinct language areas. Rather, they hoped that Belgian law would guarantee Dutch speakers the right to use their mother tongue in public life throughout the entire country. They achieved some guarantees for non-French speakers in the administration and in the courts, and a limited bilingual secondary education system in Flanders. But by the end of the nineteenth century it became obvious, even to moderate Flemish activists, that the French-speaking Walloons would not accept bilingualism. These activists hoped that Flemish would at least be accepted in dealings between Dutch-speaking citizens and the central authorities in those areas of the country where Dutch was the mother tongue of the majority. And so the Flemish activists adopted a territorial policy for "Flanders," a general name from the romantic period for the Dutch-speaking northern part of the country.[13]

In the last quarter of the nineteenth century, as a Flemish ethnic and national identity began to assert itself, a Flemish subnation emerged within the greater Belgian nation. Language was to be the most important criterion for belonging to the Flemish people, although this subnationalism had a broader agenda than simple language rights. It wanted to create a Flemish Belgian culture that would make its own unique contribution to European civilization. At the same time this subnationalism was territorially defined; it wanted Flanders to be a home for the Flemish where they could speak their own language, notwithstanding the continued existence there of a French-speaking upper class. In 1898 Flemish nationalists gained a major victory when Dutch was recognized as an official language alongside French.

Flemish subnationalism, based as it was on language and territory, was more exclusive than the broader Belgian nationalism. But for at least two reasons it could still be said to be democratic. First, it was inspired by an awareness of the need to give official status to the language of the people,

in the social and ethnic sense of the word. It therefore responded to popular (as opposed to elite) interests. Furthermore, the French-speaking
upper classes who wished to identify with the Flemish people could do so
simply by speaking Dutch in public. They were thus not excluded on ethnic grounds from membership in the "nation."

However, not all French-speaking people were willing to accommodate
the Flemish. As a reaction against language laws mandating the use of
Dutch, a counter-movement sprang up in the last decade of the nineteenth
century. This so-called Walloon movement had its main base of support
among French speakers in Flanders. It advocated freedom of language and
refused to recognize the right of the Flemish people to establish linguistic
homogeneity within their territory. In the eyes of the Flemish, the counter-
movement was seen as an imperialistic and anti-democratic effort to protect
the privileges of the elite.[14] This pattern of nationalist initiative and nationalist counter-reaction—a mutually reinforcing dynamic—is fairly typical.
It is evident in present-day Belgium as well.

Polarized as the two communities were by the end of the nineteenth
century, it was World War I that caused nationalism to lose its relative innocence. Radical nationalism was then added to the equation.[15] Radical
Flemish activists, because of their impatience with the slow Dutchification
of Flanders, accepted to reform and even divide the occupied Belgian state
with German assistance. The majority of those advocating the Flemish
cause remained loyal to Belgium, and the resulting split in Flemish nationalism has never been fully overcome. Fuelled by the *Flamenpolitik* of
the German occupier, radical activists developed a Flemish nationalism that
was overtly anti-Belgian. Although their reforms were reversed after the
war and they were tried as traitors by the Belgian courts, their anti-Belgian
Flemish ideology was kept alive by those who fled the country to the
Netherlands or to Germany, from where they prepared the revenge that
was to come in 1940–45. Here, as elsewhere in Europe, the diaspora community has been a critical factor helping to sustain a radical nationalist
agenda.

For the more radical Flemish activists, "anti-Belgianism" was the
touchstone of genuine Flemish nationalism. They wanted to destroy the
Belgian political framework, including the parliamentary system, and
linked their nationalism to fascism in the 1930s. (The more moderate
Flemish nationalists, by contrast, wanted to stick to the language laws and
work democratically within the confines of the existing Belgian state.) In
the radicals' blueprint for a new order, ethnic purity of language and not
simply use of the language was to form the criterion for membership in
the community. This type of Flemish nationalism was exclusive, ethnocentric, and racist. It emphasized the differences between "our people"
and "outsiders," and as a result turned against both Walloons and Jews
on Flemish territory. It produced a climate conducive to national socialism and to collaboration with the Nazi occupiers in World War II.[16]

In addition to the collaboration of anti-Belgian Flemish nationalism during the war, there was a left-wing-inspired revival of the Walloon national consciousness that set itself against a possible fascist Catholic Flemish domination in Belgium.[17] After the war it further manifested itself in a movement for Walloon autonomy. Among the majority of the Flemish people who did not support collaboration, meanwhile, there was a renewed respect for the Belgian nation. This was prompted by opposition to the collaboration of the anti-Belgian Flemish nationalists. Again, a Flemish Belgian movement developed that wanted to continue the strategy of protecting Dutch in Belgium by means of language laws but did not want to dismantle the Belgian state.

This pro-Belgian stance among the Flemish was not to last. It was undermined immediately after the war by the punishment of Flemish collaborators. A large number of Flemish people saw this punishment more as a generalized, and therefore unjust, repression of the Flemish intelligentsia. The credibility of the Belgian nation for younger generations of Flemish intellectuals was further undermined when a wave of Frenchification swept the country. Shortly after, a Walloon identity developed around the idea of "our own territory."[18] The distinctive pattern of socioeconomic development was in large measure responsible for this. After the war Flanders became relatively more prosperous than Wallonia, where the loss-making coal and steel industries were threatened with closure. By the mid-1960s, the Flemish were enjoying a higher per capita income than the Walloons. Unequal economic development would prove to be a fillip to nationalism elsewhere in Europe as well, notably in Italy and Yugoslavia in the late 1980s.

The government, alarmed by the strength of Walloon and Flemish nationalism, sought to contain both through a strategy of linguistic pacification. The language borders had been defined officially in the early 1960s and the provinces adjusted accordingly. Brussels, the capital, became officially bilingual, and in some municipalities close to its border, or adjacent to a language border, special arrangements were made for minority language groups. The aim was to create language areas that were as homogeneous as possible, and thus push the language question into the background.

But the language question was not so easily dispensed with. The new regulations served only to highlight the differences between the two language communities and encourage the Flemish to strive harder to make their country completely monolingual. The debate surrounding the Catholic University of Leuven in the mid-1960s was a reflection of this struggle. The university, situated in the Flemish area, had two language sections. The French speakers wanted to retain their section while the Flemish students and the majority of Flemish public opinion saw this as a threat to the (monolingual) character of the area. Flemish students therefore demanded the expulsion of the French-speaking section. The conflict reached a high point in 1966 and 1968 with Flemish student revolts that led to the fall of the government and, eventually, the splitting of the university. The

French-speaking part was transferred to Wallonia, with the autonomous Flemish University remaining in Leuven.

The forced expulsion of the French-language section from Leuven increased anti-Flemish sentiments in Wallonia and among the French speakers in Brussels. It also enhanced the attractiveness of the regional nationalist parties, among them the (Flemish) *Volksunie* and the coalition made up of the *Rassemblement Wallon* and the (Brussels) *Front des Francophones*. Toward the end of the 1960s and throughout the 1970s, these parties gained more and more support; in 1974 they captured 45 out of 212 seats in parliament—representing 22 percent of the electorate. In the same period all bilingual parties operating on a nationwide basis (Christian Democrats, Liberals, and Socialists) split along linguistic lines, making it extremely difficult to form new governments.

The government sought to introduce further reforms in response to these changing perceptions of national identity. In 1970 the constitution was amended and Belgium became a federal rather than a unitary state, comprising three Communities (French, Dutch, German) and three Regions (Flanders, Wallonia, Brussels). The Communities are concerned with the (mainly cultural) welfare of people speaking the same language, wherever they may live in Belgium. The Regions, on the other hand, are geographically defined; their institutions are responsible largely for social and economic matters.

Passage of the reform legislation required the support of the nationalist parties. In the case of the *Volksunie*, this prompted an internal crisis, with some party activists opposed to what they viewed as compromise legislation. As a consequence, the extreme right and strongly anti-Belgian section broke away and formed a new party, the *Vlaams Blok*. This party has enjoyed continuous electoral success since 1978, particularly because of its anti-immigration position, which it shares with extreme right parties elsewhere in Europe.

In 1980, further constitutional reforms led to still more autonomy for the Regions of Flanders and Wallonia, and for the Flemish and French Communities, including self-government. (The Brussels Region and the German Community were essentially untouched by these reforms.) A completion of the federalization agenda followed in 1988 and 1993 so that the Communities and Regions basically now have jurisdiction over all matters with the exception of national economic and monetary policy, justice, defense, foreign policy, social security, and the police.

The Prospects for Democratic Nationalism

It remains to be seen what effect Belgium's new federal structure, with the large degree of autonomy it affords its constituent communities, will have on nationalism. Increased autonomy, it is said, ought to allow the communities to consolidate their separate identities without the need to play the nationalist card. If the early evidence is a fair indication, however, it would appear that nationalism is not likely to lose its appeal. What kind of nationalism and whether democracy can co-exist alongside it are critical issues that Belgium will be facing in the post-Cold War period.

It is the region of the capital, Brussels, that offers the best chance for an inclusive democratic state structure. In Brussels the regional authorities have responsibility not only for local social and economic policy but also for linguistic and cultural affairs, which are normally the province of the Communities. This is contributing to the emergence of a "bicultural nationalism" as opposed to the unilingual nationalism of the Flemish and the French. Also, the official bilingualism in Brussels is so carefully institutionalized that the rights of the Flemish minority cannot be violated, and the French-speaking majority can only govern in cooperation with the Flemish living in Brussels. Moreover, Brussels appears to be developing its own identity, defined less by ethnocultural or linguistic characteristics and more by the civic institutions governing the metropolitan area and by its function as the capital of a federal state and the European Union. Since strict rules maintain the balance between the members of the French and Flemish communities within this civic polity, there are signs that the salience of ethnic nationalism is diminishing. Notwithstanding its unique position, Brussels offers a model of a multicultural framework.

It is a different story altogether with respect to Wallonia. The Walloon regional authorities are strengthening their political power to the detriment of both the Federal level and the Community level, but at the same time they are concerned about the growth of nationalism. They worry that nationalism may give rise to exclusivist and undemocratic policies. They see the task of the Walloon movement, therefore, as one of opposing nationalism, including Flemish nationalism, by supporting the liberty and rights of the individual against encroachment by the community.[19] The problem with their position is that, in the name of defending individual freedom, they would deny the Flemish nation the right to establish a monolingual space within the confines of their own community. Indeed, they offer their support, as they have in the past, to those francophones in Flanders who refuse to accept the language laws. Moreover, they continue to make demands for the incorporation into Wallonia of certain Flemish areas where there is a strong French-speaking presence. This attitude has been described by the leading Flemish historian Lode Wils as "language imperialism."[20] The Flemish and French speakers are increasingly polarized as a result. What the Flemish see as a denial of democracy, namely the refusal to abide by the language laws, the Francophones see as an expression of dissent against the denial of human rights.

The reasons for this misunderstanding lie in the differing conceptions of both the role of the state in cultural matters and the relationship between individual and collective language rights.[21] Language is fundamental to the Flemish sense of identity. It is not merely a vehicle of communication but a symbol and determinant of national identity. The Flemish attitude is that, as the nation has a well-delineated territory, all the people living within its boundaries should show respect for its language and use it in public life. For the French speakers in Belgium though, as also for the left-wing Flemish critics of nationalism, the state has no right to impose culture on its citizens. They feel that the state should be neutral in cultural matters. To this way of thinking, linguistic legislation is undemocratic.

In Canada there is a similar debate taking place, one that may shed some light on the Belgian situation. As James Tully, a Canadian political philosopher, has pointed out, "a modern constitution [cannot be] separate from culture as some liberals have suggested." He argues, furthermore, that "the politics of cultural recognition cannot be suppressed or ignored . . . for cultural recognition is a deep and abiding human need." The danger, Tully warns, is to think that "recognition and affirmation of the culturally diverse identities of modern citizens [leads to] the disunity or disintegration of modern states." To the contrary, he maintains, "The steady movement towards disunity and separation in Canada is caused by the mutual failure to recognise and accommodate the aspirations of Quebec and the First Nations, along with the just demands of the other cultural groups."[22]

One can apply this reasoning to the Belgian situation. The evolution of nationalism in Belgium, in particular the Flemish nation gaining its own state, might never have developed if, in the nineteenth century, the authorities had recognized Flemish language demands as the just demands of a cultural group within the Belgian national context. And if today the French-speaking people were to stop denying the Flemish community the right to protect its own culture and language, Flemish nationalism might not be so strong. Now, it is feared, the process of polarization is too far advanced to be able to avoid further disintegration of the Belgian state.

Despite the obstacles posed by the French, the Flemish movement has succeeded, over a century and a half, in eliminating both discrimination against Dutch speakers and the second-class citizenship of the Flemish population. It has achieved this by placing the French and Dutch languages on an equal footing at the federal level; by creating a bilingual area within the capital, Brussels, and its environs; and by defending Dutch-speaking territory, within which only one language is officially recognized. As long as Dutch speakers were discriminated against, the Flemish nationalist movement could claim legitimacy as the vanguard of the struggle for emancipation and equality, and thus for democracy. But what about today?

Today, the Flemish Community and the Flemish Region form a new Flemish (sub)state. It is a state that considers itself a nation because it has made the powers of the state congruent with an ethnic substratum based on the Dutch language and a particular Flemish culture. Through the establishment of this state structure, Flemish nationalism has taken on an official character. It has become the official ideology of the Flemish government and also of the Flemish parties and the large economic, social, and cultural bodies operating in Flemish territory. This Flemish nation is rooted in democratic principles. It has come into existence not through revolution but through reasonable compromise. It thus has a strong civic component and considers itself closer to its citizens than the older unitary Belgian state.

If the official nationalism and national polity is democratic, is it also inclusive? Yes, because it recognizes every Belgian citizen who lives in Flanders as a full Community member, without reference to ancestry and without interfering with an individual's cultural traditions. It does, however, demand that its public life be conducted in Dutch. In that sense it does make certain cultural demands of the inhabitants of Flanders. Language remains the basis of membership in the Community. This, however, is only partially exclusive. A language can be learned, and every state, even if it has no language laws, does in fact use a particular language as the official means of communication. The difference with the United States, or (even less so) with France, is that in Flanders the language is not alone a vehicle of communication. It is also a symbol of national identity. But that does not necessarily make the nation exclusive.

This democratic and more inclusive official Flemish nationalism, we have seen, is not the only tendency to claim to represent the interests of the Flemish population. There is also right-wing radical Flemish nationalism, as reflected in the political party *Vlaams Blok*. It is the inheritor of the mantle of exclusivist nationalism that first emerged during World War I and that drew new breath from its collaboration with the Nazis in World War II.[23] It has continued the anti-Belgian tradition and now embraces the French New Right ideology, rejecting the principle that all people are equal. It glorifies ethnically integral nationalism, which invokes the genealogical principle as the only criterion for membership in the nation.[24] It is fundamentally racist and therefore, by definition, undemocratic.

The choice facing Flanders is different from that facing Wallonia. It is not a question of whether the people want to build up a nation. Nation-building in Flanders is already at an advanced stage. Throughout its history, the Flemish movement has striven to set up a Flemish national state. To abolish that now, out of deference to cultural pluralism, would be to take a step backward because it would remove the civic framework from the ethnic core of Flemish nationalism and thus lead to more extremism. Within the existing Flemish nation, though, another choice has to be made. It is a choice between a more inclusive, territorial, civic, and therefore democratic nationalism, and a more exclusive genealogical, ethnic, and consequently undemocratic nationalism.

In Flanders the public debate continues about the goal of the Flemish nationalist movement. Four distinct factions are in evidence. First, there are the federalists who feel that the Flemish movement, as defender of Flemish culture, has achieved its goal and therefore need not seek any further institutional changes. Then there are the confederalists who want to increase the power of the community and regional authorities at the expense of the federal government (a position that appeals also to the Flemish government). They want to do this, principally, to prevent the French

Community authorities from promoting the interests of French speakers in Flanders and so intervening in Flemish affairs. They also wish to stop the flow of money, through the redistribution mechanism of the welfare state, from a wealthy Flanders to a poor Wallonia. Third, there are those who advocate complete independence for Flanders while wishing to maintain an open and democratic climate in the new state. Finally, there are those who advocate full independence but in addition want an exclusively nationalist regime that will "put our people first" and pursue a policy of ethnic cleansing at the expense of foreigners. This is the position of the *Vlaams Blok*.

The first two approaches appear to guarantee the continuation of the present, strongly democratic, official Flemish nationalism. The other two approaches are prescriptions for complete national independence. In the interwar period "anti-Belgianism" served as a catalyst for anti-parliamentarianism. It is very possible that complete rejection of the Belgian political tradition, following Flemish independence, would again clear the way for undemocratic experiments. Remaining as a Community within the Belgian state can serve, on the contrary, as a guarantee of democracy. Both the third and fourth solutions therefore appear to threaten democratic nationalism and should be challenged by those who wish to strengthen democracy.

There is another important factor to bear in mind. In the future, Belgium, Flanders, and Wallonia, as they define their national identities, will be increasingly confronted with the problems of a *de facto* multicultural society as Belgium becomes home to more in-migration. At present, the discussion is centered around attitudes toward the integration of the migrant community.[25] In Flanders, the *Vlaams Blok*, as a logical consequence of its ethnic genealogical nationalism, has put particular emphasis on its anti-migrant program. In so doing it has enjoyed considerable electoral success. Since the end of the 1980s, the Belgium government, too, has focused on the "migrant problem." It has opted for a policy of integration—a policy to be implemented not by the federal government but by the regional and community authorities. In Flanders, where cultural homogeneity has been taken for granted, this policy of integration, insofar as it is understood as total assimilation, has been rejected by left-wing intellectuals. They have called instead for a multicultural society that allows individuals to preserve rather than submerge their differences.

In Wallonia, by contrast, the integration debate has provoked little interest. The very idea of a migrant policy was rejected, and this even though there were more migrants living in Wallonia than in Flanders. Indeed, it was assumed that if the regional authorities were successful in their fight against the forces of economic and social decline, then all the inhabitants of Wallonia would benefit. The solution to the problems posed by a multicultural society rests in the hands of the new national or regional bodies. This will cause more difficulties in Flanders, given the strong ethnic component in the national consciousness, the tradition of safeguarding cultural homogeneity, and the zealousness of the *Vlaams Blok*. In Wallonia the situation will be a lot less fraught. The leaders of the Walloon Community expressly wish to distance themselves from nationalism, and the extreme right-wing French-speaking parties tend to favor Belgian nationalism.

So has the Belgian nation indeed reached its terminal stage? No clear answer can be given. The question is: How will the citizens of today define their national allegiances, and how will national identity evolve in the future? Recent opinion polls indicate that there is still a widespread feeling of identity with the Belgian nation and that this is not incompatible with a sense of loyalty to the Communities or Regions. If that is the case, then Belgian nationalism can perhaps survive as an idea of overarching identity for all Belgians, comparable to that provided by British nationalism for all United Kingdom inhabitants (English, Scots, Welsh, and Northern Irish).

It is possible that the trend toward increasing the powers of the Regions will continue in a federal Belgium. If that occurs, the importance of the Communities will fade and will give way to the development of both a Walloon and a Brussels region-state, each—like Flanders—with its own identity. Given that this new regional or national identity in Wallonia and Brussels will have followed the state-to-nation route, it is reasonable to suppose that these states will exhibit a stronger civic rather than ethnic character. The situation in Flanders is different. Here the nation followed a nation-to-state route, and therefore the ethnic component is very strong. But because an established democratic Flemish nationalist polity exists, it may be possible in the future—as it was in the past—to mold nationalism into a democratic and inclusive form that maintains community feeling but that at the same time is open enough to accept the contributions of people from other cultural backgrounds who want to participate in the life of the nation.

Notes

1. William Wallace, "Rescue or Retreat? The Nation State in Western Europe, 1945–93," *Political Studies*, No. 42 (Special issue 1994), p.76.

2. Ernest Gellner, *Nations and Nationalism* (Oxford: Basil Blackwell, 1983), p.1.

3. Anthony D. Smith, *The Ethnic Origins of Nations* (Oxford: Basil Blackwell, 1986). See also Anthony D. Smith, *National Identity* (London: Penguin Books, 1991).

4. Eric Hobsbawm and Terence Ranger, eds., *The Invention of Tradition* (Cambridge: Cambridge University Press, 1983).

5. Hans Kohn, *The Idea of Nationalism* (New York: Collier Books/Macmillan, 1967), Ch. 5; Smith, *The Ethnic Origins of Nations*, Ch. 6.

6. James G. Kellas, *The Politics of Nationalism and Ethnicity* (London: Macmillan, 1991), Ch. 4, p.51.

7. Frans De Wachter, "Wie is mijn volk? De verleidingen van het zachte nationalisme," in *Nationalisme: Kritische opstellen*, eds. Raymond Detrez and Jan Blommaert (Antwerp: Epo, 1994), pp.71–91.

8. That nationalism is a class-neutral element and ideologically very versatile is discussed by David L. Adamson, *Class, Ideology and Nation: A Theory of Welsh Nationalism* (Cardiff: University of Wales Press, 1991).

9. Jan Blommaert and Jef Verschueren, *Het Belgische migrantendebat: de pragmatiek van de abnormalisering* (Antwerp: IPrA/Epo, 1992); Detrez and Blommaert, op. cit.

10. Johan Degenaar, "De mythe van 'een' of 'de' Zuidafrikaanse natie," Detrez and Blommaert, op. cit., pp. 326–343.

11. For more historical background see Louis Vos, "Shifting Nationalism: Belgians, Flemings and Walloons," in *The National Question in Historical Context*, eds. Milulas Teich and Roy Porter (Cambridge: Cambridge University Press, 1993), pp. 128–147 and the critical bibliography; *The Flemish Movement: A Documentary History, 1780–1990*, eds. Theo Hermans, Louis Vos, and Lode Wils (London: The Athlone Press, 1992); Alexander B. Murphy, *The Regional Dynamics of Language Differentiation in Belgium: A Critical Study in Cultural Political Geography* (Chicago: University of Chicago, 1988); Lode Wils, *Van Clovis tot Happart: De lange weg van de naties in de lage landen* (Leuven: Garant, 1992); and Lode Wils, *Vlaanderen, België, Groot-Nederland: Mythe en geschiedenis* (Leuven: Davidsfond, 1994).

12. Lieve Gevers, *Bewogen jeugd: Ontstaan en ontwikkeling van de katholieke Vlaamse studentenbeweging. 1830–1894* (Leuven, Davidsfond, 1987); Lode Wils, *Honderd jaar Vlaamse beweging, geschiedenis van het Davidsfond*, 3 vols. (Leuven: Davidsfond, 1977, 1985, 1989).

13. The term Flanders refers to the Dutch-speaking language area north of the linguistic border that runs from west to east, Wallonia to the French-speaking area south of that line, and Brussels to the 19 municipalities forming the Brussels Region (a bilingual island surrounded by Flemish territory). Today there are 5.8 million inhabitants in Flanders, 3.3 million in Wallonia, and 1 million in Brussels. In Flanders the language is Dutch, in Wallonia French. "Flemish" refers to the region and the community, not to the language. The small German-speaking community in the eastern part of the Belgium (now a part of the Walloon Region) is a result of territorial war gains after World War I and constitutes less than one percent of the Belgium population (that is, roughly 70,000 people).

14. Chantal Kesteloot, "Mouvement Walloon et identité nationale," *Courrier Hebdomadaire du CRISP*, No. 1392 (1993).

15. Lode Wils, *Flamenpolitik en aktivisme* (Leuven. Davidsfond, 1974).

16. Bruno De Wever, *Staf de Clercq* (Brussels: Uitgeverij Grammens, 1989); Bruno De Wever, *De greep naar de macht: Vlaams-nationalisme en nieuwe orde, Het VNV 1933–1945* (Tielt-Gent: Lannoo-Perspectief Uitgaven, 1994). Louis Vos, *Bloei en ondergang van het AKVS: Geschiedenis van de katholieke Vlaamse studentenbeweging, 1914–1935* (Leuven: Davidsfond, 1982).

17. Wils, *Van Clovis tot Happart*, op. cit.

18. Kesteloot, op. cit.

19. Philippe Destatte, *L'Identité walonne, aperçu historique* (Namur: Présidence de l'Executif régional wallon, 1991).

20. Wils, *Van Clovis tot Happart*, op. cit., pp. 302–303.

21. Compare with the writings of the Canadian philosopher Charles Taylor, who advocates collective language rights. See his *Sources of the Self* (Cambridge, MA: Harvard University Press, 1989) and "Shared and divergent values," in *Reconciling the Solitudes*, ed. G. Laforest (Montreal: McGill-Queens University Press, 1993).

22. James Tully, "The Crisis of Identification: The Case of Canada," *Political Studies*, No. 42 (Special issue 1994), pp. 94–95.

23. Louis Vos, "De rechts-radicale traditie in het Vlaams-nationalisme," *Wetenschappelijke Tijdingen*, No. 52 (1993), pp. 129–149.

24. Hans De Witte, "Schijn bedriegt: Over de betekenis en de strategie van het Vlaams Blok," *De Gids op Maatschappelijk Gebied*, No. 85 (1994), pp. 243–268; Marc Spruyt, *Grove Borstels: Stel dat het Vlaams Blok morgen zijn programma realiseert, hoe zou Vlaanderen er dan uitzien* (Leuven: Uitgeverij Van Halewyck, 1995).

25. Marco Martiniello, "De communautaire kwestie en het migranten-vraagstuk in België," in Detrez and Blommaert, op. cit., pp. 172–182.

7

Nationalism and the Crisis of Liberalism

GHIA NODIA

In this chaotic fin de siècle, hopes for a "new world order" have proven both naive and short-lived. Indeed, the phrase itself has become a mockery. The promise of geopolitical stability seems ever more elusive. Liberal democratic values no longer appear to be unassailable. We seem to have entered a new epoch of international and ideological disorder.

It was the sudden collapse of communism that both promoted hopes of greater global harmony and generated an entirely new set of fears. The major force responsible for this disappointment has been a new wave of nationalism that has emerged most prominently in the former Soviet bloc. Although anti-communist dissidents were primarily inspired by Western liberal ideas, nationalism and not liberalism has become the dominant ideology of the post-communist era. Indeed, the breakup of communism has given rise to some particularly brutal forms of nationalism, including ethnic cleansing as a solution to ethno-territorial conflicts.

In 1988–89, during the initial anti-communist protests in the former Soviet bloc, the re-emergence of nationalism mainly threatened democratic prospects in countries about to be liberated from communism. Now, however, the collapse of communism has indirectly encouraged forces of nationalism within Western democracies as well. At the level of international relations, the predominant trend of the postwar democracies—to merge into a new international order—has given way to a revival of old regional rivalries. On the national level, the restoration of the nation-state spirit in the form of ethnic nationalism can be seen in aggressive anti-immigrant and anti-minority sentiment.

Perhaps the most disturbing feature of this new era is a general sense of lost, or at least faded, standards. Good and evil are no longer clearly demarcated; aggressors and victims are no longer so easily distinguished; democrats and anti-democrats often speak from the same mouth. Only model villains like Saddam Hussein can at times clarify situations, but they are not always available.

This sense of lost standards may be a sign of a metaphysical crisis—a crisis of liberal ideas. It is not only that particular politicians acting in particular circumstances fail to reach proper solutions. Rather, when it comes to problems such as fair borders between states or ethnic communities, the liberal idea can no longer provide any universally valid standards. Thus, the inability of the international community to stop the current crop of brutal atrocities, as in the former Yugoslavia, does not result from a lack of good will, resources, or international consensus (even Russia, despite a shifting foreign policy, has not disrupted consensus for quite some time). Instead, the international community is hampered ideologically. It has lost the courage of its convictions.

To be sure, the liberal idea could never provide any universally valid standards on problems such as fair borders between states or ethnic communities. Today, however, the crisis extends deeper. Having been left without real contenders in its global claims after the demise of communism, the liberal idea paradoxically appears enfeebled in its primary milieu, the West.[1] In the post-communist world, meanwhile, this crisis can be seen in an overexertion in implementing the liberal idea due to a lack of relevant social and cultural prerequisites. In both East and West, nationalism is there to fill the void.

Liberalism and Nationalism

The feebleness of the liberal idea can best be seen in the two values that have virtually come to guide Western political discourse and behavior—stability in practical politics and tolerance in the personal sphere. Both these newly ascendant values are vacuous: widely varying ways of life can be stable and peaceful, and tolerance toward others does not give much definition to one's own beliefs. Equally important, these values clash with other aspects of the liberal agenda. An emphasis on stability inevitably conflicts with the basic liberal idea of freedom, since freedom often jeopardizes stability. Excessive tolerance, meanwhile, entails a lack of conviction: in a world dominated by tolerance, true believers are regarded as unfashionable and dangerous.[2]

The priority of these values, not their substance, contradicts the initial spirit of liberalism. Certainly, the ultimate aim of a liberal-democratic order has been the stable, peaceful coexistence of reasonable people able to resolve any conflicts through rational bargaining and compromises. To impose itself as a new order, however, the liberal idea had to upset the "stability" of the *ancien régime* and be utterly intolerant of any contrary ideas. Conviction, courage, sacrifice, risk (or "creativity"), and even violence were required to promote liberalism's goals. Despite its adherence to ethnic, confessional, and social tolerance, liberalism has remained indifferent and even hostile toward those ideas that lie outside the realm of choice such as genealogy or metaphysics. The French and American revolutions starkly reveal this streak of liberal intolerance.

Once established, liberal values attained glory by historical contrast. The notion of individual autonomy certainly benefited by comparison with slavery, despotism, and blind fanaticism. So too did liberalism appear more glorious and substantial in relation to communism, a system that suppressed human freedom, that promised to expand worldwide and bury the free world. As the *anciens régimes* became distant history and communism dwindled as a serious threat to the West, liberalism ceased to draw energy from its enemies. Indeed, liberalism seemed to implode. With the French proclamation of the "death of man" in the 1960s, the world suddenly could be interpreted without assigning any special place to Man, his personal autonomy, or his creative ability. Later, with postmodernism, the Cartesian and Kantian notion of the autonomous human being was "deconstructed." As man "faded away," so too did the foundations of the Western liberal order.[3]

Western liberalism has not simply developed a new complacency or forgotten its own history. Rather, its basic values are formal to begin with and thus fail to produce answers to many of the questions raised by social life. As soon as these enemies of the free human individual disappear, liberal ideas begin to appear shallow. Freedom to do what? Openness to what? Compromise, cooperation—but toward what end? Finding these questions difficult to answer, liberalism has turned to the idea of "nature" to fill in the void. Freedom has thus become "the freedom to be natural"; openness has become "an openness to everything natural"; compromises become "avoiding conflicts between human beings and groups pursuing their natural needs." Everything "natural" then becomes the prior value: hence the sexual revolution, environmentalism, and multiculturalism—all celebrations of the "natural."

Although the concepts of "nature" and "natural" were certainly fundamental to the Western liberal order, the normative liberal understanding of autonomy is no more part of the natural order than, for instance, a traditional religious conception of a hierarchical order based on certain enshrined principles. Nor is individualism or equality "natural" in a psychological sense. The certainty of communal belonging can indeed be more attractive than the unpredictability of individual autonomy. The desire to subjugate and be subjugated can be viewed as neither more nor less "natural" than the desire for personal responsibility or mutual cooperation.

It can be argued, in fact, that the liberal order is more contrary to "nature" than any preceding system. Other political systems had been "naturally" formed as a result of struggles for power and resources; only after being established were these political systems provided an ideologi-

cal legitimacy. The ideological underpinning of the liberal order, however, was formed as a set of normative ideas in the course of cultural and
intellectual evolution—and only then materialized after a series of violent
upsurges. In this sense, the liberal order was the first ideological rather
than "natural" order.[4]

Without clear and present enemies, an entirely cohesive moral core,
or an undisputed claim to "natural" parentage, liberalism is currently on
rather shaky ground. This is where nationalism enters the equation.

Liberalism tends to reject nationalism—as an individualist doctrine opposes a collectivist one. At the same time, the liberal order often needs
the cooperation of nationalist forces to become institutionalized.[5] After
all, in the modern age, the liberal order (which assigns special privileges to
the individual) is predicated on democracy (which legitimates political
power on the basis of the collective will of the governed). Thus, the liberal-democratic order requires a cohesive body politic. Theoretically, this
polity could comprise the whole of humanity. For the moment, however,
it contains any given group of people that happens to live within borders
inherited from the *ancien régime*.

This polity (again in theory) could be kept together by a sense of participation in some general, rationally designed "social contract" in the form
of a constitution and a set of written or unwritten laws. The German
philosopher Jürgen Habermas has aptly called this force *Verfassungspatriotismus* or the patriotism of the constitution. Such an arrangement ideally
fits liberal theory. In reality, however, a body politic needs something more
to sustain unity in hard times, to make sacrifices necessary to overcome internal or external threats to the established common order, to believe that
decisions made by a majority are binding for a minority, or to have common feelings of pride and disgrace. To reach a rationally based consensus
on issues such as a constitution or the prior values on which a fair political
order should rest, a body politic should already have a pre-rational consensus. This consensus should bring together a "natural" group of people
clearly distinguishable from other groups.

Liberalism does not and cannot create this pre-rational preliminary
consensus. Instead, a controversial concept of "nation" fills the void. Despite the multiplicity of its interpretations, this concept encompasses a set
of historical, cultural, or racial features that seemingly legitimates the body
politic, at least to those who regard themselves as included.

Opponents of nationalism love to label these historical, cultural, and
racial features "created," "mythological," or "illusory." Their arguments
have some merit. After all, there is no universally valid method of determining which groups of people should be called separate political nations
that "deserve" the institutions and symbols of an independent state. If not
for certain historical contingencies, the people living in a given territory
would have different national identities, speak different tongues, willingly fight against those whom they now regard as their countrymen, and feel
kinship to those who are now foreigners if not enemies.

Still, this "mythological" way of thinking actually works. Especially annoying for a rational liberal purist, these "created" or "irrational" binding forces enable political entities to become strong and coherent enough not only to write and enact constitutions but also to construct around them a viable, politically liberal order. Such myths are critically important for the rational patriotism of the constitution.

Even those societies sometimes considered exceptions to this rule are not much different in reality. For instance, the United States seems to embody *Verfassungspatriotismus*, its nationhood derived not from ethnicity but from a common civic adherence to a certain (liberal-democratic) order manifested in the constitution. The self-awareness of the American nation has traditionally differed from typical European nationalisms in its absence of presumed mystical ties between a would-be nation and its soil. Its ethnic base was understood as broader than that of European nations.

Yet while the American nation was open to all willing to share the common constitutional ground, in reality this inclusiveness extended only to "civilized" people, that is, descendants of certain European extractions. African-Americans and Native Americans were initially out of the question; even Catholics were not beyond doubt.[6] To be sure, even these broader cultural prerequisites of the common democratic order were given much less importance than in Europe, thus making the American understanding of nation-building less ethnocultural and racial on the consciously ideological level. But this theoretical difference did not make the above prerequisites less obligatory in reality. Only after a specific image of the American nation and its political order had been established did the inclusion of blacks and Native Americans as members of the political community become part of the agenda. By this time, however, some minorities were not enthusiastic about inclusion into a pre-molded liberal order that they considered "white."

Liberal ideas emerged in a particular part of the world thanks to specific cultural and intellectual traditions. Their institutionalization in the liberal order became possible because these ideas were shared not just by intellectuals or elite groups, but by certain communities whose sense of being together had been at least in part based on particular cultural and racial features, and who were not at all willing to accept those who did not fit these criteria. These communities may become more inclusive over time—and this trend should be welcomed. But without this initial sense of commonality, of one-ness, these people would not have been able to create anything together, including liberalism.

Ethnicity and Nationhood

To understand the relationship between nationalism and liberalism, we must first distinguish between types of nationalism. Some divide nationalism geographically into "Western" versus "Eastern."[7] Gáspár Miklós Tamás delineates between the "old" nationalism of the nineteenth century and the "new" nationalism of the current era. Since they are often inter-mixed, it is not easy to divide the old from the new. Rather, particular cases fall along a continuum of nationalism; their location reflects hostil-ity toward or compatibility with the liberal spirit.[8]

However they are labeled, the first type ("Western" or nineteenth-century) should be considered essentially political. This nationalism in-spires people on a certain territory to create a strong political community and build a strong representative state. Focused on making the state the chief manifestation of the nation, this political nationalism is reasonably open and inclusive. It generally adopts a policy of assimilation toward dif-ferent ethnic or cultural groups. In the extreme, this policy strips mi-norities of their different heritages so that they become loyal members of a fairly homogeneous body politic. If full assimilation is unworkable, however, this political nationalism tolerates separate minority identities to the degree that their demands are restricted to such non-political spheres as culture, religion, or ethnic cuisine. Political nationalism is not immune to violence. States will often employ force against a problemat-ic minority that refuses to be assimilated or against a neighboring state advancing irredentist territorial claims. But exclusion of minorities is not an obligatory part of political nationalism. Anyone loyal to the state is, at least theoretically, acceptable to it.

The "Eastern" or "new" type of nationalism is usually called "ethnic nationalism." Here, nationhood is primarily defined by racial and cultur-al features. The state's chief purpose is to protect and preserve these unique qualities. Preoccupied with ethnic differences between people, this nationalism is exclusive rather than inclusive. It aims for a nation-state but conceives of its goal in terms of ethnic purity. Ethnic nationalism draws a sharp line between minorities and the core ethnic group. While de-manding special privileges for the latter, it tries to exclude the former with everything from psychological hostility aimed at making minorities feel unwelcome to "final solutions" of the Nazi variety.

By emphasizing ethnic divisions, this type of nationalism undermines even as it tries to consolidate the state. The body politic, since it is typi-cally mixed, becomes divided rather than knitted together more strongly. Moreover, the state and its symbolism—so important in generating the emotional forces of patriotism and solidarity under political nationalism—are subordinated to the ethnic "uniqueness" considered the prior bearer of nationhood.

To be sure, these are ideal types. Every real case of nationalism fea-tures elements of both varieties. Consider the case of French nationalism. On the one hand, France was created at the end of the eighteenth centu-ry as a political nation composed of a majority of people who did not speak French and would be regarded as "ethnic minorities" by today's standards (an example many would-be nations have attempted to follow with vary-ing degrees of success).[9] On the other hand, France is far from being free of ethnic nationalism, whether the anti-Semitism of the late nineteenth century or the aggressive anti-immigrant mood of the recent period.

Meanwhile, the post-communist Balkans or the Caucasus seem to provide classic examples of virulent ethnic nationalism. But they are not devoid of political nationalism as they try to fashion nation-states that at least in theory provide representation for all minorities.

Of the two varieties, political nationalism is more compatible with the liberal spirit, having cooperated from the beginning to build the strong liberal state. Political nationalism, like liberalism, viewed this state as the only possible protector of individual freedom against the force from which it craved emancipation—the traditional community.[10] As an idea, political nationalism is nothing more than a derivative of liberalism, an attempt to synthesize the basic principles of the latter with the premodern ethos of ethnicity.

Political nationalism understands the nation in much the same way that liberalism understands the individual. The basic principle of political nationalism, self-determination, is borrowed from the classical Kantian understanding of human autonomy.[11] Political autonomy is therefore as much a "natural right" of any nation as personal autonomy is that of any given individual. The fight for national independence is only legitimate because it is a particular case of the general principle—as a person's fight for individual freedom and dignity is only legitimate because it affirms the universal principle of human rights. Moreover, the nation fulfills itself by being active in history, and its worth is measured by its contribution to the common good of humanity—as an individual has to be active and contribute to the common good of the society. A nation has its individual soul or spirit (the *Geist* of German idealism) bearing a set of unique features that establishes its personal "character."

A gulf remains between the two concepts, however. While the borders of an individual's "natural" body are easily identified, the definition of the "natural" outline of a nation is much less self-evident. Throughout history populations have been mixed up, borders have been arbitrarily redrawn, many people are rather vague about their "national identity." Thus, virtually every nationalism—whether or not it tries to be political—has had (or still has) a real problem in defining exactly which ethno-territorial body is entitled to a national soul and which deserves political autonomy on a given territory. Most nationalist ideologists try to argue that national bodies are as "natural" as human ones, basing their claims on certain racial, linguistic, and historical arguments. On some occasions these arguments work, since race, language, and history are not in themselves arbitrary inventions of intellectuals or ideologists.

Yet none of these criteria can claim a universal rational validity. Occasionally these definitional problems are solved by plebiscites. Or a state succeeds in homogenizing its population through the fairly mild coercion of education and culture. In other cases, namely when nationalism slides into its ethnic variety, violent methods are used: expulsions or genocide or wars to establish "just" borders. In this controversial process of nation-building, however, most Western countries managed to avoid the violent extremities by confining their nationalism to the political variety. True, the arguments and methods used by political nationalists in the course of nation-building rarely satisfy the rigid standards of a liberal critique. But in practice liberals have usually tolerated those nationalists who haven't gone to violent extremes and have remained open to all those loyal and willing to be assimilated into the body politic.

Instead of embracing political nationalism, liberals have usually sought to build bridges to premodern forms of group loyalty. The liberal-democratic framework intentionally leaves room for activities of different communities and associations. This inclusion of collective organizations is designed to counterbalance the overly individualist and rationalist nature of the liberal order and thus make democracy more stable and effective.

While important, this inclusiveness is insufficient. Any community or association enters the general legal and political framework only as a "legal entity." The framework itself, based solely on the rationalist foundations of the "social contract," therefore lacks any communitarian element. Nationalism is indispensable in translating the age-old, "natural," "savage" forces of ethnic loyalty into the political patriotism of citizenship (a process of sublimation, Freud would say). This operation gives nationalism its political quality. In the ideal case, in which the task of nation-building is perfectly fulfilled, ethnic feelings are supposed to "melt down" and fill the mold of loyalty to one's own country and the solidarity of common citizenship. These feelings are thus neutralized and rationalized in a manner most acceptable to liberalism. While ideal cases rarely if ever occur, the history of Western Europe and North America presents some reasonably good approximations.

This operation of rechanneling the energies of ethnic loyalty into political modes of expression, however, is far from easy. It presumes the existence of liberal ideas, civil society, and the state as protector of rights and representative of interests. Where these prerequisites are lacking, ethnic rather than political nationalism predominates. Ethnic nationalism (as opposed to plain ethnic loyalty) is in itself a political derivative. It does not put forward any real alternatives to political nationalism. It is merely failed political nationalism.

This failure most often occurs in countries that tried to follow the Western model of nation-state development without having first obtained the respective level of liberal political culture. In these cases, at least initially, the countries have not opposed the Western experience of political nationalism. On the contrary, the objective all along has been to follow the Western blueprint. But lacking the political sophistication, these countries do not succeed in building strong liberal states. This sense of failure may push them toward embracing anti-Western ideologies as well.

Post-Communist Nationalism

The post-communist world has witnessed the predominance of ethnic over political nationalism. The countries of this region, after leaving communism behind and attempting to follow the Western model of modern statehood, hoped to rebuild both nation and state. They wanted a strong state legitimated by popular will and the recognition of the personal rights of citizens. But they also wanted the consolidation of the body politic as a nation based on a common cultural and historical heritage.

Post-communist countries, it turned out, rarely could achieve both these aims. In the absence of the particular economic, social, and cultural prerequisites of liberal ideology, the strong, rights-respecting state remained largely theoretical while the ethnic element dominated. The state became an instrument to preserve ethnic heritage and help exterminate any contradictory elements. The difficulty in building strong political and economic structures often led to identifying "treasonous" minorities as scapegoats. A weak civil society maintained weak ties to state structures, which in turn grew increasingly alienated from society and subsequently authoritarian. In this atmosphere, premodern feelings were less likely to be sublimated into state patriotism and the solidarity of common citizenship.

This development is rooted in the recent history of the region. Under communism, state power was completely identified with suppression, thus giving politics a reputation for being disgraceful and "dirty." The dissident movements for the most part insisted on morally resisting the oppressive regime and carefully avoided being political. Public spiritedness was only legitimate when negatively stated. The open refusal to participate left no room for a positive sense of public spirit.

Opposition movements certainly succeeded in mobilizing mass support as soon as the system loosened its grip (thanks to Gorbachev's policies). In the non-Russian republics of the Soviet Union, and to some extent in the formally independent states of the Soviet bloc, popular support was strengthened by the perception that a foreign power—the Soviet Russian Empire—blocked entry into the "civilized world." But mass support was really bolstered by populist slogans. These slogans were either based on strong anti-establishment sentiment (the "people" versus the indifferent and privileged "bureaucracy") or on nationalist sentiment. Slogans frequently substituted for a clearly defined program serving a particular constituency, since no rationally formulated interests existed under communist rule.

When the old communist regimes were formally delegitimized, new political elites seized power. (Even where former communists retook power, they too were "new" since the basis of their legitimacy and their manner of political conduct had changed.) This new elite faced tasks unprecedented in history. They could neither regard themselves as supporters of particular social forces nor claim to be encouraging social developments already under way. Only the promise and obligation of implementing a liberal-democratic model of the nation-state could truly legitimate the new governments. But to do so required garnering political will and building on civil and political traditions preserved from the pre-communist past. Those nations that had been under communist rule for a shorter time and had stronger pre-communist traditions of civil and political activities were more successful in transforming their systems.

Even for the most prepared post-communist country, however, changing drastically a way of life on such a weak basis soon led to a dissipation of reformist spirit. Public reactions of disappointment and depression multiplied, coupled with an indifference to politics and a cynicism for politicians (since politics, after all, was a "dirty" business). The media disclosed affairs scandalous enough to ruin any political career in the democratic West, but which left politicians in the East unscathed.[12] Population growth slowed catastrophically in both the more and less successful countries.[13] Four years after the fall of communism in Eastern Europe, this extremely dangerous state of depression caused by overstrain and disappointment produced more and more electoral victories for former communists (who were becoming less and less repentant about their communist past).

In countries such as Hungary or Bulgaria that already regarded themselves as nation-states and had at least formally independent status, national self-awareness under the communist regime was rather different. Although dependent on the Soviet Union in political, ideological, and economic senses, these countries still retained the symbolic elements of the nation-state. Their populations maintained separate citizenship. Their bureaucracies did not have to work in Russian. They felt themselves separated from the elder partner by real borders that could not be passed without visas. Apart from ideological restrictions, they were fairly independent in their cultural and educational policies. Unlike non-Russian Soviet republics such as Latvia or Georgia, no fears of mass migration or russification strengthened nationalist sentiment.

Thus, although anti-communist "revolutions" in Eastern Europe did promote full independence from Russia, nationalist slogans did not dominate the political scene and liberal and democratic values were still regarded as independent from nationalist rhetoric. East European liberals were from the very beginning critical of nationalists, while the latter, being divorced from the liberals, did not feel compelled to comply with Western values and therefore moved further to the right. The nationalist agenda resembled that of the former communists: capitalize on the hardships inflicted by Western liberal reformers and popularize statist programs with calls for national unity and uniqueness. Nationalism, in this environment, indeed became the "last stage of communism," as Adam Michnik has observed.

In other words, the less successful a country was in carrying out Westernizing political and economic reforms, the better the chances were that right-wing ethnic nationalism would play a significant role in society. Yugoslavia is the extreme example, but expressions of ethnic nationalism were quite strong in Bulgaria and Romania as well. At the other end of the spectrum stands the Czech Republic, one of the models of successful reform: even the divorce with Slovakia did not strengthen ethnic nationalism.

In supranational states like the Soviet Union and Yugoslavia, which viewed breakup as a decline of geopolitical vitality and tried various means to prevent movements for secession, the nationalisms of the "lead" nations—Russia and Serbia—were from the very beginning more openly and aggressively anti-Western and anti-liberal. The forces of nationalism were more clearly aligned with unrepentant and revanchist communists (the so-called "red-brown coalition" in Russia). Unity and grandeur were associated with the communist rule, while the breakup of the state was prompted by the demise of communist regimes.

For countries that regarded themselves as forcibly incorporated into these failed supranational states—the Baltic states, Georgia, Croatia—national independence was the primary item on the political agenda. National independence was included in the programs of all fronts, movements, and parties, alongside a democratic system of power, protection of human rights, market-oriented reforms, and other standard Western features. Political independence was merely the first step on the way to democratic transition. Possible contradictions between the values of independence and democracy remained purely theoretical, of interest only to intellectuals. These post-communist nationalist movements claimed to repeat the classic development of Western democracy and were clearly pro-Western.

But this pro-Western feeling was challenged by inevitable disappointments. The newly established states confidently (and naively) expected considerable Western help. After all, during the Cold War the West had supported the nationalist sentiments of "minorities" in order to weaken the communist regime. Moreover, since the fight for independence was inextricably linked to the fight for democracy, the democratic West was considered morally obliged to support pro-independence movements. The East did not realize that the West now understood the relationship between self-determination and democracy differently from the Wilsonian conception and judged cases according to pragmatic rather than idealistic considerations. Although confounding Eastern expectations, this change in Western policy did not lead to a proliferation of anti-Western sentiment. Instead, it contributed to a general sense of disarray.

In this climate of disappointed expectations, the question of ethnic minorities became the major test for these nationalist movements. According to the Western democratic ideal of political nationalism, national independence was supposed to become a joint cause for all would-be citizens regardless of ethnic origin. Majority elites would attract minorities into voluntarily joining the body politic. Stressing ethnic divisions and letting ethnic prejudice develop into open conflicts, meanwhile, would only weaken the cause of national independence.

But such conflicts, particularly in the multinational states of the former Soviet Union and former Yugoslavia, were difficult to avoid. Under communism, the legal systems in both countries required the registration of nationality based on ethnic origin (citizenship, meanwhile, was identified with allegiance to the political regime). Together with the degraded sense of political identity mentioned above, this official categorization made ethnicity the major element of a person's social identity. People schooled in this type of political awareness found it extremely difficult, after the communist regime was demolished, to marry their idea of national identity to the abstract, alien, and unemotional idea of citizenship that embraced people of different ethnic origin.

Thus, in a new atmosphere where nationalist slogans dominated the political agenda, the idea of national independence was easily ethnicized. Ethnic minorities felt a natural uneasiness, a fear that in the new nation-states they would be discriminated against as "second-class citizens." These anxieties were aggravated by both historical and contemporary circumstances, as Croats and Serbs in Croatia or Georgians, Abkhazians, and Ossetians in Georgia could readily verify.

Still, the major opponents of national self-determination were not ethnic minorities but centralist forces bent on maintaining the integrity of the Soviet and Yugoslav states. These centralists, especially in the Soviet Union, tried to defend their position with ideas acceptable to the West. But from the point of view of democratic legitimacy, their position was weak, since the separatist republics based their drive to independence on such democratic procedures as elections and plebiscites. Apart from pragmatic considerations of stability or support for Gorbachev's reforms, the only liberal principle on which the centralist forces could base their opposition to the drive of the republics to independence was the real or ostensible danger to the rights of minorities.

With this latter justification in mind, Moscow centralists encouraged minority opposition to the pro-independence movements in the secessionist republics, openly providing moral and political support and allegedly funneling covert money and arms. These organizations of minority opposition included the so-called Interfronts in the Baltic states, Polish autonomists in Lithuania, Abkhazian and Ossetian separatist movements in Georgia, and Transdniester and Gagauz separatists in Moldova. These policies heightened suspicions of ethnic minorities as the representatives of foreign interests in the country. A more open hostility from the core ethnic group and the hope of support from Russia radicalized the demands of the minority movements. This spiral of suspicions and hostility on some occasions resulted in bloody ethno-territorial war—in the Armenian enclave Nagorno-Karabakh in Azerbaijan, in the Abkhazian and South Ossetian regions of Georgia, on a smaller scale in the Russian-populated Transdniester region of Moldova, and lately in the Chechen autonomous region of the Russian federation.[14]

These conflicts between a core ethnic group and minorities did not, however, always reach this cataclysmic stage. For instance, the three Baltic countries succeeded in containing ethnic problems within certain acceptable limits. As a result, they have done reasonably well in building democratic state structures and safeguarding their political independence. Why the difference? Was the level of ethnic hostility higher in Moldova or Georgia than in Estonia, Latvia, or Lithuania?

Ethnic prejudice and suspicion, being more or less endemic to any multiethnic society, can always be driven to limits of hatred and open conflict. However, according to anecdotal evidence gathered both directly and from conversations with Russian or Western observers, the level of ethnic hostility toward Russians in the Baltic region had always been rather high compared with other regions of the former Soviet Union, at least as high as in Moldova or Georgia. Certainly Russia intentionally encouraged ethnic conflicts in Moldova and Georgia, but the same holds true for the Baltic states. While the Baltic pro-independence movements also received exceptionally strong support from the West—albeit tempered during the period of *perestroika*—it is difficult to demonstrate that this support could contain ethnic discontent within the region.

The Baltic political elites avoided bloody ethnic conflicts not because they were more internationalist. Their nationalist sentiment might be even more intense than elsewhere. But it was also more political in its mode of expression. This political element contained ethnic hostility (for both the majority and minority). Thanks to a stronger and better preserved tradition of political discourse and action, these societies were sufficiently mature to give the emotional drive for independence the form of a well-organized and disciplined political movement able to act within certain legal standards. The political elite succeeded in making the term "citizen" the keystone of state- and nation-building. Certain legal norms or political actions of the Baltic countries, especially after they gained independence, can be criticized as unreasonable and discriminating against Russian minorities. However, compared with the experience of the more southern regions of the post-communist world, the Baltic nationalist movements can serve as a model for using nationalist sentiment to build reasonably strong and fairly liberal state structures.

The Experience of Georgia

In 1989–91, the Georgian drive to independence seemed almost as strong, and sometimes even more vigorous, than the Baltic civic movements. The outcome, however, was quite different. Tensions with Abkhaz and Ossetian minorities, which developed parallel to the establishment of the Georgian independence movement, soon reached the stage of full-scale ethno-territorial wars. Thanks to the unofficial backing of Russia, as well as divisions and chaos on the Georgian side, both wars ended in the de facto secessions of the disputed regions. Moreover, territorial losses led to a civil war of Georgians against Georgians, which made the complete dissolution of the state a real possibility. Only the invitation of Russian troops offered a way out of this quagmire. Georgia thus became a strategic satellite of its northern neighbor. Its independent status in question, the nation fell victim to deep feelings of failure, frustration, and doubt.

Georgia's vision of an independent and democratic nation-state was one it shared with other East European nations. Primarily because of a low level of political culture, however, Georgia failed to live up to its ambitious vision. In other words, Georgia was Westernized enough for the model of a democratic nation-state to dominate its political agenda, but not Westernized enough to implement this model.

To be sure, whatever policies its political elite pursued, Georgia would still have had to face problems with its ethnic minorities, which constituted 30 percent of the population by the time of the breakup of the Soviet Union. The ensuing conflicts were not caused by the oppressive and discriminatory practices of Georgian nationalists, as some Russian or Western analysts prefer to think; nor were they simply stage-managed by Moscow, as many Georgians naively believe. Moreover, these conflicts did not concern "minority rights" as understood in Western democracies (the right to schools and theaters in the ethnic language, equal opportunity at the workplace, and so on).

Rather, these struggles concerned the status of certain territories and where they fit into the hierarchy of the Soviet federation. While this status would have predominantly symbolic meaning for most of the population, ethnic elites would garner important privileges in access to power. For those ethnic groups with autonomy status, an upgrade to full republic status meant secession from the would-be state—with predictable reaction from the majority population. For those with no territorial status, the demand for autonomy was perceived by the majority population as a step in the direction of final secession. Hence, any area densely populated with ethnic minorities could play host to conflict. The potential increased where minorities lived in border regions of a would-be country, enjoyed or hoped for some cross-border support, could claim a given piece of land as historically "theirs," or enjoyed some status in the Soviet hierarchy of ethno-territorial units.

In Georgia, all these factors came into play. Abkhazians, for instance, once possessed an autonomous republic and resided across the border from Russian regions populated by culturally related Circassian tribes. Ossetes once had an *oblast* and lived adjacent to their kin on the other side of the Caucasus mountains. Armenians lived in large numbers near the Georgian-Armenian border and Azeris near the border with Azerbaijan, but neither enjoyed special status in Georgia.[15] Certain of these groups have also clashed with Georgians in the past. During its brief history of independence in 1918–21, Georgia fought secessionist forces in Abkhazia and South Ossetia, and conducted a war with Armenia, which had territorial claims on Georgia. Finally, in the southwest corner of the country, Ajaria represents a special case. The Ajarians are Georgian Muslims who could once claim the only confessional autonomy in the Soviet Union. In Bosnia, territorial autonomy on a confessional basis helped to establish a separate ethnic identity. Although such an identity has yet to emerge in Ajaria, conflict may still arise between this ethnic group and the Georgian state.

In Abkhazia and South Ossetia, separatists voiced their demands early on, echoing Georgian calls for independence from the Soviet Union. Georgians accused these minorities of treason before they had even turned their aspirations into something politically tangible. It is difficult to imagine how this spiral of mutually reinforcing suspicions could have been avoided. The encouragement of Russian politicians keen on first preserving and later restoring the Soviet Union in some form greatly diminished the chances of preventing conflict. On the other hand, no Georgian politician, however liberal or internationalist, could possibly have convinced the Georgian public of the unimportance of national independence or the acceptability of an independent Abkhazia or South Ossetia. Still, the inadequate, even hysterical reactions of the Georgian political elite to these inevitable challenges from ethnic minorities greatly encouraged these conflicts.

After all, the ethnic dimension of nationalism dominated the Georgian national movement to a greater degree than in the more politically sophisticated cultures of the Baltic countries. As the Baltic experience demonstrated, putting controversial problems of ethnic politics into "cold" legal terms, without any direct reference to ethnicity, was crucial in keeping ethnic passions in check. But the Georgian elite failed to place the problem of citizenship at the center of political debate. The first Georgian president, Zviad Gamsakhurdia, pursued policies that were often regarded with good reason as the model for post-communist ethnonationalism. He had no clear approach to citizenship. The result was that the average Georgian could not sum up his or her patriotic feeling with the phrase "citizen of Georgia."

References to medieval history and blood kinship, not political notions of citizenship, completely dominated the nationalist agenda in Georgia. For instance, editorial writers who bore the decisive responsibility for shaping the Georgian national consciousness often argued that minorities were relative newcomers to the Georgian territory. If loyal to the emerging Georgian state, these minorities would be granted the right to live in peace and even have schools and theaters in their own language. If not, they would be regarded and treated as "traitors" and "ungrateful guests." Also characteristic of this premodern understanding of nationhood was a special stress on the "Christian" nature of the Georgian nation, which had formed its identity in part during medieval struggles against Muslim invaders. Such an emphasis dangerously alienated ethnically Georgian Muslims—not to mention Azeris—who by this logic could become authentic Georgians only if Christianized.

True, Gamsakhurdia at times displayed a more moderate side. Several months before the October 1990 elections, he gave up his earlier demand of abolishing the autonomous regions in Georgia. But a bloody conflict in Ossetia was already under way, and when the Ossetians declared secession from Georgia soon after he was elected, he could think of no better retaliation than formally abolishing their autonomy. The bloodshed intensified, and unable to do anything about it, Gamsakhurdia tried to capitalize on the "state of war" and the "foreign threat" to consolidate his power. He also encouraged expulsions of thousands of completely loyal Ossetians from inner parts of the country. On the other hand, Gamsakhurdia became very cautious on the Abkhazian issue, and made important concessions to minority demands, accepting the election law for the regional parliament based on ethnic quotas, which gave the ethnic Abkhazians (17 percent of the population) more seats than the ethnic Georgians (46 percent of the population).

Despite these occasional signs of moderation, Gamsakhurdia's authoritarian manners and paranoid character eventually caused a split within the ruling coalition and, later, an armed coup. With Gamsakhurdia ousted in 1992, the country remained divided, with supporters of the former president in control of some regions bordering Abkhazia. Separatist leaders representing an ethnic Abkhaz minority, who could take advantage of their slim majority in the regional parliament, were encouraged to declare de facto separation. Although new Georgian leader Eduard Shevardnadze was cautious about military solutions, in the anarchic atmosphere of the post-coup period he was too weak to prevent more radical members of his coalition from trying to tame the separatists by force. Moreover, the post-coup leadership, presiding over a divided nation, needed a unifying issue, and the war in Abkhazia could play that role.

The war that continued for more than a year ended in tragedy. The threat of territorial dissolution did not unite the nation. On the contrary, pro-Gamsakhurdia insurgents made deals with separatists in the hopes that a defeat of governmental troops would lead to Shevardnadze's ouster. With no side strong enough to win, the country seemed to go to pieces. Only thanks to a deal with Russia, in which the country gave up a substantial portion of its sovereignty, was this nightmare scenario avoided. The insurgents were defeated and a reasonable order re-established in the remaining parts of the country.

It would be misleading to say that for some cultural or psychological reasons Georgians are less tolerant than others. Georgians have traditionally boasted of a historical record of ethnic and religious tolerance and have been particularly proud to stress that the Jewish minority lived in the country for more than 2,000 years without suffering from anti-Semitism. Many Georgians still sincerely believe that if not for Moscow's provocation, ethnic wars could not possibly have broken out on Georgian soil. Both assertions could be exaggerations; but at least they show some willingness to embrace tolerance as a general value. Instead of suffering from a genetic flaw, the Georgian political elite failed to respond adequately to its ethnic challenges because of a lack of tradition in running a modern state, an isolation from Western political culture, and tragically weak structures of civil society.

Western Impact

The age-old sentiments of ethnic solidarity and hostility to foreigners from which nationalism draws most of its energy are in themselves neither political nor anti-political. They become anti-political if the society lacks the ability to think in political terms and act in a political way. Under some conditions nationalism can promote a liberal-democratic transformation;

in other circumstances, nationalism can become a serious obstacle. In the latter case, nationalism itself doesn't pose the major danger—rather the lack of a political understanding of liberal and democratic values is the greatest risk.

The more ethnic the nationalism, the more vulnerable it is to the liberal critique and the weaker it is intrinsically. Nationalism is most successful when most political, hence most compliant with liberal and democratic standards; where it becomes more ethnic, more paranoid, and as a result more extreme, it also has less chance of achieving its own goals. To put it another way, since nationalism—as "self-determination"— has emerged in the first place as an element of a more general liberal-democratic project, its success is highly dependent on the implementation of this general project.

In post-communist societies, where the social and economic basis for the liberal-democratic order is lacking or extremely weak, political nationalism can become the major force containing ethnic suspicion and hatred. It is no coincidence that the first ethnic massacres in the last years of the Soviet Union happened not in the Baltic countries where political nationalist movements were strongest but in regions such as Azerbaijan, Uzbekistan, and Kyrgyzstan that had no traditions of political nationalism to speak of. If not channeled through political action, ethnic nationalism is an amorphous destructive force that not only targets "suspicious" minorities but ultimately undermines the chances of building a viable state in the name of the majority ethnic group.

Liberal democrats may dream of an ideal society where the feelings of solidarity in ethnic or confessional communities no longer matter politically. But since such feelings remain influential, the transformation of ethnicity into political nationalism is the best option for the perpetuation of liberal-democratic ideas. As the market economy successfully channels the potentially destructive energy of selfish greed into the production of goods beneficial for society, so the channeling of the potentially dangerous energy of nationalist pride into the creation of viable state institutions has been crucial to the success of liberal democracy.

An inability or unwillingness to distinguish political from ethnic nationalisms produces policies encouraging the latter, as the case of Georgia suggests. But this inability is not simply a threat to those currently involved in so-called ethnic conflicts. The postmodern trend of depoliticization (or re-ethnicization) of nationalist sentiments, most clearly manifested in multiculturalism, poses a deadly threat to the viability of Western liberal democracy. In this situation, the basic civic solidarity of "we the people" degenerates into a patchwork of potentially hostile ethnic allegiances, and the link is severed between the cultural heritage of society and the overall regulations of the liberal-democratic state. The state becomes a soulless broker for stability while the individual trades the dignity of being a citizen for the right to represent a certain ethnic or confessional group. This new legitimization of anti-political ethnicity in the citadel of liberal democracy is ultimately more dangerous for democratic values than the failed ethnic nationalisms of the post-communist world.

The communist bloc broke up not because of external political or economic pressures on the governments. Rather, the presence of a more successful and humane Western model convinced people who lived under communist regimes that their political systems were obsolete and had to be changed. The same holds true today. The Western presence continues to be the major factor keeping post-communist societies, despite internal complications, on the track of democratic market reforms. This Western model of democratic and open nation-states also helps to prevent the emergence of fascist-like authoritarian regimes. Post-communist states want to be part of the "civilized world," which implies certain standards of ethnic politics. Once these standards are undermined, however, this critical restraining factor no longer works.

The West, therefore, must remain a strong economic and political center, acting on the basis of liberal democratic values in both internal and international politics. Programs designed to influence post-communist power elites or provide technical assistance are of secondary importance. Moreover, the West should beware of the destructive effects of short-term considerations that ultimately undercut basic values. For instance, the West eased pressure on Serbia to give Boris Yeltsin some breathing room with his domestic opposition. While this strategy may have helped Yeltsin pass certain bills in parliament, it also sent a message that certain values would not be taken too seriously, thus ultimately strengthening the anti-democratic opposition in Russia (as well as in other countries).

The West should not overestimate its power and direct influence. Nor should it intervene when it can't make a decisive difference. If the West does intervene, however, its objectives should be clearly defined and it should be confident about its moral force to achieve its ends. In this way, the West can promote its own brand of civic solidarity and help it overcome ethnic chauvinism.

Notes

1. Francis Fukuyama described this end of history—liberalism victorious after the demise of communism—in *The End of History and the Last Man* (New York: Free Press, 1992). I share his arguments that, unlike communism, which claims a universal ideological validity, those ideologies that openly reject liberal values in the post-Cold War world (ethnic nationalism, fascism, Islamic fundamentalism) have only limited scope.

2. This point is best developed by Allan Bloom, *The Closing of the American Mind* (New York: Simon and Schuster, 1987).

3. Michel Foucault, *Les Mots et les Choses: Une Archeologie des Sciences Humaines* (Paris: Gallimard, 1966).

4. I also deal with this subject in "Nationhood and Self-Recollection: Ways to Democracy after Communism," in *Towards a New Community: Culture and Pol-*

itics in Post-Totalitarian Europe, eds. Peter Duncan and Martin Rady (Hamburg and Muenster: Lit Verlag, 1993).

5. I have dealt with this question in "Nationalism and Democracy," *Journal of Democracy*, Vol. 3, No. 4 (October 1992).

6. "Noble ideals had been pronounced as if for all Americans, yet in practice they applied only to white people. Most interpretations of the national identity from Crevecoeur on were for whites only." Arthur M. Schlesinger, Jr., *The Disuniting of America* (New York: W. W. Norton & Co., 1992), p. 38.

7. Hans Kohn, *The Idea of Nationalism: A Study in the Origin and Background* (New York: Macmillan, 1944).

8. "Almost all European governments eventually took steps which homogenized their populations." Charles Tilly, "Reflections on the History of European State-Making," in *The Formation of National States in Western Europe*, ed. Charles Tilly (Princeton: Princeton University Press, 1975), p. 43.

9. Eugen Weber, *Peasants into Frenchmen: The Modernization of Rural France, 1870–1914* (Stanford: Stanford University Press, 1976).

10. Robert Nisbet, *Community and Power* (New York: Oxford University Press, 1962).

11. Elie Kedourie, *Nationalism* (London: Hutchinson University Library, 1961), p. 31.

12. Petruska Sustrova describes the situation in one of the most successful and Western-oriented post-communist states, the Czech Republic: "State institutions are not responsive to information revealed in the media. Scandals that in other countries would lead to the resignation of top government officials rarely cause a stir in the Czech Republic. . . . This inattention undermines the public's confidence in the importance of the press in a democracy. People have lost the initiative to get involved in public matters, and have come to believe that nothing has changed and that 'those on top are doing what they like anyway.' Apathy and disinterest have returned." Petruska Sustrova, "Pitfalls of the Independent Press in the Czech Republic," *Uncaptive Minds*, Vol. 6, No. 2 (Summer 1993), p. 100.

13. Nicholas Eberstadt, "Demographic Disaster," *The National Interest*, No. 36 (Summer 1994), pp. 53–58.

14. Of these, the Nagorno-Karabakh case is in some respects exceptional. No independence movement existed in this enclave before the war began; on the contrary, the war helped establish one. Moreover, the Armenians enjoyed support from Russian democrats who hastened the dissolution of the Soviet Union and not the hardliners who sought to maintain it. Only after the Soviet Union's demise did the Russian government clearly support Armenia as a strategic ally in the Caucasus. Also in Chechnya, paradoxically, Russian hardliners during the Soviet period encouraged Chechen separatism against Yeltsin's insurgent republican government.

15. To date, however, neither Armenians nor Azeris have launched movements for autonomy within Georgia.

8

The Baltic Predicament

ALEX GRIGORIEVS

From the founding of their pro-independence movements in 1988 to the Soviet interventions of 1991, the Baltic countries of Latvia, Lithuania, and Estonia were the pivot on which several important global issues hinged. Defying the Soviet superpower, these small countries tested whether Gorbachev's *perestroika* should be taken in earnest. They also established a nonviolent pattern for revolution in the region. In 1989, the "Baltic Way"—the 500-mile chain of people holding hands from Tallinn to Vilnius to protest 50 years of Soviet occupation—demonstrated not only dedication and unity in the bid for independence, but also remarkable organization and self-restraint.

In quite a different way the Baltic countries have again become important in the mid-1990s. While the more homogeneous Lithuania has successfully managed its inter-ethnic problems, Latvia and Estonia have become test cases for reconciling nationalism and citizenship in the post-communist world. A very complicated knot of ethnic, legal, and military problems is currently being untangled in these two countries. The key question, or the "Baltic predicament," is whether these small nations can preserve their identity without sacrificing democracy.

Unlike their Lithuanian neighbor, both Latvia and Estonia have come down on the side of identity. In their current laws, both countries have barred recent settlers from citizenship—ostensibly in reaction to half a century of Soviet occupation—thereby leaving up to a third of the population without civil rights. Estonia and Latvia clearly reveal the contradiction between a liberal democracy based on individual rights and the nation-state as an expression, guardian, and, in a sense, property of one ethnic community.

This predicament is neither Baltic nor Eastern European nor even particularly European in nature. No country in the world can boast of having completely resolved the tension between democracy and nationalism. At one end of the political spectrum, Afrikaaners in South Africa once preserved their identity and way of life by completely disenfranchising other ethnic groups. Now, after the fall of apartheid, they too must assert their ethnicity within new egalitarian political institutions. At the other end of the spectrum, liberal democracies have also been subject to strife. In France, for example, a concept of nation based more on shared values, language, and citizenship than on common ancestry is being undermined from several sides simultaneously. Jean-Marie Le Pen's National Front demands a *France aux Français*, with French citizenship based on *jus sanguinis* (ancestry) rather than *jus soli* (place of birth and domicile). Meanwhile, Muslim minorities defy the French concept of nation by asserting their distinctive, unassimilable identity and values.

Elsewhere, governments fall somewhere between apartheid and French civic egalitarianism. Although a liberal democracy, Israel declares itself the state of the Jewish nation. This constitutional formulation excludes Arabs (a significant minority even among citizens of Israel) but does not disenfranchise them.[1] Germany shares the Israeli concept of the state as the property of a people of common descent who claim special rights. By law, ethnic Germans have the right to German citizenship irrespective of the actual place of their birth and domicile. In the 1990s, this distinction between ethnic Germans and non-ethnic German residents of the country, combined with the non-citizen status and lack of political representation of Turks and other ethnic minorities there, appears to have compounded militant ethnonationalism and given rise to fears of resurrected national socialism.[2]

In Eastern Europe, the legal link between ethnicity and the state has been strengthened over the past few years.[3] Witness the changed preamble of the Slovak constitution. It once began with the words "We, the citizens of Slovakia." Today it reads "We, the Slovak nation," thereby ignoring the substantial Hungarian minority in southern Slovakia.

To many observers this ethnicization might seem irrational. But as the German political scientist Claus Offe has written, ethnicization has been pursued as a tool for political mobilization, both in overcoming the communist regimes and rendering the new free states cohesive after the collapse of the old.[4] Similarly, Ulrich Preuss refers to the "integrative function" of ethnicization.[5] Preuss points out, however, that "while ethnicity [can be] regarded as an integrative element of citizenship of the nation-state, it is at the same time also a divisive force. . . . To cope with this ambiguity of ethnicity is one of the most difficult tasks of the polity."[6] Indeed, the same ethnic politics that creates a cohesive society out of Slovaks alienates their ethnic Hungarian co-citizens.

The above approaches to citizenship, from the French to the former South African, are nothing more than attempts to find an ad hoc solution to the ambiguity of national identity. The difficulty is that no objective criteria exist for determining the proper balance between ethnicity and democracy. To compound the problem, the international community has been inconsistent in recognizing or censuring states for their actions in this regard. Without clearly articulated standards, international behavior very often derives from geopolitical considerations (such as Western acquiescence in strategic ally Turkey's almost all-out war on its Kurdish minority).

In the absence of adequate international standards, political elites in multiethnic societies will often use ethnic politics to further their own programs.[7] When the majority is sufficiently large, it can ignore the minority, since this alternative electorate cannot realistically challenge the ruling elite's control of the state. Where minorities are large enough to influence the result of elections, rulers can be tempted either to forgo elections altogether or disenfranchise part of the electorate. In this case, democracy continues formally but the circle of participants is significantly narrowed, as in South Africa's denial of voting rights to non-whites after 1948 and revocation of the citizenship of black Africans after 1970. Even when disenfranchisement is not a political necessity, however, the minority often serves as a convenient enemy, a perceived fifth column indispensable for political mobilization.

After independence, the ruling elites of Estonia and Latvia essentially chose the disenfranchisement option for their large Russian-speaking minorities. Ostensibly reflecting a desire to redress historic wrongs,[8] the actions of these elites have been determined to a larger degree by outside circumstances. When these circumstances have encouraged interethnic cooperation, such cooperation has been more likely to develop with the local Russians. Thus, the existence of the Soviet Union and the need for international support pushed Estonian and Latvian elites toward compromise. Early in the struggle for independence, interethnic peace and universal suffrage were perceived as conditions for international acceptance.

Unfortunately, the only way of discovering the acceptability of one's actions in the international setting is to test its limits. The recent disenfranchisement of most Russian-speakers in Estonia and Latvia has been just such a test. At the same time it has rendered interethnic cooperation unlikely as a strategy for mobilizing the electorate. The danger now is that as internal electoral fights continue to radicalize nationalist rhetoric and policies, the new divisiveness may lead to a collapse of these states, or at best to a protracted period of low-key tension that could erupt at any moment. Compromise under these conditions can only be reached by once again expanding the electorate. In the case of the Baltics, while the immediate terms of compromise will have to be reached and tested within the given countries, this electoral expansion will only be achieved if the international community presses for a politics of tolerance.

Concord Versus Discord

The most important question the Popular Fronts in Estonia and Latvia dealt with immediately after their inception in October 1988 was how to win Russian votes. Under universal suffrage and with the titular nationality composing only 62 percent and 52 percent in Estonia and Latvia respectively (compared with 80 percent in Lithuania), radical nationalists were destined for electoral failure. According to the Soviet law on elections, not only all permanent residents but even Soviet army soldiers and officers stationed in the territory could vote. Therefore, the electoral programs of the Popular Fronts were designed specifically to appeal also to local Russian-speaking residents.

The Popular Fronts in both countries stressed democratization and individual liberties for all rather than just for the ethnic majority. They portrayed Soviet communism as the enemy of all ethnic cultures, including Russians, and extoled the interethnic cooperation of the inter-war period. The Latvian Popular Front stressed the country's tradition of tolerance and multiculturalism (for instance, Latvia shared with Kazakhstan the highest percentage of inter-ethnic marriages, 25 percent, in the Soviet Union). Finally, the Front explicitly promoted ethnic minorities—not only ethnic Russians, who constituted 34 percent of the Latvian population, but also Belarusians, Ukrainians, Poles, and Lithuanians, who together made up a sizeable 11.6 percent. These non-Russians could be important electoral allies. Besides, an emphasis on the diversity of ethnic minorities allowed Latvians to feel like a plurality when they did not form a significant majority.

Latvia's Popular Front even helped organize and finance a Congress of the Peoples of Latvia. In December 1988, representatives of roughly 20 ethnic minorities, including the tiny Azeri population, discussed reviving national cultures, teaching minority languages, and establishing ties with the cultural and educational organizations of the mother countries. The concept of a multiethnic Latvia as "our common home" was introduced, where all ethnic groups could live in peace and develop their national cultures. The Russians created several widely respected and influential associations—including the Baltic-Slavic Society and the Latvian Society of Russian Culture—which regarded the Popular Front and the future independent Latvian state as a guarantor of their cultural, individual, and religious freedoms.

At the same time, the first Congress of the Peoples of Latvia endorsed certain other concepts that were not necessarily as liberal and democratic as they initially appeared. Ethnic identity was taken to be an intrinsic component of human culture and individual normalcy. It was even said to constitute a value far above all others, and people without any evident preoccupation with ethnic identity came to be viewed as abnormal, to be pitied or castigated. Curiously, this trend echoed Stalin's various anti-Semitic campaigns against "cosmopolitans." Some Latvian Jews were understandably alarmed by the connotation and defended their right to be indifferent to their own ethnic ancestry. This preoccupation with ethnicity also led to the dangerous belief that every ethnic group has a natural home where members of the group ought to live.

However, these negative tendencies of ethnicity remained dormant. At this Congress, and indeed throughout these first years of struggling for independence, the stress was laid on diversity as a source of cultural richness, on the people of Latvia (a political concept of a nation) instead of the Latvian people (an ethnic designation). These policies were not a tactical ploy but a genuine attempt to deal with the reality of an ethnically mixed population enjoying universal suffrage.

From its inception, the Popular Front of Latvia played host to two competing tendencies: one that supported the integration of all ethnic groups into a democratic state and the other that fought for an ethnically exclusive democracy. According to the nationalist tendency, only those residents of the republics who had been citizens of the pre-war states and their descendants had the right to citizenship in Estonia and Latvia. All other residents were illegal aliens. The exclusivist trend, whose slogan became "For a Latvian Latvia," was soon institutionalized as the Latvian National Independence Movement, known by its Latvian acronym LNNK. Later, competing organizations appeared even further to the right, most notably the Citizens' Congress. Yet initially these extremists were on the fringes of the movement, with the center occupied by more moderate leaders such as the Latvian Dainis Īvāns (Chairman of the Popular Front in 1988–90), the Russian Marina Kostenecka, and the Pole Jānis Jurkāns.[9] In Estonia, meanwhile, the Russian minority was large enough to be a problem but not to determine the outcome of elections. Therefore, the Citizens' Congress of Estonia, with its strategy of ignoring Russians, was a much stronger nationalist organization than its namesake in Latvia and almost surpassed in influence the Estonian Popular Front.

Many non-indigenous residents of Estonia and Latvia and, to a lesser degree, Lithuania were so scared by the rhetoric of these nationalist leaders that they rushed to support the communist-dominated and KGB-supported Interfronts. Although the names of these organizations suggest internationalism, they instead acted as conservative communist organizations supporting the preservation of the Soviet Union and the Soviet system of government. They were not particularly successful—even the largest demonstrations in Riga or Tallinn could only gather around 10,000 people compared with up to half a million for the Popular Fronts. Nonetheless, these Interfronts threatened the Popular Fronts because of their associations with the central government in Moscow, the KGB, and the Soviet Army.

The actions and rhetoric of these organizations reinforced the extreme nationalist wing of Latvian and Estonian political organizations. Thus formed a vicious circle of extremism, one that characterizes most ethnic conflicts around the world.[10] The political center of the Popular Fronts of Latvia and Estonia worked hard between 1988 and 1991 to prevent this vicious circle by developing programs that could reconcile the divergent agendas and priorities of Baltic residents. Politicians sought to guarantee civil rights for all while still assuaging fears on the part of indigenous populations that their country could be reunited with Russia.

One of the more prominent of these programs, the Popular Front of Latvia's "Theses for National Consolidation" published in 1989,[11] attempted to address the legitimate concerns of ethnic Latvians without violating the democratic rights of all people living in the country. As stated in the Theses, ethnic Latvians (the "titular ethnicity") were the *initiators* of Latvian state sovereignty while all people of the country were *guarantors* of that sovereignty. The right of ethnic Latvians to demand independent statehood was affirmed. However, only the cooperation of the entire population of Latvia could guarantee the stability and independence of the state. Moreover, the participation of non-Latvians in drafting and implementing the political, legal, and economic framework of the new independent Latvian state would guarantee the rights of non-Latvians.

Admittedly, these concepts were freighted with much symbolism, but myths and symbols are such stuff that nations are made of. Adoption of these symbols would have led to the concept of a political (French model) rather than an ethnic (German model) nation in Latvia. Citizenship would have been the result of the free choice of individuals who had lived in Latvia no less than 10 years and had a knowledge of conversational Latvian. In its 1989 law on citizenship, Lithuania adopted a similar approach, allowing all residents to opt for citizenship. Consequently, it has had far fewer problems with Russians inside and outside the country. But there, the small Russian minority (7 percent) could not affect the general outcome of the elections and did not figure much in the electoral strategies of the Lithuanian popular movement *Sajudis*.

The ideas behind the "Theses for National Consolidation" eventually made their way into the second program of the Popular Front, which aimed to establish a sort of consociational democracy in Latvia. It was a compromise based on the understanding that non-Latvians would recognize Latvian as the state language and support Latvia's independence in exchange for full citizenship rights in the restored country.

This language-and-independence for citizenship-and-civil-rights compromise appears to deny collective rights to the country's Russians as a distinctive minority. But it was nevertheless viable and acceptable to a majority of Latvians and about half of the country's non-Latvian community, according to electoral and referenda results. Massive Russian support for Baltic independence undermined communist allegations about ethnic tensions and disturbances in the Baltics. Indeed, up to 1991, the Baltic movements included almost the entire population of the area, and independence was perceived as synonymous with democracy.

The political necessity of getting as much support as possible for the Popular Front and its candidates thus promoted and institutionalized interethnic cooperation and compromise. Had these policies been implemented, quite a different set of ideas and myths about Latvia and Estonia could have replaced the official xenophobia that became state ideology by the mid–1990s.

Toward Conflict

On October 15, 1991, the Supreme Council of Latvia passed a resolution declaring that only those who were citizens at the time of Soviet occupation in 1940 and their descendants could now be citizens.[12] The parliament thus left in political limbo more than a third of the country's population. For over a month these non-Latvians could consider themselves citizens of the Soviet Union. But in December 1991 that country ceased to exist. Estonia enacted its citizenship law in February 1992, barring its Soviet-time immigrants from citizenship and rendering them stateless as well.[13]

This new legal status also transformed property rights (only citizens could own land), social security status (in Latvia retired non-citizens were entitled to 90 percent of the social benefits citizens received), the right to self-defense (only citizens could possess and bear arms), and employment (civil service became the province of citizens only). Some restrictions applied as well to non-citizens' involvement in business.

These new laws on citizenship deprived non-indigenous communities of political significance. Participation in the body politic as a guarantee of equal rights defined earlier in the "Theses for National Consolidation" was no longer a viable option. This drastic change in the composition of the electorate transformed the entire political landscape of Latvia and Estonia. The political necessity of attracting the non-indigenous vote vanished and with it disappeared the inclusive policies of the main political organizations. The Latvian citizenship act implied that a subsequent provision would enable a large part of non-citizens to naturalize. But then the ruling group in parliament and the government realized that it had already alienated its former Russian supporters; once naturalized they would not vote for the same leadership. The draft provisions for naturalization quietly died. Only under intense international pressure was a procedure on naturalization included in the 1994 Citizenship Law, with the first naturalizations taking place in spring 1995.

The disappearance of most non-indigenous voters from the electorate profoundly affected the electoral strategies, ideology, and rhetoric of the emerging political parties in Estonia and Latvia. Moderate leaders in the Popular Fronts, such as Dainis Īvāns, were gradually pushed aside. In Estonia, the moderate Popular Front government of Edgar Savisaar fell in 1993. Democratic Russian groups, which had vigorously supported the Popular Fronts in their bid for independence, felt rejected and grew increasingly critical of the national governments and the political regimes they installed. As Jurijs Abizovs, an influential author and leader of the Latvian Society for Russian Culture, told Radio Liberty in August 1993, "Before we were important and our advice and assistance were sought. We were invited to meet Gorbachev as part of the Latvian delegation to demonstrate that not ethnic Latvians alone support independence. Now we are discarded."

In elections to the Latvian and Estonian parliaments in 1992 and 1993, in which the indigenous population primarily formed the electorate, virtually all parties maintained that Estonia and Latvia were on the verge of extinction and that the Russians were to blame. A pre-election booklet for a leading party in the ruling coalition asks the question: "With so many non-ethnic Latvians in Latvia, how will the interests of ethnic Latvians be defended?" Its answer: ethnic Latvians will be protected by creating a one-community Latvian nation-state, by instituting the Latvian language as the only state language, and by adopting annual naturalization quotas for non-citizens.

Not content with the introduction of annual quotas, another member of the ruling coalition in 1993–94, the Farmers' Union, called for legislation that would limit the number of non-ethnic Latvian citizens. The Latvian National Independence Movement (LNNK) has been more precise: it has argued that non-ethnic Latvians should not exceed 25 percent of the total population and voluntary repatriation of non-Latvians should be encouraged. The even more outspoken parties in the "Freedom and Fatherland" bloc (FF) advocated a program of three d's: de-occupation (of all Russian troops and military installations), de-colonization (expulsion of non-citizens), and de-communization (barring former high-ranking communists from positions in government and education). In addition to the already existing ban on non-citizen employment in the state administration, the FF called for sharper restrictions on non-citizens in private businesses.

Once in power in Latvia and Estonia as a result of citizens-only elections, these nationalists have understandably sought to maintain their hold on political life by controlling the composition of the electorate. Aware that the international community expects the naturalization of settlers from the Soviet period, the ruling elites have sought to influence elections on at least a one-time basis by dragging their feet in adopting the necessary legislation, then by procrastinating with implementation, and then by being slow in allocating money to the institutions responsible for naturalization.

Concurrently, the Latvian government has turned a blind eye to the harassment of individuals and groups in accordance with its personnel's individual perceptions of right and wrong. For instance, the Department of Citizenship and Immigration of Latvia has been particularly active in abusing the rights of non-citizens, routinely violating the Latvian law and refusing to comply with judicial rulings.[14] Documented by the international human rights organization Helsinki Watch, these practices have included the denial of registration, which affects over 160,000 Latvian inhabitants or 7 percent of the population.[15] A registration stamp is still the only legal basis for a former Soviet citizen to stay in Latvia. Without such stamps, people living in Latvia become non-existent in the Orwellian sense of the word—they cannot work, receive social benefits, start a business, or receive medical assistance. They can also be expelled from Latvia by force. The department has already issued roughly 1,000 deportation orders, some of these to separate spouses and parents from their children. Not surprisingly, the Russian community believes that the department is implementing a covert government policy of expulsion. State Minister of Human Rights Olafs Bruveris has described the department as a political party carrying out its own program rather than an executive institution.[16]

The discrimination extends to privatization and travel. According to the new Latvian law, non-citizens cannot buy the land under the house they own. If they travel abroad, they have to pay for a return visa. Often they cannot travel abroad at all since they are not issued travel documents once their Soviet foreign travel passports have expired. Foreign embassies and consulates often compound these discriminatory measures with ones of their own. To get a British visa, for instance, a non-citizen resident of the Baltic countries must travel to Moscow. And the American embassy under Ambassador Ints Siliņš, himself an ethnic Latvian, has been reported to routinely deny U.S. visas to Latvia's non-citizens.

By contrast, Estonia's 1992 citizenship law in many ways belongs to the Popular Front era with its liberal approach to ethnic minorities and the political concept of nation. The residency requirement for naturalization is a mere two years from March 30, 1990 (changed to five years in 1995). In addition, unlike their Latvian counterparts, non-citizens in Estonia are allowed to participate in local elections, even though they are not allowed to stand for office.

However, there are some catches. The naturalization procedure requires a test of proficiency in the Estonian language. Instructions for the tests were not issued until April 1993. Consequently, in the period since the law was passed and April 1993, only 5,948 applicants out of the over 400,000-strong non-citizen community received Estonian citizenship.[17] The reasons for excluding non-citizens from the electorate are the same as in Latvia—to boost the number of voters for the parties in power and reduce the number of prospective voters who would likely vote against those currently in power. Here, nationalism was both useful and internationally accepted.

Nationalism's Vicious Circle

The vindictive attitude Estonia and Latvia demonstrate toward their minorities occurs when nationalism is transformed from an emancipatory force to an oppressive ideology unchecked by outside pressures. In a more general sense, this transformation corresponds to the pattern of revolutions described by the former Polish dissident Adam Michnik. Increasingly uneasy about the changing political mood in his own country, Michnik writes,

> Every revolution, bloody or not, has two phases. The first phase is defined by the struggle for freedom, the second by the struggle for power and revenge

on the votaries of the *ancien régime*. The struggle for freedom is beautiful. Anyone who has taken part in this struggle has felt, almost physically, how everything that is best and most precious within him was awakened. Revenge has a different psychology. Its logic is implacable. First there is a purge of yesterday's adversaries, the partisans of the old regime. Then comes the purge of yesterday's fellows of the opposition, who now oppose the idea of revenge. Finally there is a purge of those who defend them. A psychology of vengeance and hatred develops.[18]

This psychology of hatred and vengeance develops precisely because the struggle for freedom gives way to a struggle for power. The disenfranchisement of opponents on political or ethnic grounds becomes a useful tool for getting rid of rivals and mobilizing supporters. Some politicians using these tools are true believers, some unscrupulous schemers. In certain cases, former prominent communists have overemphasized nationalism as a way of legitimizing their continued power.

The psychology of vengeance encouraged by the parliaments of Latvia and Estonia has turned out embarrassing not only for liberals inside these countries but also for those abroad who actively supported the Baltic drive for independence. Russian President Boris Yeltsin is a case in point. Immediately after his election as chairman of the Supreme Council of Russia in May 1990, he spoke out in support of Baltic independence. In January 1991, when communist hardliners staged a dress rehearsal in Vilnius and Riga for a repressive coup, the arrival of Russia's leader in Tallinn turned the tide. There Yeltsin signed treaties that essentially recognized Baltic independence.

Unfortunately, almost immediately after international recognition of their renewed independence in 1991, Estonia and Latvia violated these treaties by their maltreatment of Russian minorities.[19] Russia's democrats, accustomed to allegations of maltreatment of Russians as a communist ploy to undermine Baltic aspirations for independence, initially brushed aside news of inter-ethnic problems and attempted to prove that everything was fine. Even now this miraculous transformation—of an underdog into a bully, of good guys turning bad—is an embarrassing topic for leaders of Democratic Russia. On the other hand, Russia's nationalist opposition grabbed at this opportunity to drum up patriotism and criticize Yeltsin and his government for complaisance. St. Petersburg telejournalist Aleksandr Nevzorov and Vladimir Zhirinovsky (who wants to turn the Baltic countries into a *gubernia* of Russia) are examples of such imperial populists.

Russia, too, acted with a great deal of bearish clumsiness. When Latvia passed a law that naturalization of non-citizens would only start after the withdrawal of all Russian troops, Yeltsin retaliated with a statement suspending the troop withdrawal. This statement appears to have been entirely for domestic consumption, however, since in reality the Russian army pull-out continued and was eventually completed. Some analysts attributed this discrepancy between rhetoric and action to the need at home for the comparatively well-trained Russian troops stationed in the Baltics.

These pronouncements have proved to be a blessing in disguise for the ruling nationalists in Estonia and Latvia for they could now substantiate their fears of a Russian threat to independence. Ethnic Russians within the country are portrayed as the enemy's fifth column. As non-citizens, they are increasingly discriminated against and harassed. Some of them look to Russia as a protector and guarantor of their rights. The fear of a fifth column may actually engender a fifth column.

Thus developed a vicious circle of fear encompassing both Russian and Baltic nationalists. This symbiotic kinship between two opposing nationalisms is part of the "Baltic predicament." Such vicious circles, once they appear, tend only to intensify. Asking who started the problem would get no better answer than researching the chicken-and-egg question.

Given such intensifying fears, nightmare scenarios are not difficult to imagine. The non-citizen community retreats into itself, developing a fortress mentality and acquiring the increasingly militant habits of self-defense. Confronted with increased pressure from the government and with a growing number of deportation orders carried out by force, some groups within the community may resort to violence. The government retaliates, either directly or through its armed "Home Guard," a warfare by proxy so manifestly successful in former Yugoslavia. Refugees will start to flow to Russia and Sweden with stories of harassment and oppression, followed by vociferous demands for intervention within Russia itself. It would not require a chauvinist like Zhirinovsky to lead the charge in defending ethnic brethren across the border. The politically troubled Yeltsin has already set precedents in Chechnya, Moldova, Tajikistan, and Georgia.

Crises in the "near abroad" involving Russian-speaking populations strengthen the most conservative circles in Russia. Such conflicts increase the importance of the military, slow down economic reform, and provide the military-industrial complex with a raison d'être. They direct attention and resources away from Russia's own economic, social, and political problems, thereby reducing its chances of building a viable democracy. A parallel is frequently drawn between post-Gorbachev Russia and the Weimar Republic. The two situations share at least one important feature: a sense of defeat and betrayal. The plight of Russians in the former republics of the Soviet Union, a string of Sudetenlands on Russia's rim, intensify these feelings. The Serbs have demonstrated what a strong and well-armed nation can do if it believes itself to be threatened by the whole world. Were something similar to happen in Russia, it would lead to a catastrophe on a much larger scale.

The Role of International Organizations

After being disenfranchised by Latvia and Estonia, non-citizens at first pinned their hopes on the international community and its human rights laws. Some very influential human rights organizations, most notably Helsinki Watch, immediately condemned the exclusionary Baltic laws. But soon the international community changed its course. In perhaps the most telling example, the Council of Europe treated the Baltic laws with approval. This reaction was particularly important for the Baltic states since admission into the Council of Europe was perceived as admission into Europe; "back to Europe" had been one of the most important slogans of the national liberation movements.

The Council of Europe case deserves closer scrutiny. Its confidential 1992 report[20] declares the Latvian citizenship legislation reasonable since it recognizes citizenship "for those who possessed it in 1940 and their descendants and grants it to others only through naturalization."[21] But the legislation did not *grant* citizenship to anyone; it simply spelled out the probable principles of a future law on citizenship and its conditions of naturalization. The Latvian parliament debated such a law in December 1991. However, because the Council of Europe report was perceived as an endorsement of Latvia's nationality policies, parliament abandoned the draft law and never returned to it. It was only in 1995 that the first few Russian intellectuals and ethnic Latvians from Russia were naturalized.

The Council of Europe report has done incalculable damage. It has endorsed the point of view of the radical nationalists in Latvia and Estonia. It has undermined the position of the moderate center (which argued that a restrictive attitude to citizenship would not be tolerated by the international community). It has contributed to the failure to pass a law on naturalization (even though the law had already passed the first reading). Finally, it has prompted the adoption of a restrictive citizenship law in Estonia and, as a result, promoted inter-ethnic conflict and a deterioration of Baltic-Russian relations.

Other international organizations, such as the United Nations, have shown similar insensitivity. The U.N. High Commissioner for Refugees Peter van Krieken, for instance, went so far as to accuse Baltic Russian residents of having a faulty understanding of their rights.[22] Reports on Latvia and Estonia by the U.N. Center for Human Rights, although raising objections to some administrative practices and approaches, essentially absolved the Latvian and Estonian governments of violating human rights.[23] Subsequently, international observers endorsed Estonia's citizens-only elections in September 1992. And in May 1993, Estonia gained admission as a full-fledged member of the Council of Europe.

Not surprisingly, the Estonian government interpreted this recognition of its supposedly democratic government as an endorsement of its approach to the country's non-citizens. The Estonian Law on Aliens adopted by parliament on June 21, 1993, was a direct consequence of these not entirely groundless perceptions. According to this law, all non-citizens, including those born in Estonia, were required to apply for residence permits, and it was largely up to a bureaucrat to decide whether this permit would be granted. Moreover, all residence permits were temporary and the procedure had to be repeated periodically. This law created an uproar among the country's Russians, who blocked the St. Petersburg-Tallinn highway in protest. The municipalities of predominantly Russian Narva and Silla-mae decided to hold referenda on local autonomy within the Estonian Republic.

This time not only Russia but also international organizations, including the Council of Europe and the Organization of Security and Cooperation in Europe (OSCE),[24] registered protests strongly worded enough not to be mistaken for encouragement. Under this pressure Estonian President Lennart Meri decided to send the law for analysis to experts of the Council of Europe and OSCE before implementation. OSCE High Commissioner on National Minorities Max van der Stoel reacted by stating that although several of the law's provisions could be found in the legislation of many OSCE states, "there are other articles that must be reconsidered, taking into account the fact that so many non-citizens have lived in Estonia for a considerable number of years."[25]

In response to this remonstration, the Estonian parliament did modify some provisions of the law. President Meri appointed a special council of local Russians for purposes of initiating a continuous dialogue with the Russian community. Estonian authorities have pledged to van der Stoel that they will facilitate the naturalization of non-citizens running as candidates in the forthcoming local elections. These measures, along with non-citizen representation on the local level, have created hope of a reconciliation and contributed to a dissipation, however temporary, of the crisis. In February 1995, the Estonian parliament passed a law extending required domicile from two to five years. But the new government elected one month later is likely to improve intercommunity relations.

In Latvia, meanwhile, the ruling elite continued to enjoy the indulgence of international organizations, and parliamentary elections in June 1993 were for citizens only. Although a new draft law on citizenship was criticized by both OSCE and Council of Europe experts, international observers deemed Latvia's local elections in May 1994 free and fair, despite the fact that they were citizen-only and thus more restrictive than in Estonia. Many in the ruling elite concluded that the experts' conclusions about the draft law on citizenship could be safely overlooked. In June 1994, the Latvian parliament passed a citizenship law with annual quotas that would have made naturalization of several hundred thousand non-citizens impossible. Bowing to international pressure, President Guntis Ulmanis returned the law to the parliament without signing it, as Estonian President Meri had done a year before. Under international pressure to prevent Latvia's entry into the Council of Europe, the Latvian parliament withdrew the quotas at its extraordinary session on July 21, 1994.

The debate around quotas deserves special attention. Latvian parliamentarians were openly concerned with how best to cheat the international experts. Leader of the ruling Farmers' Union faction Andris Rozentāls proposed the concept of covert quotas, so that while the word itself would not be used, its essence would be retained.[26] The pro-government daily *Diena* went even further in its editorial on June 22, 1994, calling the whole scandal a legalistic game and suggesting that the next parliament change the law again after Latvia had been admitted into the Council of Europe.[27]

Quotas by another name are already in effect. Both in the Latvian and Estonian laws, citizenship *may* rather than *must* be granted to a qualifying individual, and a state bureaucrat decides whether this or that individual qualifies. The Estonian example demonstrates that language tests, ambiguous instructions, and arbitrary implementation can indeed successfully restrict naturalization.

There is little political pressure from the current Estonian and Latvian electorates for a national reconciliation policy. The established political elite's immediate concern for an electoral victory outweighs all other considerations: the stability of the country, the preservation of ethnic and cultural identity, and even the continued existence of the sovereign state. Only international organizations such as the Council of Europe, the OSCE, and the United Nations can bring the requisite pressure to bear. Regrettably, experts from international organizations rarely have enough time to pay attention to these comparatively minor but most compelling local political circumstances. Without taking into account these considerations, however, any foreign intervention would aggravate rather than alleviate the problem, as the 1992 Council of Europe experts' report did in the Latvian case.

Reinventing the Nation

The Baltic states' different approaches to the problem of citizenship provide ample political lessons. One of these lessons is the tenacity of ethnic identity, its ability to survive against all odds and revive at the first opportunity. For the Baltics, the collapse of communism resembled the very process of nation-building a century ago. It was no mere coincidence that the upheavals of the late 1980s were named *Atmoda* ("Awakening") in Latvia and *Atgimimas* ("Rebirth") in Lithuania, both names associated with the origins of nationhood. In the twentieth century as well as in the nineteenth, however, these processes involved inventing the nation rather than *awakening* it. One key myth has been that of extinction: unless something is done *we* as an ethnic group with our specific ethnic identity will disappear. Writers and poets thus invoke heroic defenders of the nation, like the Estonian *Kalev* or the Latvian hero *Lāčplēsis* (who fell to the bottom of the river Daugava fighting the Black Knight where they continue struggling to this day).

"Inventing" the national identity does not here imply that something without basis in reality is invented. Rather, nation-building is a period of defining and debating the contents of national identity and its political consequences. Although ethnicity and nation are important concepts in contemporary politics, the indispensable ingredients of ethnic identity and of the nation are very difficult, if not impossible to define. Although many elements of ethnic identity recur in many nations (language, religion, race), none is absolutely necessary. Moreover, the contents of a given ethnic identity vary greatly over time. Indeed, a key function of culture is debating, defining, and re-defining this identity or, at least, the relative importance of its components.

All nations and all ethnic identities can be said to have a positive value, but the same is not true of all elements of ethnic identities. Ethnic identity may be composed of such elements as chauvinism and xenophobia that are incompatible with the absolute values of liberty, democracy, equality, and human rights. Chauvinism always pretends to defend the nation (a variation on the myth of extinction). In this respect, the difference is one of scope, not principle, between Hitler's *Deutschland über alles* (Germany above all others) and the Latvian draft law debated in parliament in 1992, boldly entitled "On Suspending Some Conventional Human Rights to Ensure the Survival of the Latvian Nation."

The Baltic experience also underscores the importance of understanding the political consequences of nationality, both domestically and internationally. Ruling elites are quick to grasp such consequences when supporting a concept of the nation that excludes all those who would vote against them. This political consideration often contradicts more conventional definitions of ethnicity, as when ethnic Latvians returning to Latvia from Russia were not granted citizenship until spring 1995. Their political affiliation, less exclusively nationalistic, was inconvenient to the ruling group. The criteria governing the two functions of nationalism, the integrative and the divisive, more often than not depend on political expediency. Integration of all those who belong is closely linked with expulsion of those who do not—and these decisions are made by particular political actors.

Even when divisive nationalism does not end in a massacre, as in the case of the Tutsis in Rwanda, nationalism remains dangerous for democracy. The Soviet elections of 1990, whatever their drawbacks, were a step forward for representative government in Latvia and Estonia, while the disenfranchising of almost a third of the populations in the latter countries significantly narrowed the electoral base of democracy. This raises well-grounded doubts whether the present system of governance in these countries can be described as a democracy. These doubts are further substantiated by the fact that Latvia has no acting constitution and no constitutional court.[28] One Latvian parliamentarian, praising Prime Minister Valdis Birkavs, noted that he had a very good understanding of democracy, not of a Western kind, but of one corresponding to Latvian circumstances.[29] Two hundred years ago British colonies in America went to war protesting the principle of taxation without representation. At present this principle forms a substantial part of the political system of the renewed Baltic republics of Estonia and Latvia.

The resistance of minorities is one moderating factor on the ruling majority, while pressure imposed from the outside represents another possible influence. Estonia and Latvia demonstrate how the concept of the nation was modified depending on domestic factors: the necessity of winning Russian votes in the 1989–90 elections advanced moderate leaders who promoted an inclusive concept of the nation. A comparable change of heart was prompted by international pressure in summer 1993 in Estonia and a year later in Latvia.

International factors can also work the other way. The rise of nationalism is not only the result of new "awakening" nations but also of the fact that nationalist rhetoric is currently an internationally acceptable way to voice grievances and justify policies. In other words, Latvians and Estonians did not invent the political consequences of Latvianness and Estonianness; their political elites simply complied with internationally accepted practices.

The Baltic predicament need not end pessimistically. Bowing to international pressure and responding to the demands of a more active civil society at home, Estonian and Latvian ruling elites may choose to adopt integrative policies rather than those that promote the exclusion of local non-citizens. Political leaders and organizations with experience and ideas in this field are active in both countries. With their efforts, a virtuous—as opposed to vicious—circle of nationalism could be fostered. Non-citizens would learn the local languages, many would assimilate, others would use cultural autonomy rights accorded to national minorities by current legislation. Estonian and Latvian chauvinists would be pushed to the fringes, remaining vocal but not influential. The Russian language would probably continue as one of the languages of the Baltics and the *lingua franca* of the area: too much of the area's future prosperity depends on trade with the eastern neighbor. At the same time, the integrated Baltic Russians would feel that they belong in Latvia and Estonia instead of in Russia. They would cherish the freedom and stability of Baltic politics. The Baltic countries would guarantee their rights and freedoms, and their comparatively high standard of living.

This scenario would require many changes in the attitude of the current Latvian and Estonian ruling elites toward their non-citizen communities. It would also require a very different international perspective on the relationship between democracy and nationalism. But if Estonia and Latvia are to continue they will have to modify their ethnic and political identity. As the Latvian classical poet Jānis Rainis reminds us: "*Pastāvēs kas pārvērtīsies.*" Only that which can be transformed will perpetuate.

Notes

1. Actually Israeli Arabs were not immediately recognized as citizens. This ambiguity points to the problematic character of the relationship between Arab citizens and the Jewish state.

2. This distinction recalls the Nuremberg legislation that distinguished be-

tween German citizens and German *Staatsangehörige* (citizens that are not Germans with ensuing differences of rights and status).

3. Ulrich K. Preuss, *Constitutional Aspects of the Making of Democracy in the Post-Communist Societies of East Europe* (Bremen: Center for European Law and Policy, February 1993).

4. Claus Offe, *Ethnic Politics in East European Transitions* (Bremen: Center for European Law and Policy, February 1993).

5. Preuss, op. cit. p. 30. The chapter "The Predominance of 'Communitarian' Concepts of Citizenship in East and Central Europe" (pp. 28–33) is quite pertinent to this discussion.

6. Ibid., p. 30.

7. Donald L. Horowitz, *Ethnic Groups in Conflict* (Berkeley: University of California Press, 1985).

8. I am consciously avoiding a discussion of the historic wrongs inflicted on these countries in the previous years. After all, the nationalist leaders of the Afrikaaner community also argued that they had been wronged by the British before and during the Boer Wars, in the British concentration camps, and that their community was in danger.

9. At the time I was editor-in-chief of the Russian-language weekly of the Popular Front—*Atmoda-Probuzhdenie*—which popularized these policies among the Russian voters and throughout the Soviet Union.

10. Horowitz, op. cit.

11. "Tezicy ideologicheskoy platformy NFL dlya natsionalnoy konsolidatsii jitelii raznych natsionalnostei na osnove idei nezavisimogo demokraticheskogo latviyskogo gosudarstva (Ko II siezdu NFL)." *Atmoda-Probuzhdenie*, July 17, 1989. Later these theses formed the basis for the ethnic policies outlined in the Second Program of the Popular Front.

12. "The Republic of Latvia: Human Rights Issues," Supreme Council of the Republic of Latvia (Riga: Standing Commission on Human Rights and National Questions, 1993), pp. 62–64.

13. Although it is generally true that the two countries followed the same pattern, the Estonian citizenship law adopted on February 26, 1992, established conditions of naturalization, specifying that a person who knows the Estonian language and has had lived in Estonia two years prior to March 30, 1990, and one year after the application for acquiring Estonian citizenship may be naturalized. However, the law did not spell out the necessary language requirements and naturalization could start only after April 1993, when such requirements were made public. It meant, in effect, that very few naturalized residents could participate in the referendum on a new constitution in June 1992 and in the parliamentary and presidential elections in September 1992. However, according to the law on local elections, permanent residents could vote but not run for the bodies of local authorities in the elections of 1993.

14. In November 1992, the director of the U.N. Center for Human Rights accused this department of discriminatory practices against some members of the non-ethnic Latvian population. *Summary of the Report on a Fact-Finding Mission to Latvia* (The United Nations: Secretary General, November 27, 1992), p. 3.

15. Helsinki Watch, *Violations by the Latvian Department of Citizenship and Immigration* (October 1993), pp. 4–5.

16. Interview in *The Baltic Gazette*, September 1994.

17. "Russians Pass Citizenship Hurdle," *The Baltic Independent,* April 16–22, 1993.

18. Adam Michnik, "After the Revolution," *The New Republic,* July 2, 1990, pp. 28–29.

19. Pål Kolstø, "The New Russian Diaspora: Minority Protection in the Soviet Successor States," *Journal of Peace Research,* Vol. 30, No. 2 1993, pp. 197–217. In October 1993, one of the factions in the Latvian Parliament demanded an official denunciation of the Latvian-Russian treaty on the grounds that it was never ratified by the Russian parliament. There is a vestige of specific Soviet hypocrisy to this argument since Russia's parliament refused to ratify it precisely because it had already been violated by Latvia. Noteworthy also is the retort of the ruling coalition to the demands of the right-wing opposition: there is no need to abnegate the treaty since it never legally came into force.

20. Confidential status has saved this report from all too deserved criticism. Not only was it not made available to the general public, but the leadership of the Latvian Supreme Council concealed it from its members. I learned of its contents by pure chance, although I was at the time a member of the Parliamentary Commission on Human Rights.

21. J. de Meyer and C. Rozakis, "On Human Rights in the Republic of Latvia" (Strasbourg: Council of Europe, January 20, 1992), p. 5.

22. Peter van Krieken, report distributed at a workshop on ethnic relations in Hanasaari-Hanaholm, Finland, May 1993.

23. U.N. doc. A/47/748 (1992).

24. At the time, the *Organization of* Security and Cooperation in Europe (OSCE) was the *Conference on* Security and Cooperation in Europe (CSCE).

25. CSCE Communication No. 192, Prague, July 2, 1993.

26. *Diena,* June 21, 1994.

27. "Ceļā uz Krieviju," *Diena,* June 22, 1994.

28. Officially the country returned in August 1991 to the 1922 constitution, although most of the legislation does not correspond to this constitution since it was devised to comply with the revised versions of the Constitution of the Latvian SSR of 1978. No constitutional court has been created in Latvia in violation of article 6 of the Declaration of the Supreme Council of the Latvian SSR "On the Renewal of the Independence of the Republic of Latvia." Therefore, four years after attaining independence and five years after proclaiming statehood, Latvia has no legal body capable of resolving conflicts of law.

29. *Labrīt,* July 21, 1994, p. 3.

9

Aggressive Nationalism and Immigration in Germany

JÜRGEN FIJALKOWSKI

Germany has been a special focus of world attention since 1989. First came the fall of the Berlin Wall, which had divided Europe and Germany for much of the Cold War period. Then, in 1990, Germany's two partial states became reunited. Since 1990, however, Germany has captured international attention for a less benign reason: the wave of aggressive nationalism that has swept the country and resulted in numerous violent assaults on foreigners.

In September 1991, for instance, a home of 200 asylum-seekers from Vietnam and Mozambique came under attack for five nights in the Saxon city of Hoyerswerda. The incident ended with the transfer of the asylum-seekers to other parts of Germany. In other words, despite public condemnation, the aggressive action achieved its immediate goal of "cleansing" Hoyerswerda. Another five-day assault took place in August 1992 on the Central Reception Bureau for Asylum Seekers in Lichtenhagen, a suburb of the coastal city of Rostock. Again the assault lasted five days. Just before the building was set on fire, 150 Vietnamese were rescued from the building's roof. Several hundred asylum-seekers, this time Roma (Gypsies) from Poland and Romania, were transferred to another address instead of receiving effective protection. In November 1992, arsonists targeted two buildings in Moelln inhabited by long-established Turkish families. A mother and two daughters were dreadfully burnt and 43 people lost their accommodations.[1]

The rallying cries for these right-wing extremists were "Germany for the Germans" and "Foreigners get out!" Their spokespeople justified the extremist deeds in part by invoking the symbols and writings of the Nazis. Perhaps more troubling, observers reported some obvious applause from German bystanders and onlookers. Sadly, the police reacted to the rising tide of aggression with a great deal of hesitation and uncertainty, despite the increasing brutality of neo-Nazi groups and individual perpetrators. These incidents were remarkable not only for the intensity of the acts of violence but also for their choice of victims. The perpetrators singled out not only asylum-seekers from foreign countries but also foreigners who had lived in Germany for some time.

The incidents at Hoyerswerda, Lichtenhagen, and Moelln, while attracting a great deal of media and public attention, were unfortunately only the tip of the iceberg. According to police statistics and reports from monitoring organizations, there have been hundreds of smaller but no less malicious occurrences of aggressive enmity toward foreigners and criminal offenses inspired by right-wing extremism.

For example, on a single day shortly after the 1991 assaults in Hoyerswerda more than 20 homes for asylum-seekers throughout Germany were attacked. The publicity surrounding the Hoyerswerda scandal obviously had inspired similar actions. In 1991, nearly 1,500 violent criminal offenses by right-wing extremists were registered in Germany, including at least four criminal manslaughters, 88 arson assaults, 169 bodily injuries, and 200 cases of heavy property damage. The Ministry of Interior reported on a remarkable shift during 1990 and 1991: from a decline in extremism on the left to a rise in extremism on the right.

By 1992, however, Germans were beginning to organize in response to this right-wing extremism. Supported by an increasingly outraged public, the mass media, and several established interest groups, many civic activists tried to mobilize a countermovement in support of foreigners and non-citizens (*Gegen Fremdenhass und Ausländerfeindlichkeit*). At the national level, the German government launched numerous public relations efforts to correct the negative international impressions of the new united state generated by the upsurge in violence. The federal government, as well as the governments of the *Länder* (states) and the local authorities, also made a deliberate attempt to hasten the legal prosecution of acts of violence and improve police work by reorganizing coordination to react earlier and more efficiently.

Despite these efforts by federal, *Länder,* and local authorities as well as the large candlelight demonstrations of winter 1992–93, the fire of hatred continued to smolder. In May 1993, arsonists torched an apartment building in Solingen, killing five Turkish women. On Ascension Day 1994 in Magdeburg, a gang of thugs hunted down and beat up a group of people of color. The federal government reported that the annual number of public acts of xenophobia and neo-Nazism had risen into the thousands.[2] The 1993 report of the German Board for the Protection of the Constitution registered 2,232 right-wing extremist actions—more than in 1991 but a slight decrease from 1992. According to the Ministry of the Interior, this decline resulted from the state's resolute countermeasures: the intensified efforts of the police, the more rapid prosecution of criminal cases, and the completion of debate on reforming German asylum regulations. Despite the optimism of the federal government, however, aggressive nationalism remains a troubling feature of contemporary German life.

Levels of Aggressive Nationalism

The face most often attached to aggressive nationalism is that of the skinhead. Newspaper photographs feature young men in jackboots, with angry expressions and hands extended in Nazi salutes. But the phenomenon is more complex. There are, in fact, three levels to this extremism—the perpetrators, the surrounding milieu, and the general discourse on national identity currently taking place in Germany.

At the first level, the perpetrators are generally young and involved in gangs or other underground subcultures. According to a 1993 study conducted by the University of Trier, 75 percent of the criminal offenders who victimized foreigners have been under 20 years of age and 95 percent have been male.[3] Only 10 to 15 percent—and these for the most part were educated and employed—could be proven to be politically motivated by right-wing ideologies. The remaining 85 to 90 percent of offenders lacked ideological ties, felt socially disadvantaged, and/or came from dysfunctional families.

Behind these perpetrators stand the more or less established right-wing organizations that have attempted to mobilize public attention and organize sympathizers. The German authorities responsible for protecting the constitutional order distinguish between *radical* organizations that are not irrevocably opposed to the principles of the German constitution and *extremist* organizations that actively and aggressively oppose a free democracy. The *Republikaner* Party, for instance, is generally considered merely a radical organization, although its members do engage in extremist activities. In terms of direct countermeasures, the federal government has concentrated on the extremists.

In 1993, for instance, the ministers of the interior at both the federal and *Länder* levels launched numerous police investigations and enacted seven legal bans of right-wing extremist associations, including the *Freiheitliche Deutsche Arbeiterpartei* and the *Nationale List.*[4] Also in 1993, federation-wide measures were enacted against skinhead gangs, bands, and music producers.

Still, these banned parties have attempted to resume action under different names—the banned *Deutsche Alternative*, for instance, has become the *Deutsche Nationalisten*. New groups have also emerged such as the neo-Nazi *Direkte Aktion/Mitteldeutschland*. A support organization for "national political prisoners and their relatives" represents one of the more cohesive new groups on the right-wing landscape.

Although not explicitly neo-Nazi, a number of right-wing parties such as the *Deutsche Volksunion* still aim to "not only challenge the fundamental principles of a free democracy . . . but want to reduce the value or to eliminate essential principles of this order" and therefore pursue "goals that violate the constitution."[5] The federal government is thus in its right to apply to the Constitutional Court to prohibit such organizations.

Whether extremist or merely radical, these nationalist organizations share certain features. They are organized in a strictly hierarchical manner in which members follow leaders obediently rather than engage democratically. They urge identification with the nation-state of Germany, excluding members of other nations and viewing relationships with other nations competitively. With German nationalism as their chief value, they disparage members of mere conservative parties (the Christian Democratic Party or the Christian Social Union) as being weak, open to confederal arrangements in international affairs (such as the European Union (EU)), and committed to universal human rights. Finally, they criticize the mainstream parties' stands on immigration as being indecisive and thus encouraging criminality.

Surrounding both the perpetrators and their support organizations is the general cultural milieu or *Alltagskultur*—the value orientation of the public at large. Here take place the intellectual discourses that are viewed with suspicion from outside Germany. Consider, for instance, how the political perceptions and value orientations of the public have changed over the issue of immigration.

Post-war Germany has never conceived of itself as a land of immigration. It has, however, welcomed ethnic German emigrants from the Eastern bloc (if they managed to qualify for their country's emigration allowance) as well as foreign guest workers (through an official program from 1955 to 1973). Moreover, under Article 16 of the Basic Law, formulated in 1949 in remembrance of the importance of asylum regulations for refugees from Nazism, Germany welcomed virtually all political asylum-seekers. During the 1980s, when the movement of uninvited labor-seekers as well as refugees from the crisis regions of the European periphery increased enormously, Germany embarked on a debate over these asylum procedures and its historic commitment to universal human rights. This debate led to growing political polarization and emotional outcry—both in favor of Article 16 and for restricting the inflow of foreigners. With German unification in 1990, the debate ended with an amendment to Article 16 preventing the entry of asylum-seekers to Germany from countries that respect asylum rights according to the Geneva Convention.[6]

Without a doubt, since the dissolution of the East German (GDR) regime and the unification of Germany, the new unified state is experiencing an epoch-making historical change. The current German debate is rife with discussion of historical burdens and the country's tasks in a deeply changing world order. The main participants in this debate on German identity are intellectuals, journalists, editors, talk-show moderators, church leaders, and academics. At work in this debate—as the asylum controversy demonstrated—are some unsavory representations of German nationalism: inward-looking, intolerant, xenophobic.

These three levels—perpetrators in the foreground, organizations in the surrounding milieu, and a hesitant and uncertain intellectual discourse on German identity in the background—constitute the world that spawns aggressive nationalism. When evaluating the connection between immigration and nationalism—and the appropriate policy responses—we must keep these three different levels in mind.

Immigration Pressures

Since the first target of the ugly aggressions has been applicants for asylum and visible new immigrant minorities, the question arises whether a causal relationship exists between immigration pressures and aggressive nationalism.[7] Those who advocated modifying asylum rights regulations in Germany in 1993 and hoped that they could thereby reduce nationalist aggression implicitly believed in this causal relationship. In their view, nationalist aggression was simply a reaction to the perceived influx of foreigners, particularly those asylum-seekers who did not, in fact, experience persecution in their home countries.[8]

But to what extent has Germany actually experienced immigration pressures? In 1988, two years before German unification, the balance of in- and out-migration of any kind in West Germany amounted to 550,000 immigrants.[9] In 1989 and 1990, the figures doubled to nearly a million immigrants due to open borders and waves of citizens from the GDR and ethnic Germans from Eastern Europe. In 1989, 344,000 Germans from the GDR and 377,000 ethnic Germans from Eastern Europe came to West Germany; in 1990, the figures were 197,000 and 397,000 respectively.[10]

In other words, any pressures from immigration during this period would have been caused as much by Germans as non-Germans. Asylum-seekers constituted only one of several in-migrating categories, and they were but one group that needed housing, jobs, language training, and so on. To be sure, local authorities were confronted with immense difficulties in providing shelter and instituting measures for the integration of new immigrants. However, these problems were caused by all kinds of new immigrants, not just asylum-seekers.

Nevertheless, both the absolute figures and the proportion of asylum-seekers among the total flow of border-crossing immigrants had been rising rapidly. In the years after 1988 they increased from one-fifth to about one-half the total number.[11] Applicants included both refugees and the politically persecuted, as well as migrants who left their home countries for economic or personal reasons. In addition, there was a growing number of people not actually persecuted but eager to escape the negative side effects of the social and political transformation occurring in Eastern Europe. These migration pressures are decreasing only to the degree that the new East European democracies have succeeded in coping with the stresses of post-communist adjustment.

Although in 1979, there were 6,282 Eastern European asylum-seekers registered in the EU member states, the annual figure had risen to 186,659 by 1991 and to a total of 689,549 for the entire 12-year period. Some 63 percent of the 12-year total has sought asylum in Germany; for 1991 alone, the figure stood at 76 percent.[12] Swelling the number of immigrants were the three million new expellees and refugees fleeing ethnonational conflicts, ethnic cleansing measures, and the atrocities of the war in the former Yugoslavia. Half of the 500,000 refugees currently living outside the borders of the former Yugoslavia have found formal refuge in Germany.

Not all migrants have sought permanent residency in the West, nor have they all been bound for EU countries. Short-term visits have eased pressures (e.g., the number of short-term visits from the Soviet Union to Western countries rose from 300,000 in 1985 to 3.5 million in 1990).[13] Short-term visits offer the chance to take advantage of the enormous gradations in the purchasing power of the different currencies. Much of the migration movement is also filtered and captured inside the boundaries of the former East-bloc countries. These border controls have meanwhile been improved by increased police and a series of bilateral international conventions among European countries. In the long run, the migration potentials of North Africa and the Middle East could be even more lasting than that from Eastern Europe and the Balkans, since the population in this part of the world is growing 17 times more rapidly than in the northwest European countries.[14]

On the other hand, some European countries actually have a long-term need for immigration. Immigration might be a pressure in the short term but a boon from a longer term perspective. While Great Britain, France, and Spain are not experiencing a need for immigrant labor, a negative birth rate is of concern to Italy and Denmark. Despite its current unemployment problems and housing shortage, Germany in the medium term needs at least 300,000 to 500,000 immigrants a year to compensate for its low birth rate.[15] Over the next 20 years, the number of Germans in the wage-earning age group will decrease by four million, resulting in a loss of about 10 percent of the workforce. A decline in the social product, as well as in the resources to support the pension system, could follow if no in-migration were to compensate for this loss. It is still unclear who will fill Germany's needs—ethnic Germans from abroad, citizens of other EU member states or EU-affiliated nations, or people from the more distant regions of Eastern Europe, Russia, the Balkans, the Middle East, and North Africa.

While the number of potential migrants may exceed any demand that Germany and other European countries will have, immigration pressures pose a problem only in the distant and unknowable future. Currently, migrants are not overwhelming western Europe. Therefore, it is difficult to connect rising xenophobia with increasing immigration pressures. If increased immigration is the proverbial drop of water that makes the bucket of resentment run over, it is because the bucket is already filled with resentments generated by other aspects of domestic life. Indeed, since the 1993 decision restricting asylum access to the German territories, the number of immigrants has decidedly decreased.[16] But problems with aggressive nationalism have persisted.

Immigration and Xenophobia

The sources of animosity toward foreigners and immigrants lie in the internal social problems that existed prior to the presence of foreigners and irrespective of transnational migration processes. Most important are those tendencies contributing to the formation of a "two-thirds society." In this schema, two-thirds of the population profit from the process of modernization and the expanding welfare state, while the remaining third is left behind. This remaining third runs a great risk of becoming marginalized and relegated to walks of life where there are no opportunities to gain self-esteem.[17] The aggression directed at foreign scapegoats may readily originate in the resentments of those endangered by marginalization themselves. For instance, this marginalized third often envies asylum-seekers simply because they are given shelter and support.

Right-wing movements try to mobilize and profit from these resentments. They encourage marginalized citizens to direct their own feelings of inadequacy and self-hatred toward outsiders. Slogans such as "Germany belongs to the Germans," "France for the French," and so on offer the marginalized an opportunity for group solidarity. In exerting the destructive force of aggression, the marginalized third may enjoy the last satisfaction that remains to otherwise powerless outsiders.

This frustration theory of aggression, however, is not quite sufficient to explain the phenomena. Additional conditions must be present to transform resentful attitudes into aggressive action. After all, marginalized people also have the alternative of reacting to their situation with resigned introversion or ritualized conformity. Moreover, studies demonstrate that instigators and perpetrators of aggression also come from milieus in which people are only occasionally, if at all, in danger of losing their jobs or not finding a place to live.

Thus, an analysis of the sources of enmity toward foreigners leads inevitably to the more encompassing processes of societal disintegration. Some argue, for instance, that aggressiveness lies at the very core of our rapidly modernizing societies. With traditional milieus dissolving, a ruthless preying on others in order to "succeed" becomes the chief value and prime mode of behavior.[18] Aggression against heterogeneous minorities is a reflection of the anomie that accompanies rapid social change. This problem is further aggravated when even those who successfully climb the social ladder feel insecure because of the uncertainties and discontinuities of their collective social identity—the rise of middle-class anxiety.

Anxieties are generated as well by confusion over national identity. Throughout German history, exaggerations of national identification have alternated with feelings of national deficiency, anxiety, and bad conscience. Relative to other European countries, Germany was slow in starting its historical development as a nation-state, and it became a constitutional democracy for the first time only after the military defeat of World War I. This relatively recent experience of both nationalism and democracy accounts in part for the Nazi ideology of a ruling race, the extermination of millions of Jews, and the monstrous destruction of Eastern Europe during World War II.

After the end of that war, Germany remained divided for more than a generation. Two different societies developed on its diminished territory. In the context of global and European divisions into Eastern and Western blocs, these two societies grew apart not only in the socioeconomic respects of wealth accumulation and welfare distribution, but also in political culture.

West Germany developed into a constitutional democracy. Through inclusion in European and Atlantic integration processes and with the intake of migrant workers from Europe's peripheries, it slowly began living with heterogeneous minorities who partly formed their own communities as islands within German society. East Germany, however, remained authoritarian and was restricted to the world of its bloc.

Today, the two parts of Germany are experiencing great difficulties in growing back together. The recently unified country is facing a difficult restructuring of the all but defunct East German economy. In addition, it is under pressure to come to terms with the implications of its own fundamentally changing international position. These burdens of the past and the present have resulted in a particular confusion over national identity. Germany lacks a clear notion of its historical purpose. This uncertainty concerning national identity provides the substance to the surrounding discourses of politicians and intellectuals in the mass media. While the hesitant reactions of the German authorities may be explained by a simple underestimation of the extent of the anti-immigrant problem and by the incompetence or inability of the police, confusions over national identity also no doubt contributed to muting the reaction of the elite and the public to the right-wing provocations.

While the number of criminal assaults committed by right-wing extremists and young people rose by 50 percent in 1992 to 2,285,[19] the results of public opinion surveys show that the German public effectively began to turn against the slogans of the xenophobes.[20] In November 1992, before the Moelln incidents and the deaths of three Turkish people, only 43 percent rejected the slogans. After the crime, 69 percent did so; in Berlin, the figure was 89 percent.

Moreover, Germany's acceptance and rejection of foreigners does not differ much from the EU's 1992 average. According to the annual "Eurobarometer," the European average for rejection of foreigners (103 points on a scale of 400) outweighed its acceptance (69 points). In Western Germany, the averages are 135 and 55 points, respectively. The figures from France and Great Britain are similar. The average for acceptance is greater than for rejection only in Spain, Portugal, Italy, and Ireland—countries that have far fewer foreign residents. Likewise, the results of the October 1994 elections show that right-wing extremist political parties were virtually shut out of the official political realm; more than before they are small, scattered, and divided.[21]

Policy Alternatives

To eradicate the social roots of aggressiveness against foreigners and its accompanying nationalist ideology, a comprehensive policy must be implemented. Certainly this policy must include preventive observation and surveillance as well as forceful police and legal actions. Many perpetrators and their behind-the-scenes instigators can be reached only by the enforcement instruments of the police and the courts.

But the roots of the phenomena of violence and aggressive nationalism will be addressed only by broader strategies. First, reformers must acknowledge that violence might be directed against groups other than the visible foreigners and new immigrant non-citizens—for instance, the disabled or elderly. Brutal attacks may also happen without any nationalist ideological justification. Yet, aggressive nationalist organizations also exist that translate individual hatred into a disciplined striking force.

To address these more complicated sources of aggression in individuals and groups, a comprehensive policy of social integration needs to focus on both the particular milieus of the perpetrators and the two-thirds society as a whole. Programs to provide more jobs and housing, as well as more humane working conditions, are necessary to afford the marginal layers of the employed a better chance to gain greater self-esteem. Other measures should include social work among street youths, improved training programs for youth, and improved education in schools as well as in families. Community and neighborhood initiatives might even be more important than governmental policies implemented from the top down. But of course such initiatives require the infrastructural support that can only come from governmental and legal programs. Compared to these urgent needs, a reduction in the number of immigrants achieved by excluding non-persecuted refugees will have no effect whatsoever.

It is crucial, however, that these policies of social integration be kept free of ethnonational restrictions to which they are always susceptible. In the German case, such restrictions are implied in the distinctions that are made in the regulation for citizenship, nationality, and naturalization. As a result of dominant German tradition and in accordance with the *jus sanguinis* rule—the basis for the German citizenship law (which is federal, but applied by *Länder* authorities)—a person is considered German only if he or she has at least one parent possessing German citizenship. Acquisition of German citizenship through naturalization, rather than by birth, is excluded in principle.[22] Exceptions are decided by the *Länder* authorities who examine whether the applicant was legally and continuously resident on German territories for at least 10 years and whether he or she can prove a genuine allegiance to the German culture and way of life. Access to citizenship for guestworkers officially invited into the country—and their children—has also been made somewhat easier since 1991.

But preferential treatment is still accorded ethnic Germans from Eastern Europe. The barriers to German citizenship remain much higher for long-term residents of ethnoculturally heterogeneous origin—even the second generation that is fully socialized in the dominant German culture—than for ethnic Germans steeped in the non-German dominant cultures of Eastern Europe and the former Soviet Union. Ethnic Germans, not long-term residents, are treated as "status Germans," or denizens according to Article 116 of the constitution. This provision was established shortly after the end of World War II, when millions of Germans expelled from former German territories in Eastern Europe required special legislation to be accepted into the newly constituted (West) German state. But the law, as it functions now, is a privilege based on ethnonational considerations for ethnic Germans with ordinary East European citizenship.

Thus, despite their long residence, many ethnoculturally heterogeneous families of former guestworkers, especially those from countries outside the EU, are prevented from becoming citizens. Holding fast to ethnonational privileges and keeping asylum-seekers at a distance as a means to relieve increasing immigration pressures is not an appropriate tool for fighting aggressive nationalism. Instead, it unintentionally provides grist for the nationalists' mills. It also diverts the attention of the public away from the lack of social integration in German society regardless of transnational migration. Because of this privileging of ethnic Germans, a policy of social integration that attempts to eradicate the roots of aggressive nationalism must establish a new understanding of citizenship.

Advocates of immigration reform do, as a matter of course, include ethnoculturally heterogeneous people in their conception of immigration and social integration. In the post-ethnonational, modern sense of citizenship, the concept of nationality in a pluralistic civil society rests on the assumption that people want to live together under a common government and common laws, with the implied provision of shelter for minorities, regardless of race, descent, language, gender, social class, religion, or political views. The advocates of a comprehensive immigration policy accordingly seek to gradually abolish the privileges extended to ethnic German Eastern Europeans.[23] They also hope to broaden the *jus sanguinis* rule to include elements of the *jus soli* principle, following either the French or the U.S. examples in which birth on the territory of the state confers automatic citizenship. These activists work toward the greater acceptance of dual citizenship, the shortening of the required length of residence for ethnoculturally heterogeneous residents, and the elimination of the need to proclaim devotion to the German culture as a precondition for naturalization.[24]

Keeping immigrants out of Germany and refusing foreign residents citizenship will do nothing to reduce aggressive German nationalism. Rather, the fight against this nationalism requires consistent police action against lawbreakers as well as penal prosecution of both the perpetrators and their organizations. Also crucial is a comprehensive policy of social integration designed to reduce the danger of social marginalization, which is the by-product of the division of society into haves and have-nots—the two-thirds society.

Germany desperately needs to adopt a modern understanding of citizenship and nationalism. The traditions of a nation of common descent need to be transformed into a state whose membership is characterized by equal citizens living together under the common law of constitutional democracy. Such citizens, instead of being defined by race, gender, ethnicity, descent, origin, social group, religion, or political thinking, will instead be equal political actors who look into the future for their common identity, and not the past.

Notes

1. The information on these events is all taken from German newspapers.

2. The German authorities consider right-wing extremist offenses to be not only those individual or organized assaults that are immediately directed against foreigners, but also the demonstrative public show of Nazi symbols, the public presentation of songs intended to stimulate the incitement or discrimination of foreign people and folkways, the distribution of Nazi publications, the demonstrative public denial of the mass murders of Jews and other minorities committed in Auschwitz and other Nazi concentration camps, or the violation of historic memorials to the crimes of the National Socialists.

3. *Der Tagespiegel*, June 14, 1993.

4. *Bundesamt für Verfassungsschutz* (Verfassungsschutzbericht, 1993).

5. Ibid., p. 12.

6. After lengthy and tiresome negotiations between the governing parties and the opposition, the following three amendments to Article 16 were agreed on: that the asylum title of the German constitution does not extend to those who enter Germany from countries that adhere to and implement international conventions on refugees and human rights; that the legislature will determine which countries do and do not adhere to these conventions; that the asylum decisions adopted by other states adhering to the Geneva Convention will be respected. For more information on this debate, see Douglas Klusmeyer, "Aliens, Immigrants, and Citizens: The Politics of Inclusion in the Federal Republic of Germany," *Daedalus*, Vol. 122, No. 3 (Summer 1993).

7. The following sections are based in part on Jürgen Fijalkowski, "Aggressive Nationalism, Immigration Pressure, and Asylum Policy Disputes in Contemporary Germany," *International Migration Review*, Vol. 27, No. 4 (Winter 1993).

8. See, for instance, Paul Hainsworth, ed., *The Extreme Right in Europe and the USA* (New York: St. Martin's Press, 1992) and T. Bjorgo and R. Witte, *Racist Violence in Europe* (New York: St. Martin's Press, 1993).

9. All figures in this section derive from *Bundesamt für Statistik, Statistisches Jahrbuch 1992*, and *Wirtschaft und Statistik*, No. 12 (1992).

10. Since 1991, the year after the official unification of Germany, migration from the former GDR to West Germany became a domestic matter and thus disappeared from the statistics of border-crossing movements. Moreover, the number of ethnic German resettlers from Eastern Europe was reduced again, by political measures, to about half in both 1991 and 1992 (220,000 people a year). The net balance of in- and out-migration of officially invited guestworkers and their families and of citizens of the European Union remained at a similar level of less than 200,000.

11. In 1988, a total of 103,000 people applied for asylum in Germany. Over the next four years, the figures increased to 121,000, 193,000, 256,000, and 450,000.

12. Figures taken from L. Druke, "Asylum in a European Community Without Internal Borders," presented to the Fletcher School of Law and Diplomacy, November 12, 1992; and from H. Barabass, "Statistics of the UNHCR Regional Office for the European Institutions" (Brussels: UNHCR, October 1992).

13. Figures based on J. Salt, "Current and Future International Migration Trends Affecting Europe," a contribution to the Fourth Conference of European Ministers for Migration Affairs held in Luxembourg in 1991, Council of Europe, MMG–4(91)1.

14. Ibid.

15. B. Hof, "Arbeitskräftebedarf der Wirtschaft, Arbeitsmarktchancen für Zuwanderer" in *Zuwanderung-Politik der Zukunft*, Reihe Gesprächskreis Arbeit und Soziales No. 5 (Bonn: Friedrich-Ebert Stiftung, 1992).

16. As the Ministry of the Interior reported on November 4, 1994, there were only 102,968 applications for asylum registered from January to October 1994, whereas in the same time period of 1993 it was 292,470, a reduction of 64.8 percent. *Der Tagespiegel*, November 5, 1994, p.2.

17. The term "two-thirds society" overdramatizes the quantitative proportions and belongs to the rhetoric of political debates. But it characterizes real tendencies of marginalization or the threat of marginalization, which can be observed in the change of social structure. See E. Natter and A. Riedlsperger, eds., *Zweidrittelgesellschaft* (Vienna: Europa, 1988). With regard to the German situation see R. Geissler, *Die Sozialstrukur Deutschlands* (Opladen: Westdeutsch, 1992), pp.184ff.

18. Wilhelm Heitmayer et al., *Die Bielefelder Rechtsextremismus-Studie* (Weinheim-Munich: Juventa, 1992).

19. The *Bundesamt für Verfassungsschutz* cited the figure 2,285 in a press conference of the Minister of the Interior on February 6, 1993.

20. Reported, for instance, by Ausländerbeauftragte des Senats von Berlin in a press release dated February 5, 1993. See also D. Fuchs et al., "Wir und die anderen: Ethnozentrismus in den zwölf Ländern der Europäischen Gemeinschaft," *Kölner Zeitschrift für Soziologie und Sozialpsychologie*, No. 45 (1993), pp.238–253.

21. Twenty-two parties and electoral associations took part in the 1994 German federal elections. The Christian Democratic Union and its ally, the Bavarian Christian Social Union, captured 41.5 percent of the vote. The Social Democratic Party took 36.4 percent. Far down on the list came the *Republikaner* Party, with only 1.9 percent, the highest total for any extremist party; this percentage did not translate into any seats in parliament.

22. See the introduction to K. Hailbronner and G. Renner, *Staatsangehörigkeitsrecht: Kommentar Teil I* (Munich: Beck, 1991). The legal attribution of

membership by birth takes place regardless of ethnic or racial affiliation—such affiliations are forbidden by Article 3 of the German *Grundgesetz.* Thus, the child of an African father and German mother is a German citizen. However, German nationality law combined with the relatively few cases of discretional naturalization have produced few ethnoculturally heterogeneous German citizens.

23. The initiatives originated earlier mostly from various specialists and from the Green Party. They subsequently came from the wings of all the main German parties. In February 1993, Herta Däubler-Gmelin, member of the National Committee of the Social Democratic Party, submitted a proposal for a comprehensive immigration law. Cornelia Schmalz-Jacobsen (Free Democratic Party), the Federal Commissioner for the Integration of Foreigners, submitted a draft law making naturalization easier. Even Johannes Gerster, vice president of the Christian Democratic Party in the Federal Parliament, pleaded for a more ready acceptance of dual citizenship on February 13, 1993. The discussion has been considerably stimulated by the latest assaults on Turkish families. It meanwhile became one of the subjects for the CDU-CSU-FDP coalition negotiations after the German federal elections of October 1994.

24. For a more detailed understanding, see Fijalkowski, op. cit. Also see Fijalkowski, "Nationalismus und Ausländerfeindlichkeit in Westeuropa-Sechs Thesen," in *Europa gegen den Rest der Welt?*, eds. C. Butterwegge and S. Jager (Koln: Bund, 1993).

10

Nationalism and Ethnic Minorities in Post-Communist Europe

GEORGE SCHÖPFLIN

The problem of nationhood, nationalism, and ethnic minorities in post-communist Europe has emerged with an unexpected and unpredicted virulence. Western policy, while not wholly paralyzed, is permeated by a sense of helplessness about the seemingly infinite complexity and violence engendered by these issues. As far as the West is concerned, they had been regarded as long dead and buried. In a very real sense, the era that was thought closed with the Paris Peace Settlement of 1918–20 has ended, and the solutions devised then are once again open and in question.

Furthermore, the entire communist experience has marked Central and Eastern Europe in a very different way from the experience of Western Europe. In the West, the ethnic question returned to the political agenda in the 1960s in a relatively muffled form, having at various times been successfully or unsuccessfully repressed or co-opted by processes of nation-state-building before that.[1] In the post-1945 order, Western democracies were able to absorb these old-new pressures into the democratic process, albeit with some manifest failures like Northern Ireland. This was not and, indeed, could not have been replicated in Central and Eastern Europe. The heart of the difference between the two halves of Europe is the contrasting approaches to citizenship. Whereas in the West, citizenship has been defined in such a way as to allow ethnic pressures some play within the political system and offer them a degree of representation in that system, the newly emerging democratic systems in Central and Eastern Europe have yet to construct a sufficiently sound institutional basis to make a parallel definition of citizenship feasible.

Because of the far-reaching destruction of social and institutional frameworks under communism, public identities are frequently defined by ethnonational criteria[2] regardless of whether this is appropriate to the situation or not. Thus, by way of example, while economic issues should be resolved by applying the criteria relevant to economics, there is a propensity under post-communism to define all questions by ethnic criteria. Time and again, ethnonationalists are able to use such economic issues as poverty or backwardness as a way of mobilizing support by arguing, for instance, "We are poor because aliens or foreigners have conspired against us," rather than giving economic problems explanations rooted in economics. The consequence is a confusion of agendas, with very dangerous results, because the true function of ethnicity—one of its functions at any rate—is to make provision for the collective acting out of the affective elements that exist within every society.

The proposition being offered in this analysis is that while ethnicity is an authentic experience with genuine and legitimate functions in defining identity and expressing the underlying moral codes that have a strong constitutive role in the makeup of every community, ethnicity is worse than useless when it comes to matters properly in the civic dimension of nationhood. The civic dimension comprises the rules and regulations that govern the everyday relationship between rulers and ruled and the institutional framework through which these transactions are enacted—matters of representation, taxation, the institutions that mediate between government and society, and the codes of conduct that ensure that all are treated as equal before the law.

These matters, ideally, are settled by reference to reason and rational discourse. Ethnicity by contrast appeals directly to the emotions. When questions that belong properly to the civic dimension are transferred illicitly into the realm of ethnicity, the emotionality of ethnicity pushes reason into the background and matters are decided by passion. As we cannot reiterate too often, strong emotions exclude reason.

These propositions have acquired a special urgency in the case of the post-communist countries of Central and Eastern Europe because, as already suggested, communism destroyed the nascent civil societies that were coming into being before and after World War II. The attempts to construct alternatives to Communist Party rule and develop social autonomies, like Solidarity in Poland, were structured by the conflict with the totalizing ideology and power of the communist system and, as happens so frequently, ended up adopting some of the features of the communist system, above all the emphasis on homogeneity and moralizing.

The political functions of nationhood and nationalist ideologies in the region are in any case different from those in the West. In the West, citizenship evolved before modern nationalism in the eighteenth century or grew in tandem with it and, equally, the gap between the cultural and political units was not excessively wide; east of the Elbe, however, political power and culture were severely divided.

During the nineteenth century, various sub-elites battled with ruling empires to construct their own states in the name of nations that had yet to be mobilized, so that these sub-elites were forced to rely on the one political resource that they had at their disposal—ethnicity. This historical background helps explain the strongly ethnic character of nationhood and state legitimation in the region. The subordination of Central and Eastern Europe to communism exacerbated the situation because the nations of the area by and large came to perceive communism as a new alien overlordship, and opposition to communist rule was increasingly vested in nationhood. In these circumstances, it was very difficult for any civic dimension of nationhood to emerge. Consequently, these states have made the transition to post-communism singularly unprepared for democracy.

Indeed, it could be said that the correspondence between communism and the needs of democracy could scarcely be less appropriate. Communism eliminated all possible civic institutions and codes of conduct; it turned these societies into civic deserts where the microlevel patterns of behavior were governed by mistrust and characterized by atomization.[3] It was hardly unexpected, therefore, that ethnonationalism should have acquired the saliency that it did—no other identity in the public sphere could have played this role. And some communist regimes contributed to this development by their use of nationalism. Ceauşescu in Romania was a clear example.

As a result, the democratic discourse and institutions adopted by these post-communist states to some extent remained empty forms or were filled by other, non-democratic content. A crucial aspect of this was the problem of representation. A democratic government properly speaking acts as the legatee of all its citizens and seeks to act in such a way as to meet the aspirations of the majority—that, at any rate, is the ideal. The post-communist governments, on the other hand, have a different approach to the question of representation. Either explicitly or implicitly, they tend to regard representation as something based on ethnicity and therefore to deny it or half deny it to non-members of the ethnic majority. Broadly speaking, post-communist governments take the view that they do not represent citizens but the nation. Various consequences flow from this, mostly to do with downgrading the civic dimension of nationhood and elevating ethnicity, including in areas where ethnicity has little or nothing to add other than to import a strong emotional element into public discourse and policy formation. Several of the post-communist constitutions are quite explicit in linking ethnicity and citizenship to the advantage of the majority, thereby putting a question mark over the benefits of citizenship and the chances of identification as far as the minority is concerned. The Slovak constitution comes close to being one of these.

The Case of Slovakia

The Slovak experience illustrates a number of these processes very clearly. Despite their linguistic closeness to the Czechs—the two languages are distinct but mutually comprehensible—and regardless of their historical tradition of looking toward Czech culture for some of their models, the Slovaks preferred to define their identity as something different from that of the Czechs when they entered modernity in the nineteenth century. The experience of the interwar period, when they were defined as "Czechoslovaks"—members of the same nation as the Czechs, though speaking their own language—tended to reinforce this sense of being dominated by their politically more powerful and culturally stronger neighbor. Indeed, there is a sense in which Slovaks tended to define that experience as akin to colonial domination. The Czechs might retort that without their incorporation in Czechoslovakia, the Slovaks would very probably have been assimilated by the Hungarians—the Slovak-inhabited areas had been a part of Hungary until 1918 and very substantial numbers of Slovaks had become ethnically Magyar—but this did not impede a generation of Slovak intellectuals from claiming that their status in the first republic had been subordinated to Czech agendas. Under communism, there was strong opposition to "Prague centralism" and the post-1968 dispensation gave the Slovaks a separate status and access to development funds that resulted in the rapid industrialization of Slovakia.

After the "velvet revolution," Czechs and Slovaks were committed to looking for a solution to the problems that had beset the relationship, but a workable compromise eluded both parties. The Slovaks sought a far-reaching autonomy, including a recognition of their "sovereignty," and repeatedly used their veto in the Czechoslovak federal assembly to achieve this. The 1992 elections were largely fought on the issue of the future of the relationship between the two nations. Unexpectedly, the new Czech leadership decided that it would no longer accept the anomalies of the status quo and offered the Slovaks a restricted choice—either federation, with Slovak institutions subordinated to Prague, or independence. As a result, the Slovaks found themselves with an independence that they did not particularly desire and for which they were woefully unprepared.

The new Slovak state faced a series of dilemmas. It was economically weak; it was politically inexperienced; it was short of competent administrators; and it was led by Vladimír Mečiar, a prototypical ethnic entrepreneur who was prepared to use every ethnic trick in the book to maintain himself in power. The particular ethnic agendas of the Slovaks, the lines along which ethnic mobilization could readily take place, were self-definition against the Czechs, as oppressors, and against the Hungarians, who were seen as having humiliated the Slovaks historically and, to make matters worse, a minority of whom continued to inhabit the southern strip of the country in the areas bordering Hungary.

Indeed, the dream of an ethnically pure Slovakia remained just that: roughly one-fifth of the population of the new state was made of non-Slovaks, such as Hungarians, Gypsies, and Ruthenes. Slovak nationalists resolutely set their face against this fact and sought to promote the ideal of an ethnically pure Slovakia. This dynamic underlay the constant friction with the Hungarian minority, over bilingual road signs, for example, which the Slovaks, using the administrative machinery of the state, sought to block at every turn and which brought Slovakia into conflict with the Council of Europe, a body taking an increasingly active role in the protection of ethnic minorities. Slovak self-definitions were complicated by the realization that Slovak culture was a latecomer in Central Europe, that it was relatively anemic by comparison with either Czech or Hungarian, and that a large part of the Slovak population, because it was first generation off the land, was politically and culturally very inexperienced and thus prey to every demagogic device. Concepts of ethnic tolerance and compromise were difficult to sell to a sociologically insecure population that looked for instant solutions. Friction with non-Slovaks was inevitable, as the newly promoted Slovak intelligentsia searched for homogenizing solutions. Mečiar and his party, the HZDS, as well as the Slovak National Party, were in the forefront of depicting the Hungarians as a threat to the integrity of Slovak territory, using allusive language to imply that Slovakia's problems—economic, political, social—were somehow to be attributed to the minority. This line of rhetoric appealed especially to those sections of the Slovak majority that were materially threatened by the transformation— the new urban strata recently arrived in industrialized centers like Martín, Žilina, or Banská Bystrica.

Like the Slovaks, ethnic minorities in similar situations elsewhere in Central and East Europe tend to be either entirely or largely excluded from the symbolic and affective constitution of the state[4] and to live in the state concerned in a situation of grudging toleration, in many respects as second-class citizens, even though all the civic duties (taxation, military service, etc.) exacted from other citizens fall on them equally. In these circumstances, it can easily be imagined that over time ethnic minorities grow disenchanted with the state they are citizens of but of which they do not feel they can be citizens in the same way as members of the majority can. The Russian minority in Latvia is a case of this kind, where even access to citizenship has been very difficult. The self-definition of majorities and minorities and the identities derived from these experiences will differ in a variety of ways, and the stability of a political community will depend on the extent to which the gap between the two can be bridged.

In broad terms, national majorities will tend to regard their state as exclusively theirs especially in the symbolic-affective areas. They will accept that non-members of their ethnic community may live on state territory, but even when practice is very tolerant they will be inclined to patronize the minority, regard its demands as a deviation from the norm, and insist that the majority's way of doing things is "natural." Multiculturalism is not a proposition that most members of an ethnic majority will accept automatically and even where the majority has come to terms with the presence of a minority and sees itself as ready to share in some aspects of minority culture, it will make little effort to understand minority culture and minority concerns in their entirety.[5]

The Problem of Autonomy

The question of autonomy has surfaced repeatedly in this connection. It has to be said that its impact has been overwhelmingly negative on majority-minority relations. Autonomy can be defined as operating at three levels—personal, cultural, and territorial. All three have political, cultural, legal, administrative, and other related implications. Personal autonomy suggests that the individual should be free to define his or her own ethnic identity and that the state should recognize this and use the machinery of the state in such a way as to avoid discrimination on ethnic grounds. This is broadly the situation in several West European countries.[6] There are no particular privileges or special provisions that flow from personal autonomy, but where a flourishing private sector operates, it allows individuals to run their affairs and use their money to organize schools, churches, clubs, newspapers, political parties, and so on for the maintenance and defense of ethnic activities. Personal autonomy does not imply that the ethnic group as a whole is recognized as having a collective identity or claims on the political system as a whole.

Cultural autonomy is more complex. It does involve a structured relationship between the majority and the minority and the explicit recognition by the majority that the ethnic minority has a separate legal and political persona. The precise ordering of this can vary considerably, but some kind of a recognized collective identity for the minority is a condition sine qua non for cultural autonomy. One of its central implications is that members of the minority, by virtue of that membership, can share in the benefits of the state, that their citizenship is understood as defined by loyalty to the state and to the ethnic community, and that there is no contradiction between these two. In cases of this kind, the state will make provision for schooling in the minority language, it will allow bilingual administration where this is appropriate, and, indeed, it will take care to ensure that members of the minority suffer no discrimination by virtue of their ethnicity. Cultural autonomy can be interpreted to mean that members of the minority will benefit from these provisions throughout the territory of the state, so that wherever members of the minority live, they will be entitled to education in their language if they so choose. In practice, of course, this is an ideal-typical situation and, quite apart from the expense, is often unrealistic. Furthermore, in a variety of situations, cultural autonomy will overlap with territorial autonomy.

Territorial autonomy takes the argument a stage further. It designates particular areas where an ethnic minority is concentrated and declares that in these districts the minority has the right to pursue its strategies as it chooses. This state of affairs can involve the creation of local assemblies, possibly even a presumption of minority monolingualism, all of which will be supported out of state funds on exactly the same terms as provisions for the majority. The Statute of Autonomy enjoyed by Catalonia comes close to this, as does the minority provision for Swedes in the very special case of the Aaland Islands, where members of the ethnic majority (Finns) are forbidden to settle. The Swiss system of three-tiered government—the commune, the canton, and the federation—solves the problem in another way. Almost all Swiss communes are monolingual, as are most cantons, but the state as a whole recognizes three official languages (German, French, and Italian) and special provision is made for Romansch.[7]

In post-communist Europe, on the other hand, autonomy is universally interpreted by majorities as a covert demand for secession. The proposition that a particular area should enjoy special status is anathema to members of ethnic majorities, who reject minority claims as an attack on the integrity of the state. In part, this is attributable to political inexperience and in part to the crudity of post-communist political thinking, the legacy of atomization, and the propensity to see all political contests in zero-sum terms. The aftermath of the breakup of three communist states (Czechoslovakia, Yugoslavia, and the Soviet Union) along the internal borders that the communist rulers had created has also been influential in predisposing majorities against territorial solutions. In essence, the word "autonomy" is automatically understood as a claim to territory, and the distinctions made above are dismissed as sophistry. This is explicable in the context of post-communism defined in the foregoing: the excessive but inevitable emphasis on ethnicity as the sole road to political, social, and cultural salvation; the confusion of ethnic and civic agendas; the propensity to understand the world as a series of conspiracies, a consequence of decades of powerlessness; and the deep distrust of diversity.

Diversity and the weakness of cognitive instruments to deal with it may be regarded as the core of the explanation for the difficulties caused by ethnicity in post-communist Europe. Communism was a singularly poor apprenticeship for democratic compromise and tolerance because it emphasized homogeneity, black-and-white thinking, and the kind of epistemological certainty that insisted that in each moment of choice there could be only one answer. The relativization of values, the reflexivity of modern life (the process whereby group identity is continuously restructured by the information that a community receives about itself), and the continuous construction and reconstruction of identities that are an established feature of Western life remain very alien to the post-communist mind-set.

A distinction should be made here between long-settled minority communities with a well-established area of habitation, especially minorities that have lived in a particular area since before the coming of modern nationalist mobilization, and minorities that are the result of relatively recent migration. The latter will generally encounter a variety of obstacles to integration, but it will not be regarded by the majority as a threat to the integrity of the state. Long-settled minorities associated with a particular territory, on the other hand, will generally be the object of some suspicion in the eyes of the majority, for fear that the link between the minority and the territory will result in dismemberment of the state.

This is evidently a key feature of majority attitudes in the broad area of nationhood. Closely linked to this is the reluctance to perceive minority demands as justifiable. In well-established democracies, these demands may be granted, but the majority will tend to see such concessions as derogations from a self-affirming norm. Where the majority-minority relationship is less effectively regulated by citizenship, there will be a strong tendency toward the ethnicization of the state. The state will be run overwhelmingly in the name of and for the benefit of the majority, citizenship and ethnicity will be conflated, and the minority will be excluded from the rights, though not the duties, of the former.

Minority attitudes start from the basic proposition that a minority is in a position of weakness in the face of a majority that is seen as controlling the state and, consequently, the energies of the minority will be aimed at redressing this perceived imbalance. Given that the ground rules are essentially in the hands of the majority, minority politics will tend to consist of continuous adjustment to majority initiatives unless the modus vivendi between the two parties allows the minority a good deal of autonomy.

Where the constitution of the state and its politics are reasonably open-minded, transactions between the two can take place in the civic dimension, thereby reducing the role of ethnicity in the relationship. In such cases, minority self-definitions can be partially depoliticized and the relationship between the two sides can become moderately relaxed. The way in which Welsh aspirations were confined largely to the cultural sphere by concessions over language in the 1980s is an example.[8] Wales is effectively bilingual in the official sphere regardless of whether a particular locality has Welsh-speakers or not, and the establishment of a separate Welsh-language television channel, S4C, has satisfied the expectations of the newly rising Welsh-speaking elite. Had these demands not been met, there is little doubt that Welsh activists would have intensified their campaign and polarized the situation.

Both parties, however, must understand the written and unwritten ground rules of such an arrangement. There will be invisible boundaries that neither side should cross and both will have to exercise considerable self-limitation. In the process, the minority will have to abandon certain aspirations, like full self-government and statehood, in the name of compromise and stability. The majority, for its part, will have to recognize that by incorporating the minority, it must deny itself the complete fulfillment of its particular aspirations involving the particular territory it controls. The alternative is the ethnicization of the state, which has far-reaching negative effects on both, notably mutual fear and suspicion and the threat of constant friction. Minorities in ethnicized states will, in general, lose out on both the swings and the roundabouts.

Members of such minorities will be denied access to the highest positions in politics, the armed forces, the administration, and so on, and they will probably not receive as many of the symbolic and material goods of the state as is their due. They may well conclude that the state has been ethnicized by the majority and that as a result they are permanently excluded from the benefits of citizenship. This was quite evidently what happened between the Serbs and the Albanians in the province of Kosovo after Slobodan Milošević's rise to power. The Albanians concluded that the Serbian state excluded them from both the symbolic and the material benefits of statehood and they began to devise alternative strategies, including a bid for independence.

Under post-communism, a number of factors are operating that are exacerbating these trends. One of these is what might be termed the "conflictogenic" or conflict-generating nature of post-communist politics. Given the legacy of communism and the absence of trust, individuals will start from the proposition that others, whether in the political realm or not, are potential antagonists and that only a frontal assault on their opponents can safeguard whatever interests are at issue. If both parties to a contest start from this base line, then the underlying set of shared assumptions that make compromise possible will be absent and conflict will be the inevitable outcome.

That conflict will then legitimate each of the antagonists, who in a polarized situation will find that their antagonist is essential to give them the status and power they seek. The difficulty with a state of affairs of this kind is that it promotes zero-sum games—black-and-white value systems in which minorities are almost bound to be the losers because, by virtue of being in the minority, they will lack the power to validate their interests.

Once disenchantment on the part of a minority has set in, however, the majority will see this as confirmation of their suspicions, namely that the loyalty of the minority was always suspect, that their commitment to the state was conditional, and that, in reality, the minority constituted a fifth column, a danger to the integrity of the state because their true loyalties were elsewhere. This attitude is reinforced when co-nationals of the minority live in close proximity, for instance, across the border. This, of course, is a classic example of a self-fulfilling prophecy: the majority treats the minority as a danger to the state and, by reason of their being so treated, the minority gradually turns into that danger through processes of polarization and exclusion.

At the center of the majority's fears is loss of territory. The modern European state is uniquely unable to come to terms with the idea that it might lose territory, although in premodern times this was a widespread experience. Loss of territory was not a welcome experience, but it had not acquired the near-catastrophic quality that it has today. The change has largely to do with the rise of the modern nation-state, which has sacralized territory into "national territory"—something that cannot be lost under any circumstances.

The Hungarians of Slovakia

This issue is complicated by ethnicity, but it is not purely an ethnic issue. An ethnic majority that for some reason has come to rule over territory inhabited by members of another ethnic group will automatically include that territory into its concept of the national territory and ignore, if not indeed resent, the presence of an ethnically alien minority there. Southern Slovakia illustrates this perfectly. The frontier between Slovakia and Hungary was drawn in 1920 along the Danube on the basis of strategic, not ethnic, criteria. The ethnic frontier ran well to the north of the state frontier, leaving a sizeable number of Hungarians in Slovakia.[9] Nevertheless, for Slovaks, the Danube frontier was rapidly sacralized into "national territory" and the presence of Hungarians there was regarded as a source of both symbolic and political risk.

Today, this strip of southern Slovakia has a slight Slovak majority, roughly in the proportion of eight to seven, making its reincorporation into Hungary an impossibility, quite apart from the political, economic, and cultural burdens that such reincorporation would pose. This implies that, hotheads apart, there is no serious interest in Hungary in changing the frontier between the two states, but it is very difficult to convince Slovak nationalists of this, given their assumptions about the nature of states and nations. What is especially ironic about this difficult and aggressive relationship between majority and minority is that the suspicions of the majority are almost invariably unfounded. A key distinction in this context is between integration and assimilation. Integration refers to the acceptance of the dominant political codes and procedures of a state; assimilation is the internalization of all cultural norms and the acceptance of assimilands by the assimilating majority as fully equal in all respects.

Majorities in Europe tend to underestimate the integrative capacity of the modern state and, because they define their own identity so strongly if not completely on the basis of ethnic criteria, they cannot and will not understand that a minority that has lived in a particular state for a period of time will acquire some of the civic and, for that matter, political habits of that state. One of the most striking aspects of the experience of the modern state that has emerged during the past 100 years is that even where members of an ethnic group are subjected to serious discrimination, they will only turn against that state in quite exceptional circumstances. The disintegration of the existing state is clearly one of these.

Here again the experience of the Hungarians of Slovakia is instructive. Almost all the ethnic Hungarian-inhabited territory attached to Czechoslovakia in 1920 was returned to Hungary by the First Vienna Arbitration of 1938. These ethnic Hungarians were less than overjoyed by their reintegration into the Hungarian state and would have preferred some aspects of the Czechoslovak system to be retained. The Czechoslovak identity of these Hungarians was, of course, strengthened by their reattachment to Czechoslovakia after 1945 and, despite very severe discrimination between 1945 and 1948, at no time did they consider reintegration into Hungary a desirable option; they wished to remain in Czechoslovakia. The consequences of the end of the Czechoslovak state have, however, modified this, in the sense of causing confusion about the civic identity of the Hungarians of Slovakia. This has come about overwhelmingly because the new

Slovak state has given its ethnic Hungarians little incentive to identify with Slovakia.

This implies, logically, that when a state has suddenly disappeared, the civic identities that it has inspired and generated will likewise vanish. This process results in a gap, a quest for identification with the new state to which they are now attached, and a new set of civic meanings. Unless the state in question recognizes this gap and offers the ethnic group a measure of affective identification, the minority will look to fill the gap by ethnicity. It will look to the moral and cultural values of the ethnic community to provide meanings in a moment of crisis and disorientation. Processes of this kind could be seen in Yugoslavia, Czechoslovakia, and the Soviet Union.

For the most part, minorities prefer that the political formula—the constitutive characteristics of the state—are interpreted in a broad rather than a narrow fashion so that they can be included in it.[10] Their loyalty to the state in question is generally so high that it will outweigh ethnic considerations, unless they are directly excluded and/or possibly subjected to genocide. They have learned a particular way of dealing with the state authorities, in handling matters of administration and all the thousand-and-one issues that arise in a modern state. This is very different from the relationship between the subjects of a premodern state, whose contacts with the state were few and generally negative. The Germans of Denmark and the Danes of Germany are in this category.

As far as the premodern peasantry of Central and Eastern Europe was concerned, these contacts were essentially restricted to paying taxes, being conscripted into the armed forces, and being treated badly by the gendarmerie. In a modern state, the contacts between the individual and the state are multiplied a thousandfold. For what it was worth, contacts between the individual and the communist state were particularly intense; simply because of its totalizing nature the communist state sought to impinge on every aspect of life. Not surprisingly, the relationship between the two grew in density, and members of the same ethnic group living in different states have fewer points of contact than they generally realize. By way of example, Hungarians from Romania are foreigners in Hungary and citizens of the Hungarian state increasingly regard them as such.

But if the modern state has scored a singular success in the area of integration, it has done badly in the area of assimilation. Indeed, as a general rule, it can be proposed that once an ethnic group has acquired a certain cultural consciousness of itself as a separate group, it will be all but impossible for the state (controlled by the majority) to eliminate that cultural consciousness and transform its ethnicity. The assimilation of individuals is certainly feasible, but entire communities have proved extraordinarily resilient in the face of assimilatory attempts by modern states. Even where cultural reproduction is made all but impossible—by obstacles placed in the way of a minority to develop its own intellectual stratum, for instance—assimilation does not follow. And where individuals assimilate, the possibility that their descendants may dissimilate cannot be excluded. Linguistic assimilation is generally regarded by nationalists in Central and Eastern Europe as the most effective way of ensuring that a minority should disappear. It should be noted, however, that this is not an automatic guarantee of success. The language may then be restricted to household use or even die out over time, but consciousness of a previous ethnicity will seldom disappear completely. The Kashubs of northern Poland define themselves as Poles, but they have maintained a more or less separate folkloric consciousness as well.[11]

The failure of assimilation is, as a rule, badly taken by majority nationalists, who then may attempt to quicken the pace by further repression, indeed by the elimination of all minority institutions, notably those related to education and culture. It is noteworthy that even deploying the full repressive apparatus of the totalizing communist state, as in Romania vis-à-vis the Hungarian minority, which was successful in ensuring that a sizeable section of the intellectual stratum of the minority emigrated in the 1980s, the reproduction of the minority has persisted.

There have been cases, however, where minorities—having lost the demographic game to a majority—do appear to have given up and have accepted that there is no future for them. Falling into this category are the Germans of Romania and the Serbs of Kosovo (even though the Serbian state has tried very hard to maintain the Serb population in this region). In both cases, however, the key factor seems to have been the existence of a country to which migration was possible (Germany and Serbia respectively). It seems that once a minority concludes that it cannot sustain itself demographically in the face of the majority, it will abandon what is, after all, invariably a struggle and leave.[12]

Much of this analysis would point to the desirability of majorities treating their minorities as citizens instead of subjects belonging to another ethnic group and thus to be regarded as inferior. But there is a further cluster of factors indicating the advisability of such a policy. These are concerned with domestic and international stability. It is self-evident that a contented minority, one that feels it has a stake in the state in which it lives, will be far less likely to pursue policies or survival strategies at variance with the interests of the majority. Indeed, stability based on ethnic compromise will undoubtedly strengthen a state rather than weaken it. This is a proposition that most nationalists, who approach the problem from the perspective of identity and the passions associated with identity, are likely to reject, even if the evidence points entirely in the opposite direction. Switzerland is the clearest success story in this context, but others can also be found, notably Finland and the ethno-religious Protestant minority in the Irish republic. In all these cases, the majority made significant concessions and defined citizenship by non-ethnic criteria, to the benefit of all concerned.

The international aspects of the problem parallel this state of affairs. Where an ethnic minority lives across the frontier from a state made up of its co-nationals, it will be far less likely to be attracted by irredentist policies if it is made to feel that the state in which it lives as a minority gives it equal access to both the material and the symbolic goods of the state.[13] The majority state may keep watch over the fate of its co-nationals, but it will seldom interfere in such circumstances. The Germans of South Tyrol and Austria or the Swedes of Finland and Sweden illustrate this proposition. Repressive ethnic majorities, on the other hand, have to live in an atmosphere of suspicion that their neighbor is constantly looking for opportunities to weaken it and use the minority as a Trojan horse. That in turn sets up a vicious circle of repression and suspicion that is very difficult to break. Slovakia and Hungary were at times in danger of entering this process between 1990 and 1995, as well as Poland and Lithuania.

Ethnically mixed areas pose particular problems that are at least subacute but can easily become acute, especially if the area is the scene of relatively recent in-migration or has been the focus of some other major socioeconomic transformation like industrialization. The superimposition of an authoritarian system, such as communism, aimed at creating the semblance of outward order will come to be regarded as counterproductive at the moment of relaxation, because the transformation of political legitimation will bring the meaning of the social transformation into question. In mixed areas, it is important that the cultural boundaries between the two (or more) groups be perceived as clear and secure, that each ethnic group has a sense of when it is crossing that boundary. Thus, the more markers available, the easier boundary maintenance is. While the socioeconomic change is taking place, members of ethnic groups (ethnonational, ethnoreligious) evidently need the sense of security associated with group membership, because so many of the codes of morality and behavior will be under threat from the transformation. Hence, a strong sense of some identity will acquire particular significance under conditions of transformation. Members of a group have to know who they are ethnically while the social adjustment is taking place. This matters less when such a transformation affects premodern peasantry rather than semi-modern or fully modern groups—that is, those who have already made the symbolic journey from the countryside to the city, who already have a clear consciousness of who they are. As far as the latter are concerned, this consciousness may well be called into question by their arrival in a multiethnic context that is at one and the same time different from their previous place of habitation and equally their previous socioeconomic status.

The Persistence of Boundary Markers

Ethnic groups maintain their separateness by establishing a variety of boundary markers—customs, habits, patterns of behavior, diet, speech, religion, collective memory, and so on—that they regard as uniquely their own. Virtually anything can be used as a boundary marker and, evidently, the greater the number of markers, the more difficult it is for non-members of the group to penetrate them. The density of these markers not only delimits the group, but also gives it a sense of security, inasmuch as it or its elites feel that the cultural values that give the group coherence are not easily diluted from outside.[14] When, however, two groups, each with a separate consciousness but possessing few markers, find themselves in proximity and are undergoing socioeconomic transformation, there is bound to be trouble. Precisely because the groups are close (e.g., not separated by language), they will be seen as simultaneously alike (thus governed by analogous cultural codes and moral imperatives) and unlike (thus alien). Under these conditions, the assimilation of one group by the other will appear feasible, so that both parties will define their perspectives by the other and inevitably will resent the appearance of advantages enjoyed by the other—for this is a matter of perception. Each will look to make up the advantage when the opportunity presents itself. At the same time, the leaders of each group (political, intellectual) will do everything in their power to safeguard the group's identity and persuade the group that "the other" is a source of threat—in a word, "the other" will be demonized.

As long as the superimposed order holds, this will not matter, but under the veil of tranquility, group identities will clash and resentments will accumulate, and even when the resentment is properly directed at the modernizing processes of uprooting, disruption, and the consequent disorientation of values, it will be ethnicized. Both Northern Ireland and Bosnia-Herzegovina are good illustrations of these processes.

In the case of Bosnia-Herzegovina, the boundaries between Serbs, Croats, and Muslims are weak and permeable but nonetheless are perceived as real. There is no language barrier, a high rate of intermarriage exists, and there is an urban elite that accepts integration and thus seems to have betrayed the group by disregarding the boundaries, thereby depriving the groups of their leaders and allowing the leadership to fall into the hands of marginal men, extremists, and ethnic entrepreneurs. The result is that those members of the group, the socioeconomically weak or less privileged, for whom boundary maintenance is important, will create their own new and sanguinary ways of achieving this.

However, there are other, less extreme examples than the tragedy of Bosnia-Herzegovina. Northern Ireland, while extremely unpleasant, does not begin to compare in death and destruction, but the perceived need to maintain the ethnoreligious boundary by both sides is an ever-present factor in politics.[15] On the other hand, the relationship between Jews and non-Jews in Hungary offers another illustration of the processes involved. Culturally there is nothing to differentiate the two groups, yet each is conscious of its own identity and of the different identity of the other. The characteristics attributed by members of one group to the other are not automatically negative, but they do serve to maintain boundaries in a situation that is politically tranquil.[16]

Another interesting case that might at first sight fall into this category is that of the Slovaks of the Czech Republic. In reality, this group is marked by other characteristics, and this state of affairs is unlikely to change in the future. Until the separation of the Czech and Slovak republics, the

Slovaks living in the former had no distinctive status; they were simply migrants, often living in the Czech lands for shorter or longer periods but with their home base in Slovakia. With independence, all this changed and the Slovaks of the Czech Republic found themselves in the position of a minority. The evidence to date, however, does not in any way suggest that this has given rise to any serious political difficulties. On the contrary, these Slovaks appear to have opted voluntarily to remain in the Czech Republic and thereby gradually to abandon their Slovak identity. Certainly, there was little to indicate that they would demand minority rights or establish ethnic parties, although Slovak clubs and associations have been set up in the Czech Republic. The explanation for this quiescence, this seeming readiness to abandon their Slovak identity, must be sought in historical, cultural-linguistic, and material factors. Czech-Slovak coexistence and, indeed, cultural integration have a long history, predating the establishment of Czechoslovakia. The two languages, as we have seen, are close linguistically and pose no serious boundary-crossing problem. There have been many Slovaks who have made their way in the Czech lands in the past; indeed T. G. Masaryk, the first president of Czechoslovakia, was partly of Slovak descent. Nor is religion a differentiating factor. Like the Czechs, the Slovaks are mostly Roman Catholic with a minority being Protestant.

The shared civic identities, the habits acquired by having lived in the same state since 1918, are an added factor in this respect. But probably the single most significant explanation for the low level of Slovak self-articulation was that they opted to remain in the Czech Republic voluntarily. There was no territorial issue involved; they understood what they were doing at the time when they took their decision; they knew that they would stand to benefit from that decision by choosing to live in a state with a higher standard of living and with better chance of early integration into Europe; they knew that they would retain whatever status and achievement they had acquired in terms of career and job; and they concluded that integration with probable assimilation in a couple of generations into a Czech identity would serve them better than returning to Slovakia.

Viewed from this perspective, the Slovaks of the Czech Republic are a migrant minority and not a territorial one. This raises one further point of speculation. Are the Slovaks of the Czech Republic likely to follow the dynamic of North American migrants, that after some generations they will seek to rediscover their Slovak roots and attempt to construct a Slovak culture as a subset of Czech culture? This possibility exists but is likely to happen only if the Czech majority continues to insist on maintaining a distinction between itself and the Slovaks and blocks assimilation, something for which there are no precedents. By and large, once linguistic assimilation was complete, Slovaks were fully accepted by Czechs.

Otherwise, the statistics are against the maintenance of a separate Slovak identity (there are approximately 350,000 Slovaks in a population of 10 million Czechs and many of them are in mixed marriages, implying that their offspring will be Czech). Czech identity is both strongly ethnic and civic, again implying that the fate of the Slovaks in the Czech Republic is likely to be assimilation. It is noteworthy in this connection that for the first time in their history the Czechs are living in an ethnically homogeneous state and the evidence to date, still fragmentary, suggests that the Czech majority finds it a very agreeable state of affairs that it has to make no effort to deal with diversity. Hence, rather than the North American model, one should probably look at the fate of the descendants of the Polish migrants to France as the likeliest scenario for the Slovaks; they are completely integrated into a French cultural identity and Polishness for them is only a sentimental memory. For all practical purposes, there is no serious boundary maintenance against Slovaks by Czechs.

Policy Issues

What the West has done since the collapse of communism has been to put together a series of statements and documents that can be presented as something approximating a "European standard" in the treatment of minorities. The Copenhagen Declaration of June 1991 is the most significant of these formulations. A number of issues are noteworthy here. After World War I, the West initially opted for a complex minority regime, which was supposed to be supervised by the League of Nations. This was widely seen as having failed. After 1945, minority questions simply disappeared from the broad political agenda and European integration through the Common Market mechanism was expected to resolve the ethnic issue. This did not happen, as we have seen, and the consequence has been to force the West to return to a reconsideration of ethnicity and minorities as important policy problems. However, unlike the 1918–39 period, the problem currently tends to be viewed from the perspective of international security rather than collective rights. In particular, there is a more or less explicit proposition that ethnic minority questions cannot be seen as a purely domestic political issue and that where interstate relations are affected, the international community as a whole has an interest in seeing that they are resolved peacefully.[17]

In policy terms, the question arises whether the West can do very much and, if so, what. In this connection, it is important to recognize that the lesson of the Yugoslav crisis is that the West will not intervene militarily over questions of ethnicity and conflicts deriving from disputes over the treatment of minorities. However, in situations before polarization has begun, Western pressure can be effective and useful. The West can monitor the treatment of minorities by majorities and use political influence to ensure that discrimination is curtailed. The activities of the Council of Europe and the High Commissioner for Minorities of the Organization for Security and Cooperation in Europe (OSCE) are particularly good examples. Individual Western governments can likewise offer their services as honest broker when a dispute threatens to get out of hand. It is especially important to understand that preemption is better than cure, that early intervention is likely to be far more effective than a search for ex post facto remedies. This implies that the West should maintain a watching brief over all potential and actual minority questions, that it should use private and public pressure to this end. Underlying all this is the factor that until the civic dimension in post-communist Europe is stronger and deeper, ethnicity will continue to play a far more significant and therefore dangerous role than is the case and that the West has a clear interest in preventing these from coming to a head.

Notes

1. Anya Peterson Royce, *Ethnic Identity: Strategies of Diversity* (Bloomington: Indiana University Press, 1982).

2. George De Vos and Lola Romanucci-Ross, eds., *Ethnic Identity: Cultural Continuities and Change* (Chicago: University of Chicago Press, 1982).

3. Roman Szporluk, *Communism and Nationalism: Karl Marx versus Friedrich List* (Oxford: Oxford University Press, 1988).

4. David I. Kertzer, *Ritual, Politics and Power* (New Haven: Yale University Press, 1988).

5. Gérard Chaliand, ed., *Minority Peoples in the Age of Nation-States* (London: Pluto, 1989).

6. Walker Connor, *Ethnonationalism: the Quest for Understanding* (Princeton: Princeton University Press, 1994).

7. Henry H. Kerr, Jr., *Switzerland: Social Cleavages and Partisan Conflict* (London: Sage, 1974).

8. Colin H. Williams, ed., *National Separatism* (Cardiff: University of Wales Press, 1982).

9. In 1918, there was some initial confusion as to where the southern frontier of the new Czechoslovak state with Hungary would be drawn, but this confusion was fairly rapidly resolved in favor of a strategic frontier—access to the Danube, incorporation of east-west railway lines, and annexation of a series of towns with a Hungarian majority on economic grounds. Consequently, large numbers of Hungarians found themselves on the wrong side of the state frontier. After Munich, under the First Vienna Arbitration, the ethnically Hungarian areas were reincorporated into the Hungarian state. These areas were returned to Czechoslovakia at the end the World War II. See C. A. Macartney, *Hungary and Her Successors* (Oxford: Oxford University Press, 1973).

10. Paul Brass, ed., *Ethnic Groups and the State* (London: Croom, Helm, 1985).

11. Fr. Lorentz et al., *The Cassubian Civilization* (London: Faber, 1935).

12. Gary B. Cohen—in *The Politics of Ethnic Survival: Germans in Prague 1861–1914* (Princeton: Princeton University Press, 1981)—discusses the process of abandonment. His analysis, mutatis mutandis, can be applied to several other instances.

13. Rogers Brubaker, "National Minorities, Nationalizing States, and External National Homelands in the New Europe," *Daedalus*, Vol. 124, No. 2 (Spring 1995), pp. 107–132.

14. Fredrik Barth, ed., *Ethnic Groups and Boundaries: The Social Organization of Cultural Difference* (Bergen/Oslo: Universitetsforlaget, 1969).

15. Brendan O'Leary and J. McGarry, *The Politics of Antagonism: Understanding Northern Ireland* (London: Athlone, 1993).

16. András Kovács, "Jews and Hungarians: Group Stereotypes among Hungarian University Students," *East European Jewish Affairs*, Vol. 23, No. 2 (Winter 1993), pp. 51–59.

17. Katherine Verdery, "Whither 'Nation' and 'Nationalism'?" *Daedalus*, Vol. 122, No. 3 (Summer 1993), pp. 37–46.

11

Nationalism and Sexism: Eastern Europe in Transition

ANDJELKA MILIĆ

Although they offered women equality on paper, the communist governments of Eastern Europe did not by any means construct feminist utopias. Abiding by their stated commitment to equality between the sexes and linking this equality primarily to the economic domain, the previous governments may have provided material well-being but they also brought a great deal of hardship, frustration, and denial. Making women and men equal as workers "masculinized" women and, in general, created a working class devoid of gender differences. Even this restricted equality was available to women only if they sacrificed their individuality and carried the double burdens of work and domestic duties. Where communism provided women access to modern civilization, it did so only by diktat—by imposing a uniform order on all people and by erasing, on the surface at least, gender difference as a relevant social determinant.

Because of this forced erasure of gender difference, women in Eastern Europe greeted the fall of communism in 1989 with great hopes. They hoped for the maintenance of all the benefits provided by the previous communist regimes. But they also expected the emerging new order to provide them with the right to be different, with the freedom to express and shape their own individuality, and with the autonomy to build the social institutions to guarantee their needs.

Instead, women in the region have been pushed backward in history. Huge numbers of day-care institutions have closed, access to abortion has been threatened or restricted, and unemployment has risen precipitously and disproportionately for women. Female representation in politics has declined since the elections for the first multiparty parliaments. In general, women have suffered the most from the region's general fall in living standards and deterioration in quality of life. Adding insult to injury, the guardians of the new order have claimed that this turning back of the clock is in women's own interest: to safeguard their dignity and preserve their natural function of childbearing.

If gender equality and well-run day-care centers represent the fruits of modern civilization and if the countries of Eastern Europe and the former Soviet Union have declared their intentions to join this civilization, how have these universal achievements been so easily rejected or, at least, pushed to the margin in the post-communist period?

One major factor has been what political scientist Anthony Smith has called a "new wave of nationalism" that has spread like a virus through the already diseased social fiber of post-communist countries.[1] This "new nationalism" has been visible from the very beginning of the post-communist transition, waxing and waning from country to country and taking different forms in each context.

In its earliest phase, disguised by anti-communist phraseology, this nationalism gradually won a place in the platforms of a range of political parties. In countries such as former Yugoslavia and the former Soviet Union, it has managed virtually to overwhelm all other options. Elsewhere, it has become an established force on the political landscape. Throughout the region, nationalist ideologues believe that they have all the answers to the problems of transitional hardship. Not surprisingly, they think that they have solved the "women's issue" as well.

Stated bluntly, however, nationalism is inherently sexist, openly discriminating against women and dismissive of women's needs, demands, and wants. This sexist bias derives from the very history and logic of nationalism.

"Totalitarian" nationalism, which has "soaked" into the social environment of East European societies, has traditionally been obsessed with the idea of social unity.[2] Such unity functions as a strategy to overcome the political and social discord caused by the unstable structure of nationalist ideology and the unfinished tasks of social modernization. Most often, nationalists have tried to achieve this unity by basing a sovereign nation-state on ethnic principles and drumming up considerable xenophobia toward rival ethnic groups both domestic and foreign.

In its attempt to homogenize society, nationalism demonstrates an aversion to liberal democratic values, to even the mildest form of autonomous political activity. Hence, in Eastern Europe, nationalism and feminism are at the very outset in hostile confrontation. But unlike communism, with which it shares this aversion to women's independent activity, nationalism does indeed recognize women as different. This difference, however, is exclusively sexual, a reductionism that follows from nationalism's ideological claim that biological differences between the sexes determine social destiny. This tactic of recognizing women's particularity as a distinct sex, and not as social subjects, often cleverly entraps women and their organizations.

The overall marginalization of women in post-communist societies, a goal of the new nationalists, is also supported by the region's new liberals. East European democratic capitalists generally treat the women's issue as secondary, as "icing on the cake." With liberals prioritizing markets and democratic procedures, nationalists can heighten their own appeal. After all, nationalists at least ascribe importance to women—as bearers of culture or children.

While nationalism differs from one post-communist country to the next, an examination of one case may nevertheless illuminate the above arguments. Therefore, this essay will conclude with observations on the relationship between nationalism and feminism in former Yugoslavia.

The Logic of Nationalism

Social theory has traditionally paid little attention to nations and nationalism, particularly considering the relevance of these two phenomena in the twentieth century. This avoidance of nationalism stems, first, from the fact that the concept of nation, and consequently of nationalism, is very flexible and cannot easily be confined to objective categories; like "chameleons," both concepts take on different colorings in different historical and sociocultural environments.[3] It is necessary, therefore, to distinguish between types of nations and nationalisms; so far, however, existing classifications and typologies—Hobsbawm, Smith, Gellner—are insufficient in empirical scope and accuracy.[4]

Although some argue that nations have existed since ancient Egypt or feudal China, the prevailing view is that they originated during the modern political era.[5] Nationalism, in other words, can only operate within the differentiated social structure characteristic of the modern period; though traditional, almost archaic in content, it is nevertheless modern in origin and form.

While nationalism has been instrumental in the construction of modern states, the totalitarian variety developed in Eastern Europe under the influence of German romanticism opposes the social differentiation characteristic of modernity. According to this extremist ideology, civil society must be subordinated to a unified, indivisible, and basically unchangeable national entity. All ambiguities and social tensions must be ironed out to prepare, in the extreme, for totalitarian control. To realize this project, nationalism often promotes totalitarian violence against this society. By so thoroughly denying the liberal social contract, nationalism often seems to belong more to premodern social value systems than to the modern era.

Nationalism always emerges from and expresses the singular historical heritage and ethnocultural experience of a distinct ethnonational community. Yet, paradoxically, while nationalism is particularist in this way, it nevertheless demonstrates an extreme aversion to any form of particularism within its own discourse. Nationalism reduces society to a collective, partly fictitious "imagined" entity in which ethnonational being, national community, and state sovereignty take precedence over any particular human issue or need.[6]

Thus, the political discourse of nationalism generally avoids the particular concerns of men, women, classes, occupations, or ages. When such appeals are unavoidable, they serve only to remind particular groups that their existence is conditioned by and made possible only through allegiance to a unitary fatherland or homeland. In this way, nationalism substitutes for what are in reality discrete layers of social relations and mediation. All particularities appear as mere epiphenomena of this unitary substance. Concrete human problems simply become the means to achieve the primary objective of forging national unity. According to this logic, an individual or social group can only conform to the demands of nationalist politics by subordinating interests (and even sacrificing lives) to building, maintaining, or protecting the ethnonational community.

To mobilize a mass response in favor of these metaphysical imperatives, nationalism reaches deep into the dark, unconscious layers of human nature. It hopes to awaken in both the collective and in the individual suppressed discontents, frustrations, and fantasies, and to enable their ascendancy over the conscious, rational reasoning of the subject. Thus, the ideology, symbolism, and rhetoric of nationalism exploit the inexhaustible potential of mythic prehistory, archaic customs, and national traditions in order to transform confusion, frustration, and fear into a powerful outpouring of political revolt. Nationalism builds its attractive power by invoking the ghosts of the past, by exploiting the symbolism of "blood and soil" to reduce individuals to nothing more than incarnations of a timeless cycle of national restoration.

The one particularity nationalism recognizes is the family. The family functions in nationalist discourse as a metaphor for the nation and its life-giving activity. In all major national ideologies the national community is conceived of as a Great Family. Moreover, the nation is feminine, represented as "Mother-breadwinner, whom her children should love and protect. The state is paternalized, through its Authority that is always justified and calls to arms and duty."[7] Yet, while nationalism relies exclusively on the family, Anthony Smith points out that at the same time "real families can constitute an obstacle to the ideal of a homogeneous nation wherever nationalism embraces the ideal in that extreme form."[8] In other words, family loyalty whether Habsburg or Hatfield/McCoy commands primary allegiance over any national interest.

Finally, as a modern movement emerging from the Enlightenment and embracing the values of equality and self-determination, nationalism requires the political participation of all members of the national corpus. It can not exist without the "nationalization of masses and women's suffrage."[9] Nationalism wants to be, and often is, a voice of men as well as women, young as well as old, rich as well as poor, healthy as well as ill; it aims to become the universal prefix for each and every particularity.

Attempting to appeal universally, nationalism easily deviates from democracy toward populism. In populism—frequently a continuation or even a product of nationalism—the masses are required to demonstrate their unity but not to participate as political subjects in an authentic manner. By relying on the invoked indivisibility of national interest, nationalist leaders avoid the mediation of democratic mechanisms of decision-making (parliaments, multiparty systems, elections) and establish themselves as the political monopole, the unique arbiters of national affairs. Mass participation in political life thus becomes reduced to a mere ornament legitimizing the will of the leaders or leader; it becomes ritualized as an occasional mass expression of loyalty to the Leader through fixed plebiscites or referenda that rubber-stamp his decisions.

Hence, despite its modern origin and form, nationalism strays far from modern values. Instead of individualism, it seeks collectivism; as opposed to democracy it offers populism as a "degenerate reaction to a dream about a just social order."[10] It confronts the social diversification that money and power engender with a homogenization based on a unitary ethnonational principle; it presents cultural pluralism with the monism of a closed ethnic culture; and finally, it substitutes the tolerance of democratic consensus and compromise with the authoritarian conduct of state affairs based on force rather than argument.

With these qualities, nationalism moved quickly and silently into the ideological vacuum of post-communist Europe. In Romania, the first days of liberty were followed by chauvinist hysteria in the ethnic Hungarian sections of the country. The clericalist aspects of Polish nationalism overwhelmed the civic alternatives of the Solidarity movement. German unification gave way to a wave of xenophobic and nationalistic sentiment. And Czechoslovakia and Yugoslavia, the two federal states, have been torn apart, with the latter suffering by far the greater share of bloodshed.

In this same environment, women's movements and feminism, after an initial breakthrough at the time of the general democratic awakening, lost their momentum. Although they could potentially connect to half the population, radical advocates of women's rights faced difficulties in proving themselves among all the civil movements, parties, and initiatives. In all the political consolidations within East Europe, the women's issue time and again has been a litmus test for evaluating the democratic course of social reform. Where the position of women in society has been suppressed or marginalized, the nationalist option has been the strongest and the reforms have moved furthest from democracy.

Nationalism's ultimate aversion to feminism seems at first blush to be contradicted by the experience of Nazism's "matriarchal concept"[11] or the attraction that populist movements have had for women (Francoism in Spain or Peronism in Argentina). However, as we will see, nationalism's concealed sexual paradigm in fact precludes any equal partnership with women as autonomous political actors.

Nationalism and Women

The relationship between a man and a woman represents the fundamental social division. Nationalism in ideology and practice manipulates these sexual differences in order to confirm and legitimize its own need to achieve political unity and social homogenization. By emphasizing an equilibrium between the sexes and the indispensability of the contribution of each to the whole, nationalism very successfully blurs and suppresses the sociocultural, gendered differentiation of sexes in society. By arguing that gender functions are biologically complementary, nationalism legitimates sexist relations toward women.

In nationalist ideology, the family represents a universal, a natural, an eternal entity—the "unavoidable assumption for any public development of the people" as interpreted as early as the first half of the nineteenth century.[12] By establishing gender and the family as the foundation for any individual and collective existence, nationalism counts on emotional overreaction and mass response for its support, particularly among the lowest layers of society for whom gender and the family often represent the sole source of identity. Within the family, the sex roles are interpreted in a symmetrical fashion, such that each can have meaning only in conjunction with the other. Nationalism cannot tolerate any kind of independent or separate discourse. Even the smallest assertion of the specific needs of men or women would destroy the unity of couple, family, or nation.

Nationalism does not declare itself against women as such. On the contrary, nationalism needs women, but only women constructed in a nationalist image. Nationalism thus insists on a symmetry between the sexes in the family while at the same time refuses to recognize conflicts that disturb the stability of gender relations. Nationalism is thus capable of winning women's support by making them feel as valuable as any other member of the nation. In other words, it succeeds in instilling self-esteem in women, helping them to articulate their specific identity in society. This is a game of "seduction" that nationalism plays very successfully.

Nationalism maps the paradigm of the complementary division of gender relations horizontally across the social division of labor, diminishing the importance of class and other differences. The paradigm therefore fits neatly with the definition of nation as an "imagined" community of "blood and soil," the variety of nationalism born of German romanticism. A mythic appropriation of prehistory and a fictitious continuity of national community symbolize the unity of the parental progenitors: the "father of the nation" and the "mother of the nation" whose "sons" and "daughters" share a common origin and guarantee the nation's everlasting existence.

In the community's symbolic and mystical constructions of "blood" relations, the "father of the nation" represents the soil of the ancestors—the fatherland or *patria*—that the father passes on to his male heirs. Men govern the soil, disposing of it or defending, protecting, and guarding it from enemies. Thus, the "father of the nation" unifies three functions in his domain relevant to the establishment and maintenance of economic, political, and military rule. This overwhelming male authority threatens the gender balance in the paradigmatic relationship.

The disrupted balance is, however, immediately reestablished by giving women priority through the "matricentric" symbolic representation of the national being.[13] For it is women who represent the nation as a community based on "blood." The term "nation" originates in the Latin "nasci," meaning "to give birth," "to become," "to create." Women are the mothers of the nation, both symbolically and etymologically. By the very act of giving birth, women create a permanent, consanguineous community between all members of the same ethnonation. Since blood implies stronger ties of spiritual kinship than does land, women are the "cement" of cultural identity and national continuity. Women also function symbolically as educators, transferring national tradition and culture to subsequent generations (e.g., through the "mother" tongue). Men in East European cultures that emphasize ethnic identity demonstrate a certain cult-like deference toward women in their behavior—such as the ceremonial kissing of women's hands.

Essential to this stereotyped division between men of the land and women of the blood is the synchronizing of the sexes in their separate domains. The separation or even segregation of the domains by itself does not require the domination of one over the other or the unequal valuing of the different contributions. Men and women, each in their domain, perform the tasks entrusted to them in the best possible manner and, spontaneously, the social community will be free of gender conflicts. But if women "neglect" their family, their nurturing duties, or their obligations to produce children, they do so not because of their oppressed social position but because of their own depravity. The concept of national community presupposes that its members act in harmony and unity. The alternative can only be unnatural, a malady, a pathology, a degeneration   eventually these lapses become labeled as treasonous.

The glorification of women through the symbolism of the "mother of the nation" does not, however, refer to women in general or to individual women, but to women as a sexual category (or, to be precise, women as a sexual function). Adoration of the Woman-Mother as the symbol of nationalist ideology, despite its superficial honoring of the sex, inevitably results in the humiliation of women as individual social beings. All other aspects of a woman's social being and subjective individuality must be strictly controlled by the national collective and, in extreme cases, entirely negated. Women attain equality only on condition that they give up all aspirations to social roles and responsibilities that do not derive directly from their biological nature. The abstract equation of the sexes fails to see the actual social conditions of men and women. Nationalism's basic reduction of women's being to the procreative sexual function robs women of individuality. Indeed, sexism represents the true internal essence of nationalism.

One should have no illusions, however, that men fare better within the nationalist formula. The same pattern that reduces women to "birthgiving machines" turns men into aggressive and homicidal "war machines."[14] The horrors of the war in former Yugoslavia show how nationalist strategy, by manipulating human sexuality, can lead to the brutalization of social life and sexual relations in particular. The phenomenon of rape serves as an illustration. In the nationalist-patriarchal interpretation, women as sex and birthgiving machines are the property of the national collective and hence represent its sacred inviolable borders. Violation of this common property by rape has meant symbolically trespassing on enemy territory and disrupting the blood community. This criminal act of barbarism becomes in nationalist ideology an act of honor and male sacrifice.

East European Nationalism

Feminist theoreticians agree that women in post-communist countries have experienced a decline in equal rights since 1989. After ten years of participating in the Solidarity movement, women have bitterly concluded that whereas all of Poland was once enslaved, now only Polish women are.[15] The situation following the unification of East and West Germany is comparable, as Tatiana Böhm remarks: "It is feared that the united German train will roll over the women's movement. There is much evidence that women stand to lose the most in the German unification."[16] On the other hand, women acknowledge their own failure to sustain and take advantage of the initial democratic climate. As one Czech feminist has commented, "The insignificant engagement of women in East European politics means women will miss their opportunity and uselessly repeat past mistakes."[17] The degree of oppression and the number of restrictions imposed on women during the so-far short rule of the new political forces in these countries suggest a "re-patriarchalization" of East European society.

Two ideological forces have joined hands to send women back to the kitchen and the nursery: nationalism and liberalism. According to liberalism, the prevailing state ideology in most East European countries, women's issues, since they are "secondary," should be put to one side until after the "important" questions of economic restructuring, privatization, and so on are resolved. Women's issues are thus represented as the icing on the cake,[18] the cake being a new society based on the free market and private ownership. In the interim, however, women are more frequently expected to swallow the bitter pills associated with the transition. Generally speaking, liberal politics has very little interest and understanding for the welfare state and the social services it developed under communist rule. Not surprisingly, the International Monetary Fund and World Bank have recommended cutting back these social services and throwing countless people out of work. This rise in unemployment disproportionately affects women. In supporting these austerity measures, liberals can count on political support from nationalists who would be glad to see women returned to the kitchen.

Given its recent record on women's issues in the West, liberalism's contribution to the re-patriarchalization of East European society can be viewed as temporary or simply instrumental. For resurgent nationalist forces, however, as we have discussed in the previous section, sexism resides at the very core of the ideology.

The appeal of nationalism's outdated position on women's issues is understandable. For populations deprived of individual freedoms under communist rule, nationalist politics attracts because it seemingly legitimates a retreat into the private sphere (the home, the kitchen). This protection of privacy, however, is superficial. In reality, nationalist governments do not abandon control over this sphere of human life. On the contrary, nationalism understands the private life of families to be the core of its politics. Women as the pillars of family life are obliged to sacrifice for the achievement of national goals. They are expected to repay a social debt for the recognition and adoration they receive as symbols of the glorious nation. Indeed, as Jean Bethke Elshtain points out, women have often contributed to the nationalist cause through the sacrifice of their sons, a sacrifice that defines their very citizenship.[19]

Polish sociologist Ewa Hauser explains that as nationalist forces gather strength during the building of the new democracies, their "tactic is to retard any open politicization of women: what is called for from them instead is patience, solidarity, participation and tolerance of initial hardships."[20] These insurgent political forces have not, in other words, openly opposed the more radical actions that women have undertaken. They have not sought to ban independent women's political parties in East Germany, Russia, or Serbia. On the contrary, the existence of these political parties and groups enhances the new pluralist images of these societies. Given their marginal position and their difficulty in influencing public opinion, women's political formations do not in any case present an obstacle to either liberal or nationalist forces.

But after the new governments began to feel more secure and as liberal-national coalitions consolidated on social questions, a radical change of tactic took place. Instead of widening and deepening women's equality and rights, these governments put forward demands that have limited, controlled, or even annulled women's rights and freedoms. Campaigns have been launched to ban the practice of birth control and restrict the right of abortion. Social welfare programs have been cut back, particularly in the areas of child care, social security, health services, and housing. In the employment sphere, women's opportunities for employment on equal terms, at equal wages, and with equal chances for promotion have been curtailed. The rate of women's unemployment exceeds 50 percent in all East European countries. Younger women are particularly hard hit. In countries such as Bulgaria, for example, young women under the age of 30 make up almost the majority of the unemployed.[21]

Women have also failed in the struggle for political influence in the new democratic multiparty parliamentary institutions. In Hungary, for instance, women's participation in parliament dropped from 25 to 30 percent during communist rule to only 7 percent in the post-communist era.[22] The same drop from one-quarter to less than 10 percent occurred in Poland and the former Czechoslovakia. A similar process happened in the new independent states of former Yugoslavia (Slovenia, Croatia and Serbia)—from one-fifth representation to 4 to 6 percent.[23] Even in Russia, where the Women's Party has been the most successful of its kind in the region and received 8 percent of the vote in the 1993 elections, the percentage of women in parliament still dropped from 15.7 percent in the 1989 USSR Congress of People's Deputies to 13.5 percent in the 1993 Russian Duma.[24]

With poverty growing, health care deteriorating, educational standards declining, and both unemployment and criminality on the rise, Eastern Europe is seemingly obsessed with debates, polemics, political confrontations, petitions, and resolutions circulating both for and against abortion. In Poland, for instance, until it was recently amended, the abortion law criminalized both the woman and the doctor who performed the abortion. By fighting abortion and even putting the question to the public in the form of a plebiscite (as in Poland), nationalists hope to send a clear message that no single exclusive right can exist apart from the nation and its interest, certainly not the right of a woman to govern her own body.

This assault on abortion is designed to reestablish the disturbed balance in gender relations produced by the "monstrous practice of communism." Moreover, on the abortion issue, collectivism confronts individualism, the growth of which in contemporary society nationalists view as the greatest danger to national values. By banning abortion, the nationalist state demonstrates that women do not have the right as individuals to control their bodies. Rather, the individual body is monopolized by the national collective for its own objectives. Neither life nor death ultimately belong to the individual. All belongs to the Great Family, that fusion of blood and soil, of motherland and fatherland.

The Case of Former Yugoslavia

If any single feature distinguished Yugoslav from other varieties of East European socialism, it was the tiny thread of civil society that emerged in the 1970s in the space between official politics and the everyday routine of family life and consumption. This new space was opened by a young, predominantly urban generation that was better educated and equipped to use Yugoslavia's openness for experimentation with alternative possibilities. Many informal groups were thus born, versatile in form and content and bringing a new "sensibility" into social life.[25]

Among these informal groups there developed an embryonic feminist movement. Feminism made its official appearance in 1978 at a large international meeting of feminist women in Belgrade. Following quickly on the heels of this meeting, groups emerged in the capitals of the republics (Ljubljana, Zagreb, Sarajevo). Various feminist projects were begun: a rape hotline (the SOS telephone), the translation of the work of Western feminists, the first publications of Yugoslav feminists. By the time of Yugoslavia's disintegration, many differences had appeared among the feminists of the different republics, pointing to the coming breakdown of the state. For instance, at the Third Yugoslav Feminist Congress, held in Belgrade in April 1991, the participants could not agree on a common declaration concerning the future of Yugoslavia. Feminists from Slovenia and Croatia rejected the common declaration; feminists from Serbia insisted that such a declaration was needed not only because the country's future was at stake but also to ensure the influence and power of the feminist movement. The Congress ended without any public declaration.

Still, before the first multiparty parliamentary elections in 1991, feminism was on the rise precisely at the time when interrepublic relations were worsening. In Serbia, despite the powerful superiority of the ruling Socialist Party (originally the Communist League), these elections energized the feminist movement and intensified the struggle for equal rights. For example, activists formed the Women's Lobby (*Ženski Lobi*) to coordinate women's demands within the various parties both before and after the elections. Through participation in political parties, women became more visible in the public sphere—for instance, the leading figure of the Serbian opposition Vesna Pešić—and even formed the Women's Party, ZEST.[26]

ZEST did not, however, run in the first parliamentary elections, less for financial reasons than because its members were simply not prepared to contest parliamentary seats. Regardless of this initial reticence, the party's very presence in the campaign forced other parties, particularly the Socialist Party, to turn more toward women as both active political participants and future voters. For instance, the Socialists launched an initiative in many provincial towns to establish women's political associations whose aim was to campaign independently but in fact were under the party's auspices.

Despite the surge of women into politics, the elections sent only four women to the new Serbian parliament of 250 representatives; during communist rule, women routinely captured one-fifth of the seats. In response to this dismal showing, an alternative Women's Parliament was formed (*Ženski Parlament*) to address women's problems and monitor the work of the "men's" parliament by proposing, criticizing, and submitting draft acts to the official parliament. Many of these initiatives—on social policy affecting women—were subsequently rejected, such as a proposed ministry for women. One key victory, however, was preventing the government from limiting access to abortion.

Another essential form of engagement by women was their persistent endeavor, from the very beginning of the crisis in former Yugoslavia, to search for peaceful solutions to the spiraling armed conflicts. Women formed the first groups to oppose the war clearly and loudly—they were heard as early as July 1991 in Belgrade protesting the war in Croatia. The first anti-war rally in Yugoslavia was organized by the Center for Anti-War Action, established mainly by women activists. Immediately following the outbreak of war, "Women in Black" was formed, which protested publicly against the war by holding silent vigils and dressing in black clothes that traditionally represent women's pain and grief.

The women's anti-war engagement came to public prominence during the summer of 1991 with the spontaneous protest by mothers in front of the republican parliament in Belgrade. Displeased by the deputies' refusal to meet and discuss their demands, the demonstrators eventually broke into the parliament building. The mothers demanded: an end to all armed conflicts; the release from the army of all recruits who had served their time; that military service be restricted to the conscript's republic of domicile; and that service in other republics only take place if the external borders of Yugoslavia were threatened.

Surprised by the protest's scale and the protesters' fervor, the ruling regime immediately resorted to repressive tactics. The protesters' documents were checked; several women were detained, interrogated by police, and then sentenced for misdemeanors. At the same time, the regime shifted the entire responsibility for the protested treatment of conscripts to the military authorities, and the mothers were sent for talks with the Yugoslav National Army. Feminist groups objected to this shifting of responsibility to the military. Attempts were made to establish communication and organize a joint protest at the federal level. Despite a media blockade and deteriorating communications, protesters in Sarajevo in September 1991 agreed to form a coordinating committee, its core consisting of rebellious mothers and fathers from throughout Yugoslavia. Thus, the mothers' protest grew into a family protest, as fathers, husbands, and brothers joined in.

The ruling regimes on all sides, prepared to achieve their objectives even at the cost of war, denounced the protests as anti-patriotic. In both Serbia and Croatia, new women's organizations emerged to respond to the mothers' protest by demonstrating patriotic feelings for their warring side. The mothers' protest was thus gradually strangled and isolated—reduced to personal demands by individual mothers and fathers trying to save their own children and "disregarding" the interests of the nation. Feminist groups that joined the protest with a clear anti-war stance were treated much more aggressively—with threats, office break-ins, and the tailing of activists.

With the weakening of public resistance to the war, women's political engagement has notably dropped. Disappointed and discouraged, many of the most active women during the initial democratization period have now completely abandoned party politics. Others have joined volunteer relief organizations to help the poor. The ruling establishments are delighted with this political disengagement for finally women's "hysteria" is over and matters can be dealt with "reasonably."

The Yugoslav case exemplifies many of this essay's earlier arguments. The national-political bureaucratic elites had systematically directed the crises of the socialist system toward the disintegration of the federal state. In all republics, romanticized visions of national unity overcame rational attempts to forge a democratic and multiethnic federalism. The media in the republics propagated the view that the peoples of Yugoslavia could no longer live together and that the different nationalities should band together to fight for their particular fatherlands.

This rush to nationalism was accompanied by a state-sponsored initiative to protect and defend all family members of common blood origin. This oath extended to those living in diaspora communities. Here we see evidence of *zadruga* or the traditional family organization preserved from time immemorial in the Balkans. The *zadruga* is grounded in the authoritarian rule of the collective family over its individual members. To this patriarchal logic of state functioning is added the matricentric conception of the relationship between the mother-state and the diaspora peoples. Serbs from all over are thus drawn into the warm skirt folds of *Majčica Srbija*—the diminutive form of Mother Serbia that conveys the sense of greatest love.

Under this model of parental protection, the state requires individual members to sacrifice for the collective. The state becomes the leading ethical authority and the bearer of God's justice. The individuals become children dependent on the fatherland and the maternal national state.

Nationalists in the former Yugoslavia needed women's support to consolidate power. Once in control, however, they treated women's organizations as anti-patriotic. Politically engaged at first, women have fallen into passivity. The failure of ZEST is a case in point. In the December 1993 elections in Serbia, opinion polls indicated a very high abstention rate for women, even as high as 40 percent.[27] Economic conditions have only encouraged this passivity, throwing women back into family and household tasks to compensate for material shortages and ensure the survival of the family.

Despite the success of the women's movement in mobilizing against the war, the protests still took place within the paradigm of nationalism. Women loudly and en masse entered the political scene in a role circumscribed for them by the very nationalist discourse they opposed—the role of mothers. True, as feminist theory maintains, the "personal is political." In this case, concern for children led to political protest and resistance to authorities. But the protest would not have stood a chance if it had not established itself firmly within the pattern of maternity. Instead of defining themselves, the women allowed others the task of definition. Thus, they voluntarily entered nationalism's sexist trap and made possible the regime's transformation of their general political demand for cessation of war into the individual protests of mothers saving their own children while the nation was in danger.

In the case of former Yugoslavia, nationalism has clearly manipulated women and their sexual roles in society. After a prolonged hibernation of the "women's issue" under "real" socialism, nationalism has effectively brought women onto the political scene. But this mobilization of women must be understood literally—women have been mobilized to be then assimilated into the true national consciousness. Nationalism does not expect women to remain active in political life. Rather, they are expected to nurture the national idea in their own social domain, the family. They prove themselves true members of the national collectivity by remaining in the roles of mother and transmitter of national values and ideals.

This reduction to a "natural" role in society is nationalism's major aim with respect to women. At the same time, this reduction is part of a larger pattern of blunting democracy in favor of national unity and social homogeneity. The logic of nationalism implies that the difference between the sexes is the primary human difference. If this primary difference is deprived of influence on social life, a major gap is created in the defense shield of nationalism, which becomes open to a torrent of particular demands and rights. Nationalism must therefore impose on gender relations the complementary sexual divisions based on biological function. Feminist movements, by challenging this implicit biologism, attack not only sexism, but trends toward authoritarianism in the post-communist societies of Eastern Europe.

Notes

I would like to express my deep gratitude for extended criticism and comments I received during work on this essay from Cynthia Cockburn of Great Britain and Richard Caplan and John Feffer, the editors of this book.

1. Anthony Smith, *National Identity* (Reno: University of Nevada Press, 1993).

2. Istvan Deak, "Uncovering Eastern Europe's Dark History," *Orbis*, Winter 1990.

3. Benedict Anderson, *Imagined Communities* (New York: Verso, 1983).

4. Although these analysts treat Central and East European countries, they rarely seem to acknowledge that communist rule from the very beginning had a nationalist orientation and at the same time restricted internal movements for autonomy.

5. Smith, op. cit.

6. Anderson, op. cit.

7. Edgar Morin, *Kako Mišlite Evropu* (Sarajevo: Svjetlost, 1990), p.41.

8. Smith, op. cit., p.78.

9. Ernest Gellner, *Nations and Nationalism* (New York: Oxford University Press, 1983).

10. Adam Michnik, "Priblizavanje istini," *Republika*, No. 45 (1993), p.3.

11. Jose Hermond, "Allmacht für Frauen: Faschistische Matriarchatskonzepte," *Das Argument*, Vol. 26, No. 146 (August 1984), pp.539–554.

12. H.W. Riehl, "Die Familie als Heiligtum," in *Definition und Theorie Der Familie: Die Familie in Deutschland*, ed. F. Niedhart (Leska: Opladen, 1975), p. 119.

13. Hermond, op. cit., p.550.

14. Zarana Papić, "Bivša Muškost, Bivša Ženskost, Bivših Gradjana Bivše Jugoslavije," *Republika* (March 1993).

15. Ewa Hauser et al., "Feminism in the Interstices of Politics and Culture,"

in *Gender Politics and Post-Communism*, eds. Nanette Funk and Magda Mueller (New York: Routledge, 1993), p.259.

16. Tatiana Böhm, "The Women's Question as Democratic Question: In Search of Civil Society," ibid., p.158.

17. Jiřina Šiklová, "Are Women in Central Europe Conservative?" ibid., p.74.

18. Margarita Papandreu, *The Changing Role of Women Within Changing Europe* (Den Haag: E.N.W.S., 1991), p.9.

19. Jean Bethke Elshtain, "Sovereignty, Identity and Sacrifice," in *Reimagining the Nation*, eds. Marjorie Ringrose and Adam Lerner (Buckingham: Open University Press, 1993), p.161.

20. Hauser, op. cit.

21. Eva Eberhardt and Jacqueline Heinen, eds., *Central and Eastern Europe: Women Workers in the Transitional Phase* (Report for the International Union of Foodworkers, 1992), pp.16–17.

22. Enikö Bollobás, "Totalitarian Lib: The Legacy of Communism for Hungarian Women," Funk and Mueller, op. cit., p.203.

23. Andjelka Milić, "Women and Nationalism in Former Yugoslavia," ibid., pp.118–119.

24. Wendy Slater, "Female Representation in Russian Politics," *RFE/RL Research Report* (June 3, 1994), p.29.

25. Snežana Joksimović et al., *Mladi i Neformalne Grupe* (Belgrade: Centra za idejni rad SSO, 1988).

26. Cynthia Cockburn, "A Women's Political Party for Yugoslavia: Introduction to the Serbian Feminist Manifesto," *Feminist Review*, No. 39 (Winter 1991), pp.155–160.

27. V. Goati, *Jugoslavija na Prekretnici* (Belgrade: Jugoslovenski Institut za Novina Rstvo, 1991).

12

Hibernian Endgame? Nationalism in a Divided Ireland

TOM GARVIN

The resurgence of popular nationalism in Eastern Europe and elsewhere in the world, often accompanied by horrific violence, has stunned many observers. This re-emergence of hitherto smothered collective identities has obscured the fact that the general upheavals of the past decade have had little impact on analogous collective identities in Western Europe. In the British Isles, Germany, France, Iberia, and Italy, the minor nationalities have tended toward a guarded acceptance of existing state structures, usually accompanied by the willingness of these states to modify their structures to accommodate the demands of the minorities. Ireland would seem to offer a serious exception to this generalization, although even this exception may be more apparent than real.

Arguably, the nationalist explosions in what were the communist states of Eastern Europe have been particularly violent precisely because communism repressed them so determinedly over the decades. By contrast, in Western Europe, local particularisms have tended to gain authentic institutional recognition in pragmatic, piecemeal ways. Politics has tended to replace insurrectionism, with South Tyrol being one of the earlier examples.[1] Such piecemeal solutions are rendered easier to achieve by the curious alliances that have been evolving between the interstate agencies of Brussels and the substate representative systems that sometimes express regional or national identities. The classic European nation-state is being bypassed increasingly and in ways that offer opportunities for political self-expression to local particularisms and nationalisms.

In Ireland, however, the problem historically has been that Irish nationalism received full recognition in the form of an independent state two generations ago while that same nationalism was refused recognition in the pro-Britain "unionist" area of Northern Ireland. This occurred despite the existence of a large separatist minority in the region. Gradually this uneasy situation has begun to change. While efforts to resolve the stalemate by armed conflict have failed, the growing importance of the European Union and the emergence of a Northern Irish Catholic and nationalist middle class that favors prosperity over continued strife have introduced a new dynamic into the Irish national question. The effect of these developments is likely to have far-reaching implications not only for the Irish national conflict but also for the character of Irish nationalism more generally.

Irish Divisions

To understand the Irish situation and the features of its nationalism today, one must appreciate that the Irish have always been the outlier among the nations of the British Isles; they are the least British of the British or, as they would put it themselves, the non-British of the Isles. Ireland is, most obviously, a separate island, and was the center of a distinctive Gaelic-Christian culture during the first millennium A.D. Furthermore, after the Norman and English invasions of the medieval and early modern period, whereas the bulk of the land of the island passed into the hands of newcomers from Britain, the majority of the population clung to a separate identity. Assimilation into English culture, or even acceptance of a common "British Isles" identity, did not occur, although it may have been a close-run thing.[2] Rather, in the twentieth century most Irish opted for separation and, despite its costs, have never really regretted the decision.

There are many reasons why the majority of the Irish chose to assert a national identity distinct from, and opposed to, English or British identity and why that distinctiveness persists today. From the start, religion has been the key to the Irish national consciousness. After the imposition by the English of Anglicanism as the official Irish state church and the final defeat of the Irish Catholic aristocracy at the hands of English, Scottish, and Irish Protestants in 1690, the Irish majority remained determinedly Catholic. This was due mainly to the missionary efforts of a well-organized counter-Reformation Catholic Church with secure bases in France and Spain, safe from English power. A further reason for the survival of Irish Catholicism was the underdevelopment and weakness of purpose of Irish Anglicanism: the Anglicans did not proselytize very effectively among the general population.

The Irish majority was not only Catholic, it was also dispossessed; its lands had passed forcibly into the hands of the small Protestant minority on the island. Dispossession and faith (and later nationalism) thus reinforced one another. If one were Protestant, one had more civil rights, including the right to own property. Education, where it existed in any formal fashion, tended to be a Protestant preserve, as Catholic schools were discouraged by law and public policy.

Scotland and Wales, where separatism never became as strong in modern times as it did in Ireland, afford revealing contrasts. Scotland accepted integration with the larger English nation as something positive. Scotland thus became a relatively satisfied "national substate" within the United Kingdom, retaining its national Kirk, its universities, and its legal system, while Scottish members of parliament constituted a determined and successful team of defenders of Scottish national interests. Wales, more closely linked to England, never had its own autonomous or quasi-autonomous state, unlike Scotland and Ireland. Its nationalism has nearly always confined itself to demands for religious rights and linguistic self-expression. The success of the Welsh approach can be witnessed by the continuing survival, and relative prospering, of the Welsh language.

Irish nationalism, by contrast, has been beset by profound divisions throughout its history. The Irish members at Westminster between 1801 and 1922 tended to be spokesmen for one Irish interest at the expense of another: landlord versus tenant in the early years of the Union with Britain, unionist versus nationalist in the later years. The failure to achieve successful integration with England—the "Scottish" solution—was a consequence of these divisions, exacerbated by Irish religious fanaticism and an equally rabid English political and religious bigotry. The Irish union with Great Britain was crippled from the start.

One of the sharpest Irish divisions has been between North and South, where unequal economic development laid the foundations for the partition that is the focal point of Ireland's nationalist agitations today. During the nineteenth century, restrictions on Catholic land ownership were relaxed, and in a slow, profound historical shift the land of Ireland gradually passed back from the mainly Protestant landlord class to its mainly Catholic tenantry.[3] This process was accompanied by a gradual democratization so that by the end of the century a bastard feudalism was replaced by a free-farmer democracy in embryo. But whereas Britain at this time was in the throes of an industrial revolution, a general de-industrialization occurred in Ireland as small manufacturing concerns were wiped out by British competition.[4] Only one area on the island experienced a different development in the era after 1690: the northern province of Ulster, geographically and culturally close to Scotland and subject, in the seventeenth century, to widespread colonization by Protestant settlers from Britain.

Ulster shared in the British industrial revolution, and Belfast, the capital of northeastern Ireland, mushroomed as an important industrial city in the nineteenth century, with linen manufacture, shipbuilding, and ironworking the most important activities. The rest of the island stagnated while Ulster prospered. A huge famine in the 1840s killed at least one million of the island's inhabitants, out of a total population of over eight million. Another million fled the Great Hunger, as it was called, to the

United States, there to nurse their hatred of England. Fairly or otherwise, the British were perceived as watching the catastrophe with some complacency. The resultant bitterness was to have repercussions for Irish nationalism that extend to the present. Millions more Irish people emigrated to America during subsequent decades, so that by the end of the century the population of the island had fallen to roughly four million, with about one-third in the area that was to become the Protestant-dominated province of Northern Ireland ("Ulster") in 1920.

In many ways, a huge mental gulf has grown up between North and South since then, and this goes a long way toward explaining the absence of a common purpose among Irish nationalists today. Both North and South have had utterly different political experiences, the North that of a British province under local Protestant rule, the rest of the island an independent democracy as a British Commonwealth dominion and later an independent republic. Indeed, after 1945 the North became ever more tightly attached to London whereas the South essentially forgot about the British, focusing instead on its own social and economic development. North and South have also been marked by distinct cultural experiences. Secularization has gone quite a long way in the Republic whereas Northerners are far more religiously minded. Neither part of Ireland is as post-Christian as the rest of Western Europe, but the process seems to have moved further in the South than in the North.[5]

In other significant respects, the southern republic has been evolving away from the North, indeed out of the British Isles altogether. Up to 1960, most of the Republic's trade was with Britain, and culturally it remained, as it still does, a province of the Isles. Since 1960, however, trade with the rest of the world has increased markedly, and this tendency has accelerated since both islands joined the European Community in 1973. The Republic has exchanged its historic economic dependence on Britain for a more diversified dependence on the continental mainland. This ties in rather well with the culture's long-standing Catholic links with the mainland; faith and wallet have thus joined forces and produced a marked, and very un-British, Europhilia in the Republic. At the same time, Europe has become a counterweight that Dublin can use for leverage against the otherwise overwhelming weight of Britain.[6] Once, for example, Britain could put tariffs on Irish exports; that power is now gone.

The upshot of these trends is that the Republic has essentially turned post-nationalist and consequently has dropped most of the fundamentalist rhetoric of the early period after independence, most notably in support of a united, independent Ireland. By contrast, nationalism of a traditional "faith and fatherland" kind has remained strong in parts of the Catholic areas of Northern Ireland. The Republic had developed its own national identity whereas many Northerners are unsure, and often confused, whether they are British, Irish, or both. This confusion has provided fertile ground for the pursuit of political ends through violent means.

A Question of Violence

Long before independence and partition, Irish nationalism contained with-in it a minority tradition of armed violence. This minority tradition has had to compete with a dominant tradition of democratic compromise best represented by the nineteenth-century figure of Daniel O'Connell. On occasion, this violent tradition has gained the upper hand, as it did in 1912–23 and in Northern Ireland between 1969 and 1994.

Generally speaking, violence and nationalism seem to combine most explosively when either the actual existence of the *ethnie* seems to be threatened, or when a socioeconomic interest, such as control of land, is involved. A real or imagined assault on a central set of ethnic or religious values or symbols, held to be vital to the collective well-being, can also spark extraordinary violence.

The Irish minority tradition of violent political agitation dates from the eighteenth century. Since that time there have been three great armed up-risings against British rule in Ireland and, at times, against local supporters of that rule. The first, culminating in the Rising of 1798, was inspired by the French and American Revolutions, and involved a southern Catholic and Ulster Dissenter alliance against the small Anglican landed class and their British patrons. The insurrection was put down with great brutality, with some 50,000 people killed.

The second era of armed resistance gained independence for the south-ern and western bulk of the island, now a sovereign state containing the great majority of the Catholic and nationalist population. This "Time of Trouble" lasted from 1913 to 1923, and the Anglo-Irish settlement that divided the island in 1920–23 lies behind the recent "troubles," from 1969 to 1994. Between 1913 and 1923, perhaps 6,000 people were killed on the island. British forces and Irish guerrillas fought a small war, mainly in the south of Ireland, while Catholics and Protestants in Ulster perpetrated pogroms against each other, with the Protestant pogroms being more ef-fective.[7]

After partition and independence in 1922, Protestant and British forces suppressed the Catholic minority in Northern Ireland. In the main-ly Catholic South, the guerrillas of the Irish Republican Army (IRA) split and fought a short, internecine civil war over the issue of membership in the British Commonwealth. The forces of the democratic majority won, and the South settled down to construct a liberal democracy.[8] In the North, however, the two religious groups remained in a sullen stasis, with Protestants wielding a local hegemony over the Catholic minority with British acquiescence. Northern Ireland remained part of the United King-dom but London did not supervise the local rulers. Catholics were not disenfranchised but were effectively shorn of all real political power and heavily discriminated against. The Protestant community had a built-in majority and gerrymandered the local council electoral constituencies so as to expand their natural majority even further.[9]

In return, the Catholics battened down the hatches and built a counterculture centered around their Church and Catholic/nationalist institutions. Catholics and Protestants lived cheek by jowl, often cooperated politely with each other but did not socialize much and rarely intermarried. The two communities constructed totally distinct cultural worlds, each only half-aware of the complexities inside the other. The Canadian writer Hugh MacLennan, in the context of the Quebec national question, aptly calls this a situation of "two solitudes."[10] Protestants saw Catholics as allied with the Catholic Republic in the South, in league with it to take over Northern Ireland and, perhaps, to drive Protestants out ("back to Scotland"). They commonly saw Catholicism as a superstitious and even evil religion. Catholics, for their part, saw Protestants as richer, bigoted, and having the might of Britain—the local superpower—behind them. Catholics developed a victim psychology, seeing their own woes far more vividly than those of the other side. Protestants similarly were often blind to the condition of Catholics.[11] It is against this backdrop that the third era of armed resistance began in the late 1960s.

Like so much else in modern Ireland, the political process that destabilized the post-1923 standoff in Ireland was imported from America. It consisted of a series of campaigns mounted by young, mainly Catholic leaders and activists for civil rights, modeled on the Black civil rights campaign of that time in the United States. In effect, the Catholics, echoing eighteenth-century predecessors, said to the Protestant government of Northern Ireland: "You say we are all British, you refuse to permit us to join the independent Republic, and you deny our Irish identity. Very well, then, give us the rights of Britons."

This argument fell on sympathetic ears, not only in the southern republic but in Britain and the United States. London was belatedly embarrassed by the fruit of its own malign negligence and rushed to make amends. However, it was too late; Protestant terrorists tried to provoke action by the authorities against the Catholics by faking IRA bombings. Rioting in late 1969, in which the Protestant police took a conspicuous part, resulted in mass attacks on Catholic ghettos in Belfast and Derry. The British sent in the army in an attempt, temporarily successful, to quell the fighting. However, distrust between the soldiers and the Catholics grew, and, after a few years, a new Provisional Irish Republican Army started to murder soldiers, Protestant civilians, and Catholic dissidents.[12] IRA bombing and killing reached its height in 1972 and London, in response, abolished the Belfast parliament and introduced Direct Rule.

Direct Rule did little to stop the violence. Over 3,000 people have lost their lives in Northern Ireland in the past quarter of a century because of the Troubles. Most of the killing, however, has been concentrated in small areas inside Northern Ireland, though occasionally Protestant bombers have made excursions to Dublin and IRA bombers to London. By and large the IRA and its Protestant, notionally pro-British equivalents have killed civilians, car-bombed pubs and supermarkets, and murdered people going to work, essentially because the assassins were certain, or thought they were certain, of the victims' religion.[13] Each side has tended to deny the centrality of religious denomination; in fact, it is commonly said that to suggest the conflict in Northern Ireland is about religion is a gross oversimplification. In reality it is no oversimplification at all.

For many years Irish insurrectionists benefited from the support of Irish-Americans, just as diaspora communities have supported more radical expressions of nationalism elsewhere in Europe (for instance, in Croatia, Armenia, and the Baltics). IRA propaganda, to the effect that the Dublin government was a British puppet, fell on uninformed and receptive ears in Boston and New York. Thus, although Irish democracy had won the Civil War in Ireland, it lost it in parts of Irish America. After all, many emigrants from Ireland to the United States in the 1920s had been involved in the defeated side of the Irish Civil War and their descendants continue to harbor bitter resentment. The allegiance of Irish-Americans has been gradually shifting, however, to the constitutionalist cause represented by Dublin, as all parties to the conflict become persuaded of the futility of seeking to resolve the national question through violent means.

Hibernian Endgame?

What is happening in Ireland today is a slow but relentless triumph of politics over physical force, as the IRA and the British each realize what Dublin has long understood: that there can be no victory in this apparently endless war. On the IRA side, the demise of the Soviet Union has removed an important ally; for years Irish nationalist insurgency was encouraged by Soviet moral and financial support, usually furnished indirectly. This paralleled Soviet encouragement to Islamic and anti-Zionist groups in the Middle East and North Africa. Similarly, Irish-American support for the IRA has diminished, due in part to effective diplomatic activity by the Republic. The IRA has become increasingly isolated internationally.

A further factor working in favor of politics over violence is that Dublin and London no longer regard Northern Ireland as a bone of contention but as a common problem for which a political solution can and must be found. The British and Irish democracies have to deal with Ulster *together* and both now know this. The IRA and the Protestant paramilitaries also, belatedly, have come to understand this.

The IRA started to put out feelers to both the British and Irish governments in the mid-1980s, once it became clear that few on the island sympathized with the IRA's particular fusion of violent means and political ends. The Anglo-Irish accord of 1985 and the joint Dublin-London Downing Street Declaration of late 1993 made it clear that the Republic wished no union with the North against the wishes of the Northern majority and, similarly, that London had no desire to hold onto the North against the wishes of that majority. In August and September 1994, the IRA and the Protestant paramilitaries declared cease-fires after 25 years of violence.

In the early years of the Ulster Troubles, there had been fears of an all-Ireland conflagration. Many commentators, most notably Conor Cruise O'Brien, warned of such a disaster—what in hindsight might be called an "Irish Bosnia"—with tribal warfare engulfing all of Ireland. The crucial difference between the Irish situation and that of Bosnia, however, is the overwhelming might of Britain, which has been capable of holding all of Ireland together. Only a precipitate British withdrawal from the North could conceivably destabilize both Irish polities. If that were to happen, the heavily armed Protestants—with the support of the Ulster police, the British-organized militia, and many British army veterans—might try to set up their own state in eastern Ulster, drive the Catholics west of the River Bann, and take in Protestant refugees from the west of Northern Ireland. The Republic's army might then be drawn in to come to the aid of its Catholic countrymen. The Republic would thus very probably behave as Serbia has, and the Ulster Protestants like Slovenia, or worse, Croatia. This was the scenario, incidentally, that the IRA—fascistic and romantic in its deeper instincts—long dreamed of but would never admit to: the wrecking of democratic Ireland. The result would be, as O'Brien once suggested, a new and more malign partition, between a smaller, deeply Orange (i.e., Protestant) state in the northeast, and a slightly larger, "Greener," mainly Catholic, militarized Republic on the rest of the island.[14]

This scenario, it is now evident, is a fantasy. It is unlikely ever to materialize, partly because the horrors are fairly well understood by populations who live in democratic and quasi-democratic cultures in both parts of Ireland. The Republic has a tiny army, and that army is there to ensure that no IRA coup ever occurs in the Republic; in 1922–23, after all, it destroyed the old IRA in eight months, with the quiet approval of the general population. The Republic has no stomach for war; it is one of the most demilitarized societies in Europe, partly in reaction to the exaggerated militarism of its founding fathers and partly a reflection of the popular revulsion to the brutality of the IRA. This brutality has done more to render the partition of Ireland popular in the Republic than anything else. Ironically, the IRA, by alienating so many southern Irish, may end up in the history books as the force that made Irish partition permanent.

A far more likely alternative to this nightmare scenario is the evolution of a series of pragmatic agreements between London and Dublin, between Northern nationalist elected representatives and both governments, between unionist politicians and both governments and, more covertly, between the paramilitaries and the legal authorities. Seen from this vantage point, the August 1994 IRA cease-fire is an admission of the obsolescence of the IRA world view.

It may be that a Basque rather than a Bosnian scenario prefigures the Irish future. Since 1976, Madrid has given up trying to repress Basque identity. Instead, it has devolved extensive powers to the Basque provinces, recognized Basque culture officially, and subsidized the area. The armed paramilitary police, the *Guardia Civil,* has assumed a low profile, and a set of civilianized police forces directs traffic and investigates ordinary crime. As a consequence of this increased autonomy, the Basque guerrillas have experienced a substantial erosion of support.

A further factor working against militant nationalism in Ireland is that here, as elsewhere in Western Europe, the sovereign nation-state has lost much of its logic. Multinational companies and multinational governments have had the effect of making the classic sovereign state seem inadequate, if not irrelevant. On the island of Ireland, economies, popular cultures, state services, and transport systems are increasingly trans-frontier and transcend the British-Irish state system created two generations ago. A sort of re-unification by osmosis is occurring, and a potent agent of this process is the dynamic of European integration. Against this backdrop, nationalist and unionist violence appears increasingly pointless, with the nation-state having lost much of its attractiveness as something to be aspired to.

A shift in public attitudes is reinforcing this trend. This shift has occurred in tandem with the development of a Catholic and post-nationalist middle class in both parts of Ireland, but particularly in the North. It is not clear that the Ulster Catholic middle class is all that keen on a formal reunification of the island. The Republic is, after all, relatively poor, and Northern Catholics have done well out of the artificial and heavily subsidized economy that London has created in Northern Ireland. It could be that British money has created a form of Green unionism.

Northern middle-class Catholics, although appreciative of the moral support provided by the very existence of the Republic, do not necessarily see their short-term future as being inextricably bound up with the South. Their political influence in Northern Ireland has grown considerably, and a certain guarded acceptance of some aspects of the Northern state has evolved among them. In particular, lower taxation and better social services have a powerful appeal. Certainly a wholesale dismemberment of Northern Ireland, combined with its amalgamation with the Republic, as traditionally dreamed of by the IRA, is not on their agenda. To some extent Northern Irish nationalists see the possibility of gaining political clout through the British institutions of Northern Ireland as well as through the institutions of the Republic, Europe, and the United States. Ireland, in short, is going global.

Ulster Protestantism seems to feel that it has lost the psychological upper hand it enjoyed a generation ago. (One mark of change: southern Protestants, small in numbers, have thrown in their lot with the Republic. They have generally little political sympathy with their Northern co-religionists.) Irish nationalists make natural politicians, rather than soldiers, and the Republic has played its hand slowly and rather cleverly over the two decades, lining up domestic and foreign forces on its side. British leaders seem nowadays to get on better with Dublin leaders than with whatever leadership might be generated by Protestant Belfast.

In the final analysis, the London-enforced experiment of anti-Catholic Protestant rule in Northern Ireland simply did not work. The bigotry, incompetence, and overconfidence of Protestant leaders in the North after 1920 had much to do with this failure. The kind of politics suited to an imperial dependency just would not do in a post-imperial era where the ex-colonies sat at the same council tables as their former masters, sometimes with even more clout. Unionist leaders, or, more accurately, their followers, have been slow to grasp the fact that they stand among equals and are certainly in no position of unassailable political or cultural superiority. Furthermore, they find it difficult to internalize the proposition that they actually have no real enemies. A bargain cut now, in the mid–1990s, will be better for them than one cut in 10 years' time; the bargain will be a good one and will give them most of what they want: formal recognition by the Republic of the North's "otherness." Irish Prime Minister Albert Reynolds, leader of Fianna Fail, the most nationalist of the Republic's political parties between 1992 and 1994, displayed great political courage in late 1994 when he declared unequivocally that Ireland cannot be reunited without the consent of a Northern majority—that is, the Protestants. The realization that the nationalist siege, always partly imaginary, has ended is only now descending on the democratic representatives of Orange Ireland and their followers.

The historical experience of the Irish, in contrast with that of the English, underlines a proposition put forward by Dubliner George Bernard Shaw three quarters of a century ago. In effect he argued that if a people do not achieve a means of national and/or cultural self-expression, it will find it difficult to think of anything else until that urge is satisfied in a tolerable, even if imperfect, way.[15] Recognizing substate nationalisms, granting authority to local institutions, and confronting cultural differences can help satisfy that urge. Above all, the demotion of physical force in favor of political negotiation, as a means of settling relationships between those ill-fitting entities called nations and states, does offer a palliative that can, surprisingly, also become a solution.

We are witnessing the slow triumph of politics over insurrectionism in Ireland. The nationalist Irish are very willing to settle with the unionist Irish. It remains to be seen whether the unionist Irish have yet come to the conclusion that a settlement is necessary. It also remains to be seen if British, Irish, and European political institutions have sufficiently transcended the old nation-state formula to permit them to do so.

Notes

1. South Tyrol, formerly part of the Austro-Hungarian empire, was annexed by Italy after World War I and the claims of the majority German-speaking population were denied. In a series of negotiations in the 1960s and 1970s, the Italian government recognized German as a local official language and made general arrangements for the recognition of Austrian identity in the area. See Marion Toscano, *Alto Adige/South Tyrol* (Baltimore and London: Johns Hopkins University Press, 1975), passim.

2. On the "Britishness" and "Irishness" of the Irish, see John A. Murphy, "Ireland: Identity and Relationships," in *National Identities*, ed. Bernard Crick (Oxford: Blackwell, 1991), pp. 79–89.

3. Paul Bew, *Land and the National Question in Ireland*, (Dublin: Gill and Macmillan, 1979); Samuel Clark, *The Social Origins of the Irish Land War* (Princeton: Princeton University Press, 1979).

4. Kieran Kennedy, Thomas Giblin, and Deirdre McHugh, *The Economic Development of Ireland in the Twentieth Century* (London: Routledge, 1988), pp. 3–12.

5. On the cultural shift in the Republic on nationalist issues, see *Revising the Rising*, eds. Mairín ní Dhonnchadha and Theo Dorgan, (Derry: Field Day, 1991). On secularism in the Republic, see in particular Niamh Hardiman and Christopher T. Whelan, "Politics and Democratic Values" and "Values and Political Participation," in *Values and Social Change in Ireland*, ed. C.T. Whelan (Dublin: Gill and Macmillan, 1994), pp. 100–186.

6. Tom Garvin, "Wealth, Poverty and Development: Reflections on Our Current Discontents," *Studies*, Vol. 78, No. 311 (1978), pp. 312–325.

7. Charles Townshend, *The British Campaign in Ireland, 1919–21* (Oxford: Oxford University Press, 1975), passim.

8. Joseph Curran, *The Birth of the Irish Free State* (Birmingham: University of Alabama Press, 1982), passim.

9. Conor Cruise O'Brien, *States of Ireland* (London: Panther, 1974), pp. 263–283 and passim.

10. Hugh MacLennan, *Two Solitudes* (New York: Duell, Sloan and Pearce: 1945), passim.

11. For a fascinating informal picture of the cultural shift in Catholic Northern Ireland, see Finuola O'Connor, *In Search of a State* (Belfast: Blackstaff, 1993).

12. O'Brien, op. cit., passim.

13. On the IRA in general, see Patrick Bishop and Eamonn Mallie, *The Provisional IRA* (London: Heinemann, 1987).

14. O'Brien, op. cit., pp. 263–283.

15. George Bernard Shaw, *The Matter with Ireland* (London: Hart-Davis, 1962), pp. 55–56.

13

Reconciling Identities
in Conflict

DAN SMITH

If we talk about nationalism and ethnic politics in Europe today, we will soon start talking about war. Bosnia, the scene of Europe's most violent nationalist conflict in the post-Cold War period, springs immediately to mind. But it is not the only example. Elsewhere in ex-Yugoslavia, there is the frustration of Serbia's oppressed Albanian community, the domestic and regional tensions surrounding Macedonian independence, and the unresolved conflicts between Croatia and Serbia. In the Caucasus, similarly, all meaningful politics is nationalist and the level of violence is extremely high. The war between Armenia and Azerbaijan over the Nagorno-Karabakh enclave, Moscow's war against Chechnya, the expulsion of over 60,000 Ingush from North Ossetia, and the Abkhazian and South Ossetian wars of secession from Georgia—though they have not all received equal media coverage—all attest to the salience of nationalism and ethnic politics.

Nationalism has been one of the most potent political forces, not always violent, in Eastern Europe and the former Soviet Union since the last years of the Cold War—in creating the new states of the Czech Republic and Slovakia; in Hungary and in the large Hungarian diaspora; in the Baltic states of Estonia, Latvia, and Lithuania; in Moldova and Ukraine, in Poland, and not least in Russia. On the other hand, nationalist conflict—violent and otherwise—is not limited to Eastern Europe and the former Soviet Union. The unity of the United Kingdom has been challenged not only by the long and debilitating war fought in the name of two competing nationalisms—Irish nationalism and Ulster Unionism—

but also by Scottish and Welsh nationalisms, neither of which has a political strategy of violence. In Spain, Basque separatism has at times been violent but Catalan autonomism has been largely nonviolent and largely successful. In France, Breton nationalism has now declined but Corsican nationalism, though gaining narrow support at the polls, remains strong and occasionally violent. In Italy, the South Tyrol separatist movement was violent in the late 1980s and early 1990s; most of the outstanding issues were settled peacefully in 1992. Finally, in Belgium, the former violence of Flemish-Walloon relations has gone but tensions occasionally run high.

The Western news media have provided some facile and mostly misleading descriptions of nationalist conflict in Europe today. Among them is the claim that these conflicts are purely the result of the end of the Cold War. It is true that in some countries—the Soviet Union, Czechoslovakia, and Hungary—it was impossible for nationalist movements to operate freely under Soviet control. The weakening and eventual ending of that control made it possible for nationalist agendas to be picked up again after a long historic interruption. But in Western Europe and the Balkans, the reassertion of nationalism has not primarily been a consequence of the Cold War's end. (The main exception is Germany, whose unification was impossible during the Cold War.) The wars of Yugoslavia's disintegration are not products of the end of the Cold War. The breakup gathered momentum from about 1985, aided by the development of the U.S.–Soviet détente that began in 1987. But the principal reasons are internal—relating to the failures of economic policy, the weak legitimacy of the post-Tito leadership, and severe regional discrepancies in economic prosperity that coincided roughly with ethnic divisions.

Though nationalism does not always produce violent conflict, it generates and feeds off an emotional intensity that can both detonate sudden violence and endure through long periods until hate becomes a part of the culture. This combination of explosiveness and durability makes so many ethnonationalist conflicts seem intractable. It makes it hard to discuss the prospects for establishing peace in nationalist conflicts without descending into a dark and disabling pessimism. And it casts a shadow over attempts to find constructive approaches that can be taken by outside parties—the topic of this essay.

Two major bodies of research are relevant to this inquiry. One concerns conflict resolution, the other nationalism. Theorists and practitioners of conflict resolution often emphasize that their work is fundamentally about reconciling identities in conflict. Similarly, most leading writers on nationalism come to a point in their argument where they put a great deal of emphasis on identity. I wish to address this intersection between these two fields, with the modest hope of helping to identify some broad principles useful for the resolution of ethnonationalist disputes and for constructive intervention by third parties.

Conflict Resolution

The conflicts under consideration here involve open, organized, politically motivated violence—that is, war—fought to fulfill a nationalist agenda. Conflict resolution, on the other hand, is a general term, relating to a field that many writers treat as more or less homogeneous—from individual to industrial to international conflicts.

As long as the terms remain general, the main concepts are relevant to just about any kind of conflict, nationalist or otherwise, though they often do little more than reflect common sense. For example, it is important that disputants learn to listen to each other, respect each other's point of view, and recognize that problems look different from different perspectives. In many conflicts, progress can be made only if the parties see resolution as an unfolding process, with agreement proceeding step by step from relatively easy to progressively more contentious issues. Equally, a good mediator or facilitator will always know how to listen and learn. More than that, the third party needs to avoid getting drawn into the political issues in a conflict or revealing strong sympathies with either side. The mediator's most effective moral stance is empathy for the victims.

These are general, rather obvious guidelines. The more specific the discussion of conflict and conflict resolution becomes, the less transferable are the main ideas. In the end, individuals representing great powers or warring groups do not think and behave as if they only represented themselves. For that reason, the more therapeutic techniques of conflict resolution—role reversal, exercises that are supposed to build trust, and so on—are unconvincing if one is considering how to facilitate the early resolution of an armed conflict. They can play a part in a slow (perhaps decades-long) laying of foundations for a more peaceable political atmosphere. But in the short term it is hard to see nationalist leaders from the Balkans or the Caucasus trusting each other enough even to start engaging in trust-building exercises.

Oddly, or so it might seem, a key issue of debate in the general literature on conflict resolution is whether it is possible or even desirable to resolve conflict. Conflict can be valuable, the driving force for necessary social and political change. If the response to injustice causes conflict, it is better to eliminate the injustice than resolve the conflict. But the conflict, one can reasonably argue, should not cause large-scale death and misery, itself an injustice. Thus, the point is not to resolve but to transform conflict. Historic enemies need not love each other as long as they simply decide to stop inflicting and risking death and misery.

Even the transformation as opposed to the resolution of a conflict will require outside mediators to dig to the roots of a dispute, which often are very deep indeed. As John Burton, a former Australian diplomat, has written:

[A]fter observing major powers being defeated in wars with small nations and central authorities failing to control religious and ethnic conflicts within their boundaries, it became clear to me that conflicts of this kind were not generated primarily—or even at all—by shortages of material goods, or even by claims to territory. There were fundamental issues in all cases, issues touching on personal and group security, identity and recognition, and especially a sense of control over political processes that affected security, identity and recognition. The power of human needs was greater than military might.[1]

Visible in this paragraph is a progression up a hierarchy of conflict causes, which to some extent mirrors the trajectory of Burton's own work over the years. There is conflict over interests, which can be transformed by a bargaining process aimed at finding the point where the calculations of interests on each side become compatible. The breakthrough comes, as a study of rapprochement between three pairs of long-standing international rivals (East and West Germany, China and the United States, Egypt and Israel) has shown, if and when the adversaries can cease insisting on unilateral advantage and instead identify "genuine mutual advantage in their bilateral relations."[2]

But this model of conflict and conflict resolution may be most (and perhaps only) applicable to diplomacy between rival powers. Conflict resolution can only begin when the parties start to want peace. That desire is not always enough by itself, which is why third-party mediation and facilitation of negotiations can be helpful. Either side may have a faction that rejects negotiation and compromise. The most important negotiations are not always between the conflicting parties but within them—the syndrome of the war party versus the peace party. There may be more subtle tactical and strategic disagreements, as there were for years between Sinn Fein and the Irish Republican Army over the relative merits of electoral politics and armed struggle in Northern Ireland. Years of conflict, moreover, instill instincts of mutual distrust and hostility. All these obstacles must be surmounted if interests are to be negotiated.

However, in many armed conflicts the issues concern—on one side at least—not interests but needs. Needs are much harder to negotiate than interests and the bargaining process must go further yet be more delicate. The point where the calculations match becomes that much harder to find and the possibility of negotiations breaking down is that much greater. Yet this bargaining process may still not reflect the actual motivations on either side, whether among leaders, activists, supporters, or the general population (which, though affected, is more or less passive). The needs at stake are not necessarily wholly or even primarily material. The stakes may involve identity—especially in a nationalist conflict—and how can people be expected to bargain over who they are?

When needs and identity are at stake, resolution requires political leadership of the caliber that was shown, to take two outstanding examples from outside Europe, in the end of apartheid in South Africa and the accord between Israel and the Palestine Liberation Organization signed in August 1993. In both cases, the advantages of a peaceful settlement have entailed considerable risk-taking on the part of leaders of communities at war with one another—personal risks whose extent was made clear by the assassination of Prime Minister Yitzhak Rabin in November 1995. These steps have been all the more difficult because they have required large numbers of people to assume a new understanding of their collective identity. It has meant white South Africans accepting that to be a white South African no longer had to mean brutalizing black South Africans. Many whites proved unable to make this change. In Israel, it has meant the majority distancing itself from the militant spirit of the West Bank settlers, even though that spirit has much in common with the *kibbutzim* that were important in Israel's foundation and central to its self-understanding. These transformations have been far from easy and in Israel the process is particularly fragile: among both Palestinians and Israelis, militant groups reject the accord and any peace process that includes compromise. In the same way, resolving or transforming the conflicts in ex-Yugoslavia means significant numbers of Serbs and Croatians accepting that, to be Serb and Croatian, it is not essential to hate the other group. Even with a political leader of the stature and vision of a Nelson Mandela, overcoming the deep roots of ethnonationalist conflict would be difficult. Without such a leader, blatantly lacking in ex-Yugoslavia and in the many disputes in the former Soviet Union, the task is all the greater.

When an interim resolution is achieved—a cease-fire that lasts, an agreement to hold elections—a considerable amount of expertise is available to help administer the process. It is to be found in various U.N. bureaucracies, some government aid agencies, and in many nongovernmental organizations. However, medium-term success involves not just U.N. Blue Helmets monitoring cease fires and international teams observing elections but international aid to build up the social infrastructure (such as clean water supplies, transport, education, health care, etc.) and investment to lay the groundwork for long-term economic viability. The prospect of aid can itself be an inducement for adversaries to settle or at least cool their disputes.

Of course, these programs face enormous difficulties as inadequate resources are deployed to meet daunting objectives. But the technicalities of how an agreement is implemented are not the real issue of conflict resolution. The real problem is getting an agreement in the first place, one that sticks. The real problem lies not in finding inducements that appeal to self-interest but solutions that address need and identity. It is because these issues are so central to nationalist politics that the conflicts it fosters seem so difficult to settle. A close examination of the components of nationalism is necessary if we are to understand the dynamics of ethnonationalist conflicts and identify avenues to resolving them.

Understanding Nationalism

Although we employ the terms "nation" and "nationhood" quite readily, they in fact elude easy definition. Joseph Stalin, in his *Marxism and the National Question*, offered what in many ways is a representative definition: "A nation is a historically evolved, stable community of language, territory, economic life and psychological make-up manifested in a community of culture."[3] Yet rather than clarify, this definition, like so many others, demonstrates how difficult it is to gain a firm understanding of fundamental concepts. Each element of Stalin's definition is contestable. To begin with, not all nations are historically evolved. Likewise, linguistic unity is neither a sufficient nor even a necessary condition for nationhood.[4] Language itself is a fluid and elusive category. The distinction between a dialect and a language is wholly political and the boundaries between the languages are often blurred. Dialect continua cover large areas; in them, the inhabitants of neighboring villages understand each other easily but a traveler journeying across a complete continuum would encounter several different languages.[5] As to the supposed unity between nation and territory, it is actually the non-congruence between claimed territory and claimed nations that is half the basis of ethnonationalist conflicts. The evidence lies in ex-Yugoslavia and, equally, the patchwork revealed by any ethnographic map. Lastly, cultural unity is also a construct; it masks the diversity in most cultures of rites, rituals, customs, and manners, while it systematically ignores obvious cultural affinities that do not fit the nationalist logic.

It is impossible to formulate a general definition of what constitutes a nation that fits all accepted nations. This understanding lies behind the pragmatic approach Hugh Seton-Watson adopts at the start of his magisterial history, *Nations and States*: "All that I can find to say is that a nation exists when a significant number of people in a community consider themselves to form a nation, or behave as if they formed one."[6] Because the creation of a nation often requires the assertion of power, Seton-Watson's definition would benefit from the addition of a clause: "If they can get away with it."

The trouble with this definition, however, is that it is useless for judging whether justice lies more with one group or another in a dispute about who has the right to govern a particular territory or whether a community deserves formal recognition. This is not surprising. The problems we are discussing are political. The nation is a political idea and nationalism is a political movement. A nation's claims may draw heavily on ideas of justice but their substance ultimately is political. It simply is not possible to adjudicate between competing national claims on the basis of general, legal principles.

The violence of the wars in Croatia and Bosnia-Herzegovina, the chauvinism of politicians such as Russia's Vladimir Zhirinovsky, and the emotional response of crowds moved by appeals to national pride lead us to emphasize the visceral element of nationalism. It is easy to depict nationalism—implicitly if not explicitly—as brutal, uncivilized, irrational, and inherently violent and destructive. But this is incomplete, inaccurate, and, ultimately, unhelpful.

Nationalism is not just a visceral urge; it is also a political doctrine and a movement. It has its evidently non-rational side but that is not the whole story. Ernest Gellner's definition of nationalism emphasizes the doctrinal, programmatic aspect: "Nationalism is primarily a political principle, which holds that the political and the national unit should be congruent."[7] As such it functions as a principle of political legitimation of the modern state. Anthony Smith embraces this within a more inclusive definition of nationalism as "an ideological movement, for the attainment and maintenance of self-government on behalf of a group, some of whose members conceive it to constitute an actual or potential 'nation' like others."[8] He thus includes both the doctrine and its political vector and indicates the salience of nationalism before and after achieving nationhood. In both definitions, nationalism is goal-oriented—that is, irrespective of any moral judgment, it is rational. A different emphasis comes through in John Plamenatz's argument that "[N]ationalism is a reaction of peoples who feel culturally at a disadvantage."[9] These three definitions each highlight different aspects. They are not mutually exclusive. The problem is not to analyze nationalism as a political doctrine, as an ideological movement, or as a cultural reaction; the problem is to analyze it as all these things. The challenge is not to understand nationalism as rational politics or as a non-rational social force but as both.

One needs, therefore, to understand not only the obvious negative sides of nationalism but also its benefits. Historically, as Tom Nairn has argued, "Far from being an irrational obstacle to development, [nationalism] was for most societies the only feasible way into the developmental race—the only way in which they could compete without being either colonised or annihilated."[10] In three major phases of economic development—nineteenth-century industrialization, post-1945 economic reconstruction, and the most successful cases of post-colonial development—the competitive advantage has lain with politically cohesive and economically forward-looking states. They both regulated and created markets. They mobilized, educated, and disciplined the labor force. They ensured the growth of a qualified managerial and professional class. They drew executive logic, administrative stability, political identity and legitimacy, as well as ideological appeal, from a national basis. Indeed, one way of looking at nationalism is as an ideology that turns an economic strategy into a principle worth dying for.

Today, the benefits of nationalism can be listed under three headings. First, it protects cultural diversity against a homogenizing world culture. Not much else seems capable of doing this. This theme is present in much of the discourse of those who opposed the Maastricht treaty on European Union (EU) in the debates of 1992 and 1993 and now resist further EU integration. It was perhaps even more prominent in campaigns against accession to the EU in the Nordic countries in 1994, especially in Norway. But it can also be found in nationalisms that have supported European integration, such as Scottish nationalism and Catalan autonomism.

Second, nationalism is a reasonable defense against the all-conquering ideology of the all-powerful market. Though largely untested in this respect, nationalism has at least as much chance as environmentalism (and probably more) of mustering sufficient political strength to place effective constraints on the power of multinational corporations.

Third, in an age of growing alienation from the political process, nationalism often has the advantage of offering political arenas of human scale and reasonably manageable size. This particularly benefits certain regions of multiethnic states—Scotland in the United Kingdom, Catalonia in Spain, Slovenia in former Yugoslavia, and many republics of the former Soviet Union. In seeking smaller political units, nationalism has changed direction in this century. The project of European nationalism in the nineteenth century was not only national independence (e.g., of Norway from Sweden, and of subjugated nations in the Habsburg and Ottoman empires) but also national unification (as in Germany and Italy) as well as cultural integration within politically unified states such as France and the United Kingdom. Today, most nationalist movements are not integrative but divisive, seeking not larger but smaller political units, which may be more responsive to democratic pressures and more likely to engage the political energies of their citizens.

Of course these benefits are not without their complications. An argument that nationalism has benefits is not necessarily an argument *for* nationalism. Today's small nationalism can be defended as potentially more democratic but it is often in fact based on fear of the other, the strange, the different, against which it is by turns defensive and aggressive. It has a built-in tendency to ethnonationalist chauvinism. Tom Nairn has put this well:

> [A]ll nationalism is both healthy and morbid. Both progress and regress are inscribed in its genetic code from the start. This is a structural fact about it. And it is a fact to which there are no exceptions: in this sense, it is an exact (not a rhetorical) statement about nationalism to say that it is by nature ambivalent.[11]

There are not good and bad nationalisms—nice Scottish and nasty Serbian nationalism, for instance. Rather, there is good and bad in all nationalism. Neal Ascherson, a Scottish nationalist, like Nairn, has made a particularly telling analysis of the dual moral quality of Polish nationalism. He points out that there are two equally intense versions, one that went so far as to call itself "National Egoism" upheld by the National Democrat movement in the early years of this century. It not only asserted Polish interests over all others but defined the true Poland as Catholic and Slav, and therefore identified all the ethnic minorities—Jews, Belarusians, Ukrainians, Lithuanians, Germans—as threats to Polish identity. The other version, associated with Józef Piłsudski, the dominant figure in Polish politics between the two world wars, yearned for a multinational Poland, recreating the late medieval Polish-Lithuanian Commonwealth. According to Ascherson, then-Polish President Lech Wałęsa—along with the rest of the old Solidarity leadership—adhered to the Piłsudski version but the most common kind of nationalism in Poland is closer to "National Egoism" and contains a lot of crude xenophobia and anti-Semitism.[12]

At the heart of the ambivalence lies the historic truth that nationalism began in the late eighteenth and early nineteenth centuries as a fundamentally democratic ideology because it asserted that the legitimacy of government derived from the people and not, for example, from dynasty or the will of God. But the real challenge is to identify the health in Serbian and Croatian nationalism or in Zhirinovsky's variety of Russian nationalism that, according to Nairn, inevitably accompanies their evident morbidity.

Nationalism's Appeal

If there is to be a possibility of bringing peace to ethnic and nationalist conflicts, a crucial first step is to understand how and why the idea of nationalism has become so widespread and so strong—to understand its appeal. One important element is that it is a highly communicable idea: one nationalist initiative inspires another, whether in emulation, competition, or self-defense. On a deeper level, however, large numbers of people feel that the doctrine and program of contemporary nationalist movements offer an effective response to their needs. Among those needs are economic ones. Nationalist movements consistently claim that the fulfillment of their programs will bring prosperity. Similarly, nationalist leaders often represent particular social groups who stand to benefit from national independence—for instance, the educated middle class often frustrated in commerce or in their professional careers because of ethnic, religious, or national discrimination.[13] The drive for independence in Slovenia and Croatia derived in part from a perception in these two republics that their wealth was subsidizing the "lazier" inhabitants of the southern republics of Yugoslavia. Major disputes arose over the Federal Fund for the Accelerated Development of the Underdeveloped Republics and Kosovo, which was set up in 1965 to finance development in the south. Far from being an instrument of cooperation, it became a cause of division, pushing the republics to act on their own interests, which, in time, were increasingly defined in ethnonationalist terms.[14]

The resentment of Slovenian and Croatian nationalists exemplified a classic pattern: the more prosperous units of a multiethnic state or empire assert nationhood to avoid further subsidizing the poorer parts. In the former Soviet Union, the pressure for independence from the three Baltic republics exhibited a similar pattern. The process can also work in the opposite direction. "We are being held back by our exploiters" is a familiar refrain among leaders of less prosperous ethnic and national groups, as it was, for instance, among Slovak leaders in former Czecho- slovakia.

The issue of needs has additional and more subtle depths. Nationalism is, in part, a response to the impact of major social and economic change, often felt in a multitude of painful, personal ways as established commu- nities fall apart. It is an ideological invention that seems to provide some degree of cultural stability in the midst of disorienting social change. Sev- eral scholars are scornful of this process of invention. Ernest Gellner, for example, emphasizes the fraudulence of the project of nationalism: "Its myths invert reality: it claims to defend folk culture while in fact it is forg- ing a high culture; it claims to protect an old folk society while in fact helping to build up an anonymous mass society."[15] The traditions that nationalism seems to revive and offers to protect often turn out on clos- er inspection to be relatively new. The Scottish tartan and the kilt, for in- stance, popularly believed to date from time immemorial, in fact arise from the eighteenth century; clan tartans were an English invention.[16]

Though of recent vintage, these "traditions" often evoke strong feel- ings and a sense of political commitment. Allegiance to them is one reason why nationalism seems to offer stability, even when the nationalist move- ment itself often has a revolutionary agenda. The discovery of a national past—whether real or imagined—binds fractured communities together by giving them a new sense of common heritage. History, whether false or true, offers a sense of continuity amid change. Tom Nairn aptly depicts na- tionalism as a "modern Janus"—the Roman god with two faces—looking back to an idealized past in which it finds the strength to face the future.[17]

Closely related to stability is the issue of group identity, which is rou- tinely at the forefront of analyses of nationalism. Isolation appears pro- foundly frightening. It is the cost of elevating individuality over group identity in the modern age. Relationships, including those within the family, may offer some relief, but they may not be enough. Further re- lief comes from a network of personal relations and family connections in a small community. Even that may not suffice. A more abstract set of connections builds to a larger community of people with common ways of living, common ways of approaching the basic problems of life and death, and shared assumptions about ethics and social organization. Under the impact of major social change—modernity in the nineteenth century, globalization in the late twentieth—group identities may cease to be viable. People must then seek new handholds for their sense not only of themselves but of the groups to which they belong or wish to belong.

Why do they then turn to the nation for identity and to nationalist movements for a political program? Although nationalism invents tradi- tion, it does not invent just any tradition. To work, to have appeal, to be able to mobilize people and offer them a sense of continuity and stability, the historical myths and symbols that nationalism projects have to be rec- ognizable. A nationalist movement must speak for identity formations that are already understood and widely accepted. This has led some scholars to look at the "ethnic origins of nations" and the phenomenon of "nations before nationalism."[18] This is not to suggest that there is a primordial basis for nations and nationalism—that nations are somehow in our blood. Nations are built on foundations that are themselves constructed, not given. Ethnicity is not a racial category, let alone a genetic or so-called natural category; it is a social category. It is constructed on the basis of the often slowly evolving mechanisms of group and community identity. Its defining fulcrum lies in the core myths that mobilize groups and give them their internal cohesion, identity, and self-perception. On these myths of core identity nationalism builds.

Individual identity is highly situational, whereas collective identity is pervasive and persistent. On the individual level, we all have many identities we may choose among (consciously or not), given the particular situation in which we find ourselves. On the collective level, however, we cannot make these identification choices if the object we would identify with is constantly shifting. In an increasingly rich literature on identity and the politics of identity, it is now commonplace to recognize that collective, social identity functions on multiple and overlapping levels. No level of identity is exclusive of another though, at each level, each category of identity may be exclusive. For example, national identity overlaps with smaller and larger frameworks: one may be Norwegian (but not also Swedish), Scandinavian (but not also Mediterranean), white (but not also black), middle class (but not also working class), Catholic (but not also Protestant), and socialist (but not also conservative).

Nationalism intervenes persuasively in this process. Its emphasis on staking claims about a place (this land is ours) and the past gives both individuals and groups a sense of their geographical and historical location. In those cases where nationalism is closely related to religious differences (e.g., Ireland, ex-Yugoslavia, and some parts of the Caucasus), it offers people a sense of their place not only in this world but the next.

Starting from Identity

Any effort to intervene constructively in nationalist conflicts—whether by suggesting possible solutions or through actual involvement in negotiations and conflict resolution—means addressing the depth of emotion that characterizes nationalism. It needs a strategy that takes account of nationalism's capacity to meet human needs and therefore uses identity as its starting point. The consequences of not doing so have been vividly demonstrated in ex-Yugoslavia.

Nationalist leaders, because they operate with a different calculus of risk, seem ready to take chances that would make other politicians quake. For West European governments, judiciously weighing the risks involved in stepping up their military commitment in ex-Yugoslavia during 1993 and 1994, issues like credibility and strategic stability were at stake. In

Bosnia, meanwhile, the contending parties fought for who they are. This discrepancy does much to explain why the Bosnian Serb leaders constantly seemed to have the tactical advantage. West European and U.S. leaders, and those who brief them, appeared not to recognize this fact, which is why their measures had so little effect for so long on Croatian and Serbian aims and policies.

Within a multiparty conflict of great complexity and fast-changing military and political fronts, the major nationalist leaders of Bosnia, Croatia, and Serbia have attempted to do what they perceive is in their best interests. In so doing they have made rational calculations. Although there are stories about some military leaders in these wars that suggest they may indeed be psychotic or close to it, there is no reason to believe that the political leaders have acted irrationally. Nor should one assume that they necessarily prefer a strategy based on conflict to one that is peaceful. The challenge, then, is to find this peaceful solution. The place to seek it is not within the logic of each parties' interests but in the logic of their identity needs.

But how is it possible to get at identity and make it the starting point for conflict resolution? One option is to take a second look at the fact that, although traditions are invented, there is often still an intense emotional attachment to them. The converse is equally valid: though the emotional attachment is intense, the tradition is invented. We are dealing with the results of social construction. And what can be socially constructed can also be unmade.

A different route to the same conclusion is to look at the determinants of identity. The anthropological literature is rich in this regard and it is from the Norwegian anthropologist Fredrik Barth that the basic insight comes that social identity depends not on innate or natural qualities but on relations between groups.[19] However, Richard Jenkins argues that, in exploring how identity is shaped, anthropologists have tended to miss the role of power in the external pressures that shape identity.[20] One implication of this observation is that externally shaped elements of social identity can be influenced by deliberate strategy. This is not to suggest that we can negotiate identity; in a direct sense identity remains non-negotiable. But that is different from saying that it is unchangeable.

One element of conflict could be called "identity pressure." In Bosnia-Herzegovina and in some parts of the Caucasus, neighbors turn against each other and snipers take aim at old school friends. This shocks the civilized mind. Yet there is nothing original in the insight that insecurity breeds assertiveness and even aggression among individuals and between groups. A safe and secure identity formation is not likely to generate conflict; it is the threatened identity that tends to produce violence. And once violent conflict has begun, the possibility of defeat is a further threat to social identity. A productive negotiating process is one that attempts to relieve identity pressures on both sides.

This is what was so wrong about the approach taken in the Vance-Owen and Owen-Stoltenberg negotiations that sought to settle the wars of ex-Yugoslavia from 1992 to 1994. They were not a process of conflict resolution. This is not wisdom after the fact of failed and broken agreements; it is a judgment that would be justified even if the agreements had been respected. The negotiations mainly involved the parties examining a map and declaring which towns, villages, roads, and countryside belonged to them. Far from resolving the conflict, it was simply the continuation of conflict around a conference table, with every incentive to grab another few towns and roads. These negotiations, moreover, were conducted against a backdrop of offers of aid and threats of military action. For most commentators the problem was that the threats were not backed up by action until 1994, and then only sporadically, so that they were never credible. But that was not the real problem. For if the threats had been implemented and the parties forced into an agreement, that would not have led to peace. It would simply have deferred war, perhaps until the West's attention had been engaged elsewhere, at which point the violence would have erupted with renewed ferocity. Sooner or later, putting on the pressure risks being self-defeating.

When the U.S.-sponsored Dayton negotiations on the wars in Croatia and Bosnia-Herzegovina began in November 1995, the immediate background was NATO's summer bombing campaign and the spectacular military successes of the Bosnian and Croat armies, taking back territory and expelling large numbers of Serb civilians. Consequently, regardless of any formal agreement, there was a permanent potential for renewed violence at a later date. The Bosnian government's own dissatisfaction with any agreement to divide its country was a further sign that U.S. diplomacy and pressure could get the parties to the table but could not make them want peace—at least, not at any price. An agreement produced under such circumstances cannot conclude a conflict; it is merely a strategic pause, which is valuable or not depending on whether it offers a breathing space for a new arms buildup or for a more wide-ranging effort to deal with the underlying causes of conflict. Writing about the role of the facilitator, John Burton says:

> Options must evolve from the specific needs and interests of the parties . . . [who], however, are usually too caught up in their own problems to consider alternative solutions. Usually they do not have the background knowledge to design innovative approaches. . . . [Facilitators] must assume responsibility for putting forward a range of possible options for discussion without putting forward any firm proposals.[21]

This delicate process of negotiation can wend its way through interests and material needs but will probably arrive at identity sooner or later. Third-party mediators and facilitators (and, equally, anybody who is trying to produce ideas about how to resolve a particular conflict) have to find options that work on soft spots in each party's assumptions about their own identity, using them as a starting point for a logic that leads to a peaceful outcome.

For example, a common cultural element among several ethnic groups and nationalities in southern and southeastern Europe is a pairing of qualities that may strike northwestern Europeans as rather odd: an emphasis on revenge and retaliation is balanced, or at least counterpointed, by an equal emphasis on hospitality, generosity, social responsibility, and protection of the weak in a community. It is the task of diplomats, facilitators, and mediators to encourage parties to treat their antagonist generously. For the side that is in a position of advantage, this means showing mercy; for the side at a disadvantage, it involves showing forgiveness. The third party has to find options for resolving a conflict that coaxes out these aspects of social identity.

In many cases, including ex-Yugoslavia and the Caucasus, the negotiation process needs to find a way to provide security for the side that has the power and the position of advantage. This may seem like a reversal of both logic and justice. It may seem like taking sides with the winner. But only if there is a way of providing some degree of security will it be possible to win concessions from the stronger party. And certainly, if the negotiating process can offer no security, there is no reason why the stronger side should surrender any part of its advantage.

This does not mean providing military security, however, through arms transfers, alliances, or security guarantees. That is both illusory and likely to be distorted into the exercise of military power. It is identity that should be made secure—and there military power is irrelevant. Achieving this goal requires listening carefully and open-mindedly, even to those to whom it is often very hard to listen and who do not themselves pay the same respect. In 1991, the Serbs of the Krajina region and other Serbs living in Croatia had reason to fear the consequences of Croatian independence for their own communities. The Tudjman government began by kicking Serbs out of government jobs; it looked like anti-Serbianism, pure and simple. And the Croatian nationalist movement used symbols also employed by Croatian fascists, perpetrators of genocide against the Serbs in World War II. In 1992, the Bosnian Serbs likewise had reason to fear the consequences of independence for Bosnia-Herzegovina, as it was being pursued by a governing party that identified itself as Muslim, in alliance with a Croat national party. Those reasons do not justify wars of aggression, atrocities, the shelling of civilians, or ethnic cleansing. But in attempting to resolve the conflicts, it will be worth listening to those fears and exploring those reasons. The effort is important, for successfully finding a peaceful way to make identities secure will effectively disrupt the logic that leads from a desire for freedom to support for a strong state.

A different tactic for a third party in negotiations is to hold out the prospect of entering the modern world. At one level this simply means offering material inducements for peaceful behavior: sign the cease-fire and get the aid. But the issue often has unconsidered subtleties of both presentation and substance. A likely soft point is ethnic pride. To offer a different source of pride than a strong state, the best inducement may not be business investment but, depending on the circumstances, a modern education system and comprehensive literacy program, or an effective health-care system, or a transport system that connects the region with the rest of the world. In the Balkans and the Caucasus, it is feasible, though expensive, to implement such programs. They offer communities a chance to care for their own without brutalizing the alien other. Offered as an alternative to conflict, they demand an implicit reordering within multiple identities.

Beyond Negotiations

Conflict resolution and the role of third parties need not be confined to negotiating an agreement to end the current conflict. They can also attend to what must happen to minimize the possibility of conflict returning once an agreement has been signed.

The issues raised by a consideration of social and political identities center on the need for and nature of membership in a community, indicated by, for example, nationality and/or citizenship. One element of citizenship is civic identity—the emotional significance of membership in a political community. Some research on the political psychology of citizen identity indicates ways in which it is shaped by social experience. At the risk of simplification, one broad conclusion is that the greater the degree of privilege, the more independent and individualistic the citizen identity will be; conversely, underprivilege is associated with a more interdependent identity. And the evidence is that the "more interdependent the self, the more likely a person is to have the kinds of psychological predispositions that facilitate a rich practice of citizenship."[22] This finding is consistent with the generalizations above about the ways in which national identities and nationalist movements become important to social identity.

The downside of this, however, is that the same study shows that interdependency is inversely related to political tolerance. That is, a strong citizen identity, produced in part by a sense of social disadvantage, risks being an intolerant one. When the sense of disadvantage is felt along ethnic or national lines, the intolerance is inevitably ethnic or nationalist.

This relationship between civic participation and intolerance seems to offer a bleak view of humanity and modern society. In conflict resolution, however, the downside almost always has an upside. If the other side of the coin of ethnic prejudice and nationalist chauvinism is a strong sense of citizen identity and a sense of psychological interdependence, an aim of conflict resolution should be to make the interdependence more inclusive and to make the citizen identity focus less on ethnic difference. The focal points for such an effort are in education and cultural policy.

In the longer term, as Hugh Seton-Watson suggests, nationalism would not produce nearly so much tragedy if it aimed for something other than the state.[23] He was rightly pessimistic about the possibilities of developing practical politics on that basis but it would be well worth exploring the idea of stateless nations and nationless states. This does not mean doing away with states but, rather, exploring two perspectives that could be influential because they speak directly to the identity logic of nationalism.

The first is that defending cultural identity may be best done by disengaging it from political power.[24] States are, after all, the carriers of almost every influence that can diminish or change ethnic and communal identity. Out of this we could perhaps recapture a more open-ended definition of nationhood that is less tightly linked to statehood. For this to work, a sense is needed of the possibility of active citizenship in multinational societies.

This leads to the second perspective, which would seek to influence the link between cultural identity and politics—the link between ethnicity or nation and state—by a combination of regional economic integration with local political autonomy. John Burton argues that in disputes involving communities, "resolution may be achieved only by a break from traditional institutional forms of government and a consideration of forms of decentralization or zonal systems that border on separation."[25] This could lead to what one writer has called "soft forms of nationhood,"[26] which could also be thought of as strong forms of autonomy. Perhaps Catalonia offers a model here.

There are places where this approach does not go far enough—parts of Croatia and of Bosnia-Herzegovina, for example, as well as much of the Russian Caucasus. Here, the truth is that any reasonably sized administrative unit will contain ethnic minorities with their own identity needs. Declaring through the area's name, therefore, that it belongs to one ethnic group could always be the cause of conflict. Indeed, as is shown by the way the old Chechen-Ingush autonomous republic broke up (when the Chechen part led by General Dzhokar Dudaev decided in 1991 to secede from Russia), it can be a mistake to give an area even a combination of ethnic names. In these cases, administrative units have to be detached from ethnic possession. A model for this approach is to be found in almost every state in the United States.

In some ways, this detachment of state and nation, culture and politics, is also the prospect held out by advocates of regional integration. Of course, precisely at a time when the European Union is offering its members and would-be member states a soft form of nationhood through restricted sovereignty, there is a nationalist backlash in Western Europe. That is cause enough for awareness that this prospect is not straightforward. Yet the world system is increasingly interdependent. A growing number of states are members of international organizations that, to some degree, regulate their activities and impinge on their sovereignty, often in non-dramatic, unspectacular ways. It seems inevitable that this debate will continue.

There are modes of conflict resolution that, by coming to grips with the deeper levels of conflicts, can offer some hope in even the grimmest of

Europe's ethnonationalist wars today. Beyond that, there is some hope of developing the more peaceful sides of ethnic and national cultures. And beyond that, in the long term, we neither can nor should evade a discussion about what are more peaceful forms of government.

Notes

1. John W. Burton in *Conflict: Human Needs Theory* (New York: St. Martin's Press, 1990), p. xv.

2. Tony Armstrong, *Breaking the Ice* (Washington, DC: United States Institute of Peace, 1993), p. 142.

3. J. V. Stalin, *Marxism and the National Question* (1913). Cited in E. J. Hobsbawm, *Nations and Nationalism Since 1780* (Cambridge: Cambridge University Press, 1991), p. 5.

4. Anthony D. Smith, *Theories of Nationalism*, 2nd ed. (London: Duckworth, 1983), pp. 180–185.

5. David Crystal, *The Cambridge Encyclopedia of Language* (Cambridge: Cambridge University Press, 1987), p. 25.

6. Hugh Seton-Watson, *Nations and States* (London: Methuen, 1977), p. 5.

7. Ernest Gellner, *Nations and Nationalism* (Oxford: Basil Blackwell, 1983), p. 1.

8. Smith, op. cit., p. 171.

9. John Plamenatz, "Two Types of Nationalism," in *Nationalism: The Nature and Evolution of an Idea*, ed. Eugene Kamenka (London: Edward Arnold, 1976), p. 27.

10. Tom Nairn, "Demonising Nationalism," *London Review of Books*, February 25, 1993, p. 6.

11. Tom Nairn, *The Break-Up of Britain* (London: New Left Books, 1977), pp. 347–348.

12. Neal Ascherson, "The Borderlands," *Granta 30* (London: Faber & Faber, 1990), pp. 55–57.

13. Miroslav Hroch, *Social Preconditions of National Revival in Europe* (Cambridge: Cambridge University Press, 1985).

14. Sabrina P. Ramet, *Nationalism and Federalism in Yugoslavia 1962–1991* (Bloomington: Indiana University Press, 1992).

15. Gellner, op. cit., p. 124.

16. Eric Hobsbawm and Terence Ranger, eds., *The Invention of Tradition* (Cambridge: Cambridge University Press, 1983).

17. Nairn, *The Break-Up of Britain*, ch. 9.

18. Anthony D. Smith, *The Ethnic Origins of Nations* (Oxford: Basil Blackwell, 1986); and John Armstrong, *Nations Before Nationalism* (Chapel Hill: University of North Carolina Press, 1983).

19. Fredrik Barth, "Introduction," in *Ethnic Groups and Boundaries* (Boston: Little, Brown, 1969).

20. Richard Jenkins, "Rethinking Ethnicity: Identity, Categorization, and Power," *Ethnic and Racial Studies*, Vol. 17, No. 2 (April 1994).

21. John Burton, *Resolving Deep-Rooted Conflict* (London: University Press of America, 1987), p. 66.

22. Pamela Johnston Conover, "Citizen Identities and Conceptions of the Self," *Journal of Political Philosophy*, Vol. 3 (June 1995), pp. 133–165.

23. Seton-Watson, op. cit., p. 469.

24. Thomas Hylland Eriksen, "Ethnicity versus Nationalism," *Journal of Peace Research*, Vol. 28, No. 3 (August 1991).

25. Burton, *Resolving Deep-Rooted Conflict*, p. 66.

26. Gidon Gottlieb, "Nations Without States," *Foreign Affairs*, Vol. 73, No. 3 (May/June 1994).

14

Nationalism and
Toleration

MICHAEL IGNATIEFF

In 1917, in the course of an essay on "The Taboo of Virginity," Freud observed in passing that "it is precisely the minor differences in people who are otherwise alike that form the basis of feelings of strangeness and hostility between them." He went on, "it would be tempting to pursue this idea and to derive from this 'narcissism of minor differences' the hostility which in every human relation we see fighting against feelings of fellowship and overpowering the commandment that all men should love one another."[1]

Freud is illuminating a paradox at the root of the psychology of intolerance: it is not the common elements humans share with each other that inform their sense of identity but the marginal "minor" elements separating them. In the first instance, Freud had in mind gender difference. Men and women share the same genetic endowment, down to a chromosome or two, yet when deriving their sense of identity they focus exclusively on the minor sexual differences between them. What Marx called "species being"—our identity as members of the same species—counts for relatively little in the formation of our self-image. Male identity, for example, does not begin from a perception of our essential similarity with females. This in itself is not surprising since all identities are formed by differentiation. What is puzzling is why this differentiation should be accompanied by such large amounts of anxiety. Why is it that men's identities depend on the constitution of women as an object not merely of desire but of fear? "Perhaps this dread is based on the fact that woman is different from man, forever incomprehensible and mysterious, strange and therefore apparently hostile.

The man is afraid of being weakened by the woman, infected with her femininity and of then showing himself incapable."[2] Strange, and therefore hostile: why is it that minor differences should be strange and *therefore* hostile? Why is it that, sharing so much, we humans should fear our minor differences so intensely?

When Freud returned to the "narcissism of minor differences" five years later, in "Group Psychology and the Analysis of the Ego," the focus of his analysis had shifted from the differences between men and women to the antagonisms dividing social groups. Even in intimate groups— "friendship, marriage, the relations between parents and children"—emotions of hostility and suspicion compete with feelings of human kinship. Here too "species identity" and even long-standing emotional bonds are never sufficient to overcome feelings of hostility. The emotional result is ambivalence, and it arises not, Freud thinks, primarily because of conflicts of interest, but because of the intrinsically antipathetic and aggressive character of all identity formation.

Both in the family and in larger social and political units, Freud argued, the closer the relation between human beings the more hostile they are likely to be toward each other:

> Of two neighbouring towns each is the other's most jealous rival; every little canton looks down upon the others with contempt. Closely related races keep one another at arm's length; the South German cannot endure the North German, the Englishman casts every kind of aspersion upon the Scot, the Spaniard despises the Portuguese. We are no longer astonished that greater differences should lead to an almost insuperable repugnance, such as the Gallic people feel for the German, the Aryan for the Semite and the white races for the coloured.[3]

Freud then goes on to suggest that such hostility is connected to "narcissism":

> In the undisguised antipathies and aversion which people feel towards strangers with whom they have to do we may recognize the expression of self-love—of narcissism. This self-love works for the preservation of the individual, and behaves as though the occurrence of any divergence from his own particular lines of development involved a criticism of them and a demand for their alteration.[4]

The facts of difference themselves are neutral. It is the narcissist who turns them into a judgment on himself. Narcissistic anxiety expresses itself chiefly in passive self-absorption and epistemological closure. A narcissist is incurious about others except to the extent that they reflect back on himself. What is different is rejected if it fails to confirm the narcissist in his or her own self-opinion.

Freud does not explain why some forms of narcissism are essentially passive, others more aggressive. In the original Greek myth, after all, Narcissus is an archetype of passive self-absorption. He stares at his own reflection, oblivious to the world. Freud does not explain why it is that the same self-absorbed figure can suddenly come awake from his daze of self-love and attack those who break into his reverie. But in connecting self-absorption to a capacity for aggression, Freud helps us to detect an unseen connection between the aggressive forms of narcissism and intolerance. One observable characteristic of intolerant people is that they are actively uninterested in learning about those they purport to despise. Freud helps us to see this form of closure as a narcissistic defense of their own identities. On this reading, intolerance is a self-referential circuit in which a narcissist uses the external world only to reproduce confirmation of his or her essential beliefs. It is the narcissistic investment in intolerant belief that makes it so uniquely unresponsive to rational argument.

Likewise, and once again by extrapolating a little from Freud, it becomes possible to think of nationalism as a kind of narcissism. A nationalist takes the neutral facts about a people—their language, habitat, culture, tradition, and history—and turns these facts into a narrative whose purpose is to illuminate the self-consciousness of a group, to enable them to think of themselves as a nation, with a destiny, a vocation, and a claim to self-determination. A nationalist, in other words, takes "minor differences"—indifferent in themselves—and transforms them into major differences. Nationalism is a distorting mirror in which believers see their simple ethnic, religious, or territorial attributes turned into glorious qualities. Though Freud does not explain exactly how this happens, the systematic overvaluation of the self results in the systematic devaluation of strangers and outsiders. In this way narcissistic self-regard depends on and in turn exacerbates intolerance.

If intolerance and narcissism are connected, one immediate and practical conclusion might seem to be that we are only likely to love others more if we also learn to love ourselves a little less. Breaking down stereotypical images of others is only likely to work if we also break down the fantastic elements in our own self-regard. The root of intolerance seems to be found in our tendency to overvalue ourselves.

How can we correct this without falling into excessive self-abasement? Presumably by learning to regard ourselves with a cold eye, see ourselves as others see us, and awaken from the protective cocoon of our narcissism. Freud's therapeutic process—the talking cure—was conceived as a struggle to emancipate oneself from deluded self-images by a process of self-distancing, by standing apart and seeing ourselves through the eyes of others. Such an ideal is difficult enough for individuals to practice. Is such a "talking cure" conceivable for groups, for nations? Actually, the idea is not as far-fetched as it might seem, but one does have to imagine a country having a conversation with itself, in a million competing voices. It is just possible that such a conversation occurred in West Germany after World War II, a talking through of the relation between nationalism and intolerance that left most, though not all members of society, thinking and behaving differently after the conversation had been concluded.

The fact that being Jewish—a simple, surely minor difference—could, in the case of Nazi Germany, be turned into a major "biological" gulf raises the critical question of which differences count as major, which as minor. Freud himself appears to have imbibed the fantasies of his own time, to the effect that racial difference was major, while breaking with his time in maintaining that gender differences were minor. Yet in the light of the substantial elements that all humans share with each other, it could be said that all human difference is minor, or, more precisely, pales in significance beside the elements we share.

One could argue, in fact, that the differences that matter are those between individuals within groups, not between the groups themselves. Genetic research seems to suggest that no significant variations exist in the distribution of intelligence or cognitive ability among racial, ethnic, or gender-based groups, but that there are significant variations among individuals within these groups.

Intolerance customarily fixes on group differences as the ones that are salient and tends to ignore the differences between individuals in the loathed group. Indeed, in most forms of intolerance, the individuality of the person despised is all but ignored; what counts is merely his or her membership in the group. Not only are intolerant people fundamentally incurious—uninterested in the groups they despise except insofar as their behavior confirms their prejudices—they are also uninterested in the individuals who compose despised groups: indeed they hardly see "them" as individuals at all. What matters is the constitution of a primal opposition between "them" and "us." Individuality only complicates the picture; it makes prejudice more difficult to sustain, since it is at the individual level that forms of identification and affection can arise to subvert the primal opposition of "them" and "us."

It is worth speculating that if intolerant groups are unable or unwilling to perceive those they despise as individuals, it is because intolerant individuals are unable or unwilling to perceive themselves as such either. Their own identities are too insecure to permit individuation: they cannot see themselves as the makers of their individualities and hence they cannot see others as makers of theirs either. In their intolerance, they allow themselves to be spoken for by the collective discourses that have taken them over; they do not, as it were, speak in their own right. On this account, the narcissism of minor differences is a leap into collective fantasy that enables threatened or anxious individuals to avoid the burden of thinking for themselves or even of thinking of themselves as individuals. Why these identities should be so vulnerable, it can be shown, will depend on who they are and what threatens them.

Types of Nationalism

One can illuminate these general considerations with some practical examples drawn from contemporary European nationalism. In particular, one can distinguish between the types of nationalism and their relation to intolerance.

It is a truism to say that nationalism leads necessarily to intolerance. Like all truisms, this one is not necessarily true: some stridently nationalistic societies—America, for example—are not obviously more intolerant than more quietly nationalistic ones, like Britain. It all depends on the type of nationalism and the type of society. The question is which particular kinds of nationalism, in which particular situations, are most likely to breed intolerance? Or, to put it another way, why it is that certain forms of intensely nationalistic society find the practice of tolerance toward neighboring ethnic societies or ethnic minorities within their own society not merely difficult but actually repugnant?

The kind of intolerance that concerns us here is the kind not directed against beliefs, doctrines, practices, or actions. It is not the intolerance with which the classical texts of the liberal tradition were concerned. Locke was writing against intolerance toward specific doctrine and belief, maintaining that it was strictly irrational to compel individuals to abandon propositions they believed to be true, since the psychic state of being persuaded of propositions does not and cannot depend on the will. "Such is the nature of the understanding that it cannot be compelled to the belief of anything by outward force."[5] The intolerance that concerns us here is directed toward who people are—that is, to the totality of those signs (skin color, religious ritual, language, dietary customs, dress, and behavior) that demarcate them as different, and that, crucially, are also not subject to their individual wills. Such intolerance, it should be noted, shares the irrationality that Locke identified in relation to those forms of intolerance directed at belief. Individuals are blamed and condemned for being something that is not in their power to alter.

The intolerance that interests us is the one that claims that it is impossible and undesirable for different ethnic groups to "live and let live"—that is, to share the same state, territory, and resources. This is the intolerance that insists on the necessity and the right of each ethnic group to follow what the South African apartheid regime used to call "separate development." This is an intolerance expressed in terms of an extreme moral and cultural relativism. It insists that group identities are so all-shaping that they create moral worlds unintelligible to each other, and that groups therefore are incapable of living together in peace within the same territorial and political space. This form of intolerance underpins ethnic cleansing in Bosnia, Christian-Muslim conflict in the south Caucasus, and terrorist firebombing in Northern Ireland. This intolerance often tacitly presumes the superiority of a particular group but is more often relativist and separatist; it may only insist on the impossibility of sharing civic space with other groups.

One might have expected such intolerance to be most prevalent where two ethnic groups differ most, in terms of language, religion, culture, or style of life. The narcissism of minor difference makes us realize that the opposite is just as likely. In Bosnia, for example, there are three groups—Muslim, Croat, and Serb—who have come to resemble each other so close-

ly over the past three generations that it cannot be said that they are at all
ethnically distinct. Yet all are actively engaged in the late twentieth century's most odious, certainly most publicized, form of intolerance: ethnic
cleansing. The question is why ethnic cleansing appears where it does, and
what role nationalist beliefs play in making ethnic cleansing possible. It is
a truism to say that ethnic cleansing is a "result" of nationalism. Yet in
what sense is this truism true?

In popular parlance, nationalism has almost become a synonym for
intolerance; at the very least, nationalism is seen as an intolerant form of
patriotism. The distinction between patriotism and nationalism is not
easy to draw: one person's patriotism is another's nationalism. We often
call societies nationalistic when all that we mean is that they are intensely
patriotic. In principle, at least, the two are distinguishable. Patriotism is
love of a country one can take for granted as one's own; it is love for a
country whose borders are settled, whose identity is more or less secure,
and which does not have large groups of its own people subject to the
domination or control of another country. The intense love of country
one encounters in the United States, or occasionally in Britain in time of
war, is more properly called patriotism than nationalism. As an uncontest-
ed emotion, patriotism can be, though it is not always, free of intolerant
aggression toward other nations or peoples. Nationalism, by contrast, is
love of a country that happens to belong to someone else. Nationalists
frequently belong to nations that do not have a state of their own, either
because they are ruled by some colonial or imperial power, or because they
are a subjugated national minority in the state of another national group.
Nationalism, by definition, is a contested claim to self-determination, and
because it is contested it is often a source of conflict and intolerance. It arises, typically, where ethnic difference has been overlaid with domination—
that is, where one group has ruled another, where ethnicity has conferred
political, economic, or cultural authority over another. It is a history of
domination, characteristically, that turns the simple facts of ethnic difference into an abyss of narcissism in the dominant group, and wounded pride
and resentment on the part of the dominated group.

Although popular usage treats nationalism as a set of emotions, it is in
fact a political doctrine with three essential components: that the peoples
of the world naturally divide into nations; that these nations should have
the right to rule themselves; and that this exercise in self-determination
should, in most cases, result in each nation having a sovereign state of its
own. Since there are several thousand groups of people who call themselves nations, and under 200 recognized states, the number of unmet
nationalist claims in the world, and therefore potential sources of conflict and intolerance, is very large.

There are herbivore and carnivore nationalisms: nationalisms whose
chief manifestation is love of one's own, and those where love of one's own
seems inseparable from hatred of others; those nationalisms that are linked
to intolerance and those that are not. One can connect these distinctions

to two basic criteria—civic or ethnic—according to which nations define who belongs to them.[6] Civic nationalism—of the French, British, and American type—defines the nation not in terms of ethnicity but in terms of willingness to adhere to its civic values. Allegiance is essentially directed toward the state and its civic institutions and values. Ethnic nationalism—of the German and Polish type—defines the nation in terms of ethnic origins and birth. Allegiance is directed primarily at the nation, at the traditions, values, and cultures incarnated in a people's history.

In societies of a civic nationalist type, belonging is not tied to ethnic origin, yet forms of national patriotic sentiment, as we have seen, can be extremely strong. Indeed, in the American case, the more heterogeneous the ethnic composition of the republic, the more insistently patriotic its discourse becomes, or, rather, the more central to that discourse becomes the claim that the nation-state is capable of giving a home and a welcome to all. Civic nationalist societies are not always tolerant places: the patriotic consensus can become so overbearing that the right to differ may be overrun. And when demagogues succeed in convincing people that the country is in danger, as Senator McCarthy did in the 1950s, patriotism easily turns into paranoia. Yet a society anchored in a culture of individual rights and liberties is more easily returned to the practice of toleration than one where social allegiance is invested in ethnicity.

Societies premised on ethnic nationalist criteria of belonging have a different record in relation to tolerance of ethnic difference. Of course not all ethnically homogeneous states are intolerant: the Finns, Hungarians, Norwegians, Swedes, and Czechs are more or less ethnically unified and yet do not appear to be substantially intolerant societies. But in some societies, like the German, there has been a strong historical connection between anti-Semitic intolerance and the definition of nationality by *jus sanguinis*, by birth and Germanity rather than residence and choice. Polish anti-Semitism, likewise, may owe much to the essentially ethnoreligious basis of Polish national sentiment. Thus, it may not be ethnic homogeneity or an ethnic basis for citizenship alone that creates conditions for intolerance. Additional historical experiences of national humiliation may be necessary to turn ethnic consciousness into ethnic paranoia: in the Polish case, the humiliation of an extinguished statehood, from the eighteenth-century partitions to the Treaty of Versailles; in the German case, war-time defeat, an onerous peace settlement, recent and therefore insecure national unification coupled with a particularly messianic and universalizing conception of German cultural mission.

Serbia offers another example of the same pattern. An ethnically homogeneous nation with a proud, self-aggrandizing history but a historically weak state, the Serbs are intensely conscious of themselves as the historical leaders of the Balkan peoples: going down to glorious defeat against the Turks in Kosovo field in 1389 and then becoming the first people in the Ottoman Empire to wage a successful nationalist struggle of liberation in the early nineteenth century. This made them the Piedmontese of the

Balkans, the people who took on themselves the historical task of unifying the South Slavs and freeing them from the Ottoman and Austro-Hungarian yokes. The Serbs think of themselves as the warrior defenders of the border reaches of European Christendom against the Muslim foe. Yet they are a numerically small people, struggling for statehood in a region that historically has been the major point of intersection and conflict between the Christian and Islamic empires in Europe. A nationalism forged in the crucible of imperial conflict must necessarily have memories of humiliation and defeat, from Kosovo in 1389 to the heroic but catastrophic winter retreat of the Serbian armies into Montenegro and Albania in 1915. Serbia is a case of a small nation with grandiose dreams that it is not strong enough to realize: chief among these dreams is the reunification of all Serbs within one contiguous territorial state. Serbia is also a case of a small nation that feels it has fought for Europe on its border regions with the Islamic world, but has never been rewarded or acknowledged by Europe for its sacrifices.

Yet as Serbia longs for European recognition, it also doubts whether it actually belongs to Europe. As an Eastern Orthodox people, it feels, like the Russians, that its very belonging to Europe is in question. Is it of the East or of the West? These uncertainties and weaknesses in its identity as a nation render it especially vulnerable to paranoia and intolerance, and its populace prone to a demagoguery that insists that nobody understands them but themselves. This form of "epistemological closure" may be a common feature of "intolerant" nationalisms, by which is meant a conviction that their history locks them into a situation that can only be understood from the inside, never from the outside; that all outsiders, especially those from the great powers, who have so often presided over or witnessed their humiliation, can never be true or reliable friends.

Croatian nationalism shares similar characteristics with the Serb variety: Croats think of themselves as a small people with a great vocation, a frontier people at the border between East and West, Christianity and Islam; a colonized people whose great dreams of nationhood have been continually frustrated by outside powers. Yet while Serbs have gloried in fighting alone for statehood, Croats have always collaborated with outside powers to attain their nationalist designs. They quarried out a domain of autonomy within the Austro-Hungarian empire, and then, less defensibly, aligned themselves with the fascist occupiers in World War II to create their own independent state. It is central to Croatian nationalist consciousness to believe that they belong to Western Catholic European civilization, while Serbs are Orthodox, Eastern, and "Balkan," in all that is pejorative in the term.[7]

Usually the terms "Europe" and "nationalism" are seen as antitheses. Europe stands for the values of a civilization, chief among them being tolerance, which transcend national divisions. In reality, "Europe" figures constantly within nationalist consciousness as a neuralgic element of national pride, resentment, and, above all, self-differentiation with other neighbors held to be "less" European. Thus, Croats think of themselves as "better Europeans" than Serbs; Serbs bitterly resent that they are not considered "good Europeans." In Western Europe, too, there remains a strongly competitive element in each nation's attempt to define European values for itself. Moreover, East Europeans mean something very different by the term than West Europeans. Both Serbs and Croats thus use European as a synonym for "non-Muslim," a usage that has impeccable historical credentials but ones that most West Europeans have forgotten, at least, that is, until the Iranian Revolution and the Salman Rushdie affair. Given that Europe is supposed to stand for tolerant supranationalism, it is ironic, if not also depressing, that the competition to be thought more "European" than one's neighbors is a central source of intolerant nationalist emotion right across the continent.

As a matter of historical fact, Europe does not stand for toleration any more than it stands for ethnic cleansing. The doctrine of toleration *is* a European invention, but so is the concentration camp. Since the religious massacres of the Reformation and Counter-Reformation, ethnic or confessional cleansing has been as central an element of European behavior as the practices of toleration and the doctrine of universal human rights. Yet the Europe that all these post-communist states are rushing to join is all too frequently conceived, imaginatively, as a history-free Disneyland of tolerance.

As for toleration, if it is a specifically West European value, it arose in specific historical circumstances that are not easily replicated. It can be seen as the answer produced by seventeenth-century jurists, philosophers, and statesmen to the question created by the Reformation and the breakup of the unity of Christendom in the sixteenth century: how to ensure civil peace within societies that do not have confessional uniformity. This breakup of Christendom gave enormous impetus to the philosophical attempt to understand how society itself cohered. If everyone no longer believed the same things, how did such organisms hold together? From Hobbes through Locke and Adam Smith, the theory of society as an order of free, contracting individuals uniting together to guarantee each other's security, liberty, and prosperity began to take shape. This attempt to theorize social order in individualistic terms meant doing away with the premise of ethnic and confessional homogeneity as the principle of social coherence. Toleration emerges as a doctrine, therefore, within the context of a reconceptualization of society itself, as an organism bound together, not by ties of birth and ascription, be they ethnic or confessional, but by the new ties of interest, property, and rights. In this sense, toleration as a doctrine, practice, and habit of mind emerges with and in turn presumes a society of free, contractual individuals.

What practical implications follow from this historical point? It might just be that toleration depends on a civic order in which the rights of the individual are held to be prior to and constitutive of the social order. It cannot function in "organicist" societies, where the social order is prior to and constitutive of individual rights. This may be the "European" invention of which we are so proud: and the question arises whether toleration can sink roots in societies that do not have rights-based, individualistic cultures like our own. The point is not that toleration is alien to Eastern Europe or that it is futile to insist on human rights standards in such societies. The problem is that before you can have tolerance, as a social practice, you have to create a political culture in which human identity itself is seen as individual and civic, rather than ethnic and collective. Transition to democratic regimes can occur almost overnight. The transition to a tolerant culture, tragically, requires time, peace, and prosperity, and all three are in short supply in Eastern Europe.

The Cain and Abel Syndrome

If both Serbian and Croatian nationalism belong to that particular category of intolerant nationalisms—that is, nationalisms with a strong ethnic component mixed in with memories of humiliation and defeat—what still has to be explained is why they should become enemies of each other. Why, in other words, should such extreme and violent intolerance arise between two peoples who share so much, including a common language? From 1918 to 1989, Serbs and Croats spoke a language called Serbo-Croatian. In dialect, pronunciation, vocabulary, and orthography, there are differences in how each group uses the language, but these differences are minor. Since 1989, nationalists on both sides have insisted that there is a Serbian language, in a Cyrillic alphabet with a distinctive vocabulary and pronunciation, and Croat nationalists for their part are busy purging the Croatian language of apparently foreign or Orthodox Slavic impurities. Here is a classic example of the processes of narcissism magnifying a minor difference into a major one.

But it might be argued that the differences between the two peoples are actually quite significant. It is certainly true that the Croatian culture is Catholic in origin, the Serb culture Orthodox, and that these two peoples live on the historic frontier between West European Catholicism and Eastern Orthodoxy. Samuel Huntington and others have seen nationalist conflict as a subset of a much larger and more elemental encounter between opposing civilizations: Muslim, Catholic, and Orthodox.[8] Yet this ignores the fact that confessional observance has waned on all sides of the battle-front so that for the vast majority of the population, by 1990, religion had become a merely nominal rather than real marker of identity. Substantial intermarriage has further blurred the confessional markers. Yet as war enveloped the Slavonian plains in 1991, fighters on each side took to wearing Orthodox and Catholic crosses, although few of these young men could have ever been in their respective churches since baptism. Here is a case where narcissism leads the two groups to reinvent differences that had all but disappeared.

In addition, these processes are occurring in a society that since 1960 has been undergoing rapid modernization. Serbs, Muslims, and Croats all benefited from the development that occurred in Tito's Yugoslavia in the 1960s, and which for a time made the country the most prosperous and free in the communist world. Both Serbs and Croats had the opportunity to work as *Gastarbeiter* in northern Europe, and both were able to return, with their incomes and their Mercedes, and construct villas for themselves. A substantial convergence in the lifestyles and aspirations of these ethnic groups occurred over the past 30 years, yet it is precisely here that the most violent ethnic warfare in Europe has exploded. It is these Mercedes and these villas that both sides share and that both sides are so intent to destroy. In other words, modernization and a convergence of forms and styles of life to a West European model have done nothing to abate, indeed may even have exacerbated, ethnic conflict. Thus, it might be true that when ethnicity was genuinely primitive, backward, "tribal," and rooted in local Balkan village life, it was relatively peaceful. When it has become modern, open to the world of modern media, travel, and exposure to the outside world, it has become murderous. How are we to explain these paradoxes? Is nationalist intolerance a reaction against the convergence and homogenization represented by modernization? That is certainly Ernest Gellner's account of nationalism.[9] Instead of seeing nationalism as an atavistic resurgence of the primordial and tribal, he interprets it as a fundamentally modern attempt to reinvent forms of community and belonging and identity in the face of the loss of traditional expressions of these values in the course of modernization. But if this is so, how exactly does it happen? Why is it that the opening to the world represented by modernization seems only to produce the closure of ethnic particularism and conflict?

Two elements proved fatal in the Balkan case. The first was the nature of the narcissistic fantasy to which the Serbian and Croatian political elite succumbed: the idea that state and nation could coincide in one contiguous territory. This was a fantasy for the simple reason that one-third of the Serb population lives outside the border of Serbia, and a substantial proportion of the Croatian population lives beyond Croatia. National unification, or the fusing of state and nation, could only occur at the cost of substantial territorial aggrandizement and ethnic cleansing. That is, the nationalist fantasy violently contradicted the objective realities of the Balkans. Again, one can only explain the inability of the actors to see what was staring them in the face if one gives due emphasis to nationalism as a form of narcissism, as a self-image so alluring that, as in the fable of Narcissus itself, it lures those who fall for it to their deaths.

The second crucial element was the collapse of the Titoist state. Mutual toleration between ethnic groups is always possible provided there is an overarching state that, both nominally and practically, affords all equal protection before the law, or, to put it another way, protects each ethnic group against the other. In a situation like the Balkans where, over substantial areas like Bosnia, no one ethnic group has an overwhelming demographic advantage—where all groups are more or less equally pow-

erful minorities—a superordinate state is the very condition of mutual toleration. In the Yugoslav case, however, the postwar state was built on two
pillars, both made of sand: one-party hegemony and the personal charis-
ma of a dictator. When these two pillars collapsed, as they were bound to
do, ethnic groups were then delivered into the Hobbesian war of all against
all. In this situation, it ceased to be rational for individuals to practice the
forms of interethnic accommodation and tolerance that had grown up
under the aegis of the Titoist state. As demagogues began to mobilize the
population along nationalist lines and as the state order began to fragment,
it became rational, instead, for individuals to look to their group for protection. As they did so, the seductions of narcissistic identification became
harder to resist. But we should not forget that if they ended up impris-
oned inside ethnic narcissism, they were driven there, fundamentally, by
the collapse of the state, and by the fear and terror that followed. The central point is that as individuals, Serbs and Croats were only too aware that
it was deeply irrational, in a society of densely interwoven ethnic accommodation and intermarriage, for each ethnic group to look to their own
for protection. As individuals, they knew it was far better to live with each
other in peace. But once the state collapsed, once there was no institution
capable of providing protection for all, toleration ceased to be a rational
strategy; instead everyone ran to the protection of their own.

The essential dynamic in the Yugoslav case is quite specific to the
Balkans: to the extremely diffuse and splintered patterns of ethnic settlement in the region and to the Hobbesian conflict likely to break out there
once state authority disintegrates. Yet many key elements in the Yugoslav
case, notably the way in which modernization heightens the narcissism of
minor differences, can be observed elsewhere in Europe. In Turkey, for example, an authoritarian secular state has devoted 70 years to extirpating—
by force—the difference between Kurds and Turks. These two peoples may
appear to outsiders as nearly indistinguishable; most Turkish Kurds, for
example, only speak Turkish. Yet the forcible modernization and integration of Turkey has only exacerbated the conflict between the two peoples,
so that now, southern Turkey is a war-zone, a battleground between the
intolerant, unitary nationalism of Kemal Ataturk and the insurgent populist nationalism of the Kurdish PKK.

Ukraine, likewise, illustrates the same theme: that as modernization
reduces the salient differences between ethnic groups, nationalism emerges
to inflame the minor differences that remain. In Ukraine, ethnic Russians
and Ukrainians appear to share common linguistic, cultural, and religious
elements, and, where they differ, they differ at the margins: Ukrainian Uni-
ate Catholicism can be considered a variety of Orthodoxy just as the Ukrainian language can be considered a variant, though a significant variant, of
Russian. In the Soviet period, moreover, both Russians and Ukrainians
were hammered together by Soviet power, an artificially created famine,
and the suppression of nationalist difference in the name of socialist brotherhood and unity. The net effect, paradoxically, is that as the communist

yoke collapsed, nationalist consciousness, far from being eroded over the previous 75 years of enforced Stalinist modernization, came back more strongly than ever. Now, as economic catastrophe stares both ethnic Ukrainians and ethnic Russians in the face—in other words, as the economics of their common plight suggests the necessity of cooperation—there are elements on both sides driving their peoples toward civil war within Ukraine. How can this be happening when both peoples have sound historical reasons to consider themselves "brothers"?

Indeed, as the reference to brothers suggests, it may be that the appropriate title for the paradox we have been exploring is the Cain and Abel syndrome: the ironic fact that intolerance between brothers is often stronger than that between strangers. The analytical question, therefore, is how the essential elements of similarity that make groups "brothers" are denied and reconstrued so that the two groups confront each other as "strangers."

This same syndrome can be illustrated in Northern Ireland, where what has to be explained is why patterns of intolerance, inherited from a religious era, should have been exacerbated, rather than reduced, as both communities modernize and secularize. The Troubles are presented as an ethnoreligious conflict, yet neither the ethnic nor the religious elements in the identity of each side are unambiguous markers of difference. Attempts are made, on the Catholic side, to construe the Protestants as an alien group, as settlers, colonists of Scottish, English ethnic origin; on the Protestant side, attempts are made to construe the Catholics as equally alien, "bog Irish" primitives, tied to such un-British superstitions as the doctrine of papal supremacy.

In reality, both sides have lived on the same spot for more than 300 years, and there are substantial tendencies to intermarriage, just as there are in the Serb and Croat cases. The reality is that both Ulstermen and Republicans have equal claim to calling themselves Irish. As in the Serb and Croat cases, though to a markedly smaller degree, confessional observance is declining and religion functions as a community marker rather than as a lived element of identity. As responsible figures on both sides never tire of saying, though to little effect, the confessional differences between Protestantism and Catholicism cannot obscure the fact that the two religions preach tolerance as both a private and a public virtue. Both sides, moreover, inhabit a substantially disadvantaged region, and one might have expected that common economic hardship would create shared bonds of class or economic interest. Finally, the substantial elements of disadvantage in the Catholic community—second-class housing, job discrimination, police harassment—are less salient as causes of discontent and as a marker of difference than they once were.

And yet, despite all the elements that ought to bring the two sides together, the conflict, if anything, has hardened the two communities' identities into frozen masks of uncompromising intolerance. And as the two antagonists frequently admit, no one understands the other as well as they do: they are truly brother enemies, and an outsider who cannot tell a Protestant and a Catholic apart, from accent, dress, or deportment, will soon become aware that each side has developed an extraordinarily elaborate code, relating to personal names, place of residence, modes of transport, favorite pubs, and so on, to figure out who is actually who. What appears to be happening is a fanatically ingenious, creative, and elaborate attempt by elements within the two communities to deny the common interests on which a regime of mutual tolerance might be erected.

A final example of this process might be seen in Scotland. Scottish nationalism is essentially a modern, late twentieth-century phenomenon, not an ancestral survival from the days of the clans. As David McCrone and others have argued, Scottish national consciousness has increased as the markers of Scottish economic, social, and cultural distinctiveness have waned—in other words, as Scotland's demographic, economic, and social patterns have converged toward standard U.K. patterns.[10] The Scots are becoming more like the rest of "us" and it is this, precisely, that is driving them toward a more insistent emphasis on Scottish self-determination.

Although modernization and "progress" thus may exacerbate relations between ethnic groups and lead to an increase in intolerance, this should not be construed as an argument against taking economic disadvantage seriously: things might have been worse in Northern Ireland had the British government not addressed both the sectional grievances of Catholics and the general economic disadvantage of the province. The analytical point to be made is that toleration is more dependent on values, culture, and perception than on the facts of difference. A reduction of "objective" difference between competing groups does not necessarily, and by itself, lead to a reduction in "subjective" suspicion. Indeed, as groups converge "objectively," their mutual intolerance may grow.

Individual Versus Collective Identities

The same dynamic of intolerance that can be observed with respect to ethnic difference is apparent in the case of race. Skin color is a relatively minor difference; it certainly is no carrier of differences of ability, talent, or application. Economic differences within groups of identical skin color can be much more decisive in determining the life chances of individuals than differences between racial groups. Indeed, as the economic conditions of two racial groups converge toward each other, one might expect their interests to converge and their mutual identification to increase. The narcissism of minor differences teaches us to expect a different result.

One could mention the example of wage-laboring whites in the American South after the Civil War. As their economic condition declined, their conditions of life began to converge with the poverty of most blacks, though of course a significant gap remained. Marxist and socialist labor organizers, from the 1930s to the 1960s, sought to persuade whites and blacks to recognize the convergence of their economic and social interests.

In other words, they sought to persuade them that their common "class" interests transcended the "racial" suspicions that divided them. These attempts did not succeed. As economic conditions converged, suspicions among the "red necks" increased: it might even be the case that as the elements of personal dignity and pride connected to economic performance were summarily stripped away by the operations of the capitalist market, dignity and pride came to repose exclusively in the one, unloseable marker of identity, which was skin color.

The same paradoxical relation between economic and racial markers of identity is observable among the declining section of the white working class in Europe. It is precisely as economic pressures force the convergence of white and black patterns of life that white racial hostility becomes most explosive. Economic competition for jobs, and the divide-and-rule policies of employers, cannot explain this re-emphasis on skin color as a marker of identity between groups. Whiteness is above all understood culturally and historically as the badge of privilege and superiority, and hence as a marker of dignity and pride. In the imperial heyday these meanings went unchallenged; in a post-colonial, post-imperial world, the more these meanings are challenged, the more they are insisted on. Why should this be so? It may be that among economically disadvantaged groups there are relatively fewer ways of achieving dignity, status, and pride as individuals. Just as adherence to trade unions was once based on the sound intuition that economic advance could only be achieved collectively, not individually, so as class institutions of solidarity decay, and individual means of achievement remain blocked, the available sources of pride in neighborhoods increasingly inhabited by "foreign" people return to the collective element of skin color. When white skin is then tattooed with national flags, as it often is, skin color and national symbols are bonded together into an identity that insists that nationality is or ought to be a function of race alone. In the Europe of the 1990s, such flags can be seen on male, and sometimes female, biceps from Wolverhampton to Leipzig. It could be argued that they are to be seen wherever individuals are forced, by economic circumstances, into exclusively collective routes for the assertion of personal identity and pride. Racism, on this account, is the pride of those trapped in collective identities.

It would follow that racism might diminish if the trapped were freed, if the trapped had the means to pursue individual lives that would accord them measures and markers of achievement and pride. There must be some truth in this, though with the proviso already entered that reduction of "subjective" feelings of intolerance does not necessarily follow from reduction of "objective" barriers between groups. Yet it might be true that toleration bears some relation to the possibility for individuation and individual achievement. A German man who can show you his house, his car, and a family as measures of his own pride rather than just his white skin may be less likely to wish to torch an immigrant hostel.

Yet the capacity to individuate oneself depends on much more than having a job and a home of one's own. It also means learning the capacity to think for oneself: that is, being able to cease absorbing collective identities without reflection; becoming self-conscious that one's personal identity may be different from the collective identity of color. In this sense education is important, not simply as an avenue of mobility and individual achievement but as a means of teaching self-reflexivity and critical thought, the tools for distancing the self from the collective identity.

All of this analysis runs counter to the proposition that intolerance is a consequence of modern competitive individualism and emerges in conditions of capitalist market anomie. On the contrary, it seems that the culture of individualism is the only reliable solvent of the hold of group identities and the racisms that go with them. To be sure, if the market fails, as it is failing upwards of 20 million unemployed young people in Europe alone, then it does create the conditions in which individuals may turn to group hatreds in order to assert and defend their identities. But, in principle, a culture that insists on individual responsibility, that links identity not to group ascription but to individual achievement, is much less likely to produce intolerance than one that continually reinscribes the individual in the group and that insists that the sources of the self's worth are all to be found in the collective.

The point here is somewhat paradoxical: the habits of mind necessary to toleration may have just as much to do with how people view themselves and their relation to their own collective identities as they do with their attitudes toward others. The essential task in teaching toleration is to help people see themselves as individuals, and then to see others as such; that is, to make problematic that unthought, unconsidered fusion of personal and group identity on which racism depends.

For racism and intolerance are, at a conceptual level, procedures of abstraction in which actual, real individuals in all their specificity are depersonalized and turned into ciphers or carriers of hated group characteristics. Often, indeed, such processes of abstraction have to struggle against the obdurate likableness of the individual. Thus, the notorious phrase, "Some of my best friends are Jews but . . . ," which recognizes, in ironic form, the uncomfortable lack of consonance between the actual Jews one knows and the abstracted stereotypes one persists in believing. When Othello is tormented by jealousy toward Desdemona—a jealousy at once sexual and racial—he finds himself struggling, in effect, with a process of abstraction, in which the Desdemona he loves is successively reduced, by cancerous paranoia, from the particular woman he passionately loves to a white woman it is conventional for black men to hate. Only when such a reduction of her individuality is complete, when the object of his vengeance is an abstracted cipher, can he accomplish the vengeance his paranoia desires.

Intolerance, as a sentiment of collective prejudice, has to struggle against, and eventually deny, more elementary patterns of human recognition and fellowship that function at the individual level. This would suggest that intolerance is a form of divided consciousness, in which abstract, conceptual, ideological hatred vanquishes concrete, real, and individual moments of identification. This pattern of struggle is familiar enough and has a familiar ending: the Nazi camp commandant who falls in love with his Jewish maid, only to dispatch her to the gas chambers; the white slave owner who maintains tender relations with individual slaves, only to insist the more vehemently that slaves are not persons but property; the British racialist who has individual relations with Pakistani restaurant owners or shopkeepers but believes, nonetheless, that Pakistanis in general should be sent "home."

What appears to be happening in these familiar, even clichéd instances, is that a moment of intrahuman recognition, which abolishes the difference between them, is violently denied by the stronger party and an abstracted, "ideological" difference is reinstated in order to maintain the dignity and power of the oppressor. For, from the oppressor's point of view, the moment of human recognition decisively threatens both his identity and power: a camp commandant who begins to spare his Jewish lovers will not be a camp commandant very long; a slave owner who decides slaves are persons may not be able to retain his estate very long; a racialist who admits he rather likes Pakistanis and values the services they provide might have to consider the possibility that whiteness of skin does not confer the right to decide who deserves to call themselves British. In this sense, therefore, an "individualized" encounter between oppressor and oppressed, ruler and ruled, racialist and victim, is so fraught with possibilities of loss that one side at least has a standing interest in keeping relations enclosed within the abstraction of collective prejudice. For the abstracted, collective plane of intolerance keeps power relations as they are: it is intended to prevent those moments of human recognition that make intolerance ashamed.

Against such collective abstraction, victims of intolerance have always made a double appeal: to their own individuality and humanity. The two claims are distinct. In situations of extremity, a victim who recognizes an individual among the group of his oppressors will desperately seek to evoke their former relations in the hope that the particular oppressor may exempt him from the general fate and make an exception in his case. Failing that, the victim will appeal, not to his individuality, but to the common human identity he shares with the oppressor. "Hath a Jew not eyes?" is the general form of such appeals.

Since it is, needless to say, more than evident that a Jew hath eyes, the question is why intolerant beliefs that deny this evidence should retain such plausibility. Why is it that the victim's twin appeal—to individuality and common humanity—so often falls on deaf ears? The narcissism of minor differences does help us to explain why this failure of human recognition occurs so perennially.

Modern liberal societies operate systems of distributive justice that value, reward, promote, or punish individual difference, and juridically, at least, ignore collective differences. The law is nominally blind to differences of race, color, creed, ethnicity, gender, and sexual orientation, and is highly discriminatory in relation to individual difference at the level of action and intention. Likewise, our systems of reward and promotion sift minute differences in individual ability and attempt to deny the salience of collective difference; or if they take collective difference into account—as in systems of positive discrimination—they do so, not in order to advance groups but to level the playing field of competition for disadvantaged individuals.

The utopia at which such liberal societies aim is a fully tolerant world. While it is obvious that such a world would be desirable, the question is whether it is psychologically plausible. For a moment, let us imagine what such a world might look like. It would not be a world that had banished anger, hatred, suspicion, or dislike. It would merely be a world in which all angers, hatreds, suspicions, or dislikes would be purely private or between individuals. That is, if one disliked people it would be entirely because of their characteristics as individuals: their moral, aesthetic characteristics or their opinions. You would not dislike them because they were black or white, rich or poor, female or male, homosexual or heterosexual, German or Chinese, but simply because they were, as individuals, boring, untrustworthy, vain, stupid, or whatever. In such a liberal utopia, in other words, interpersonal aggression would have an outlet, but it would be directed at real individuals, as opposed to aggregated, abstracted collective entities called races, classes, genders, and so on. This utopia helps us to make clear at least that a tolerant world is not necessarily a world free of invidious comparison, still less a world free of hatred and aggression. It is merely a place in which individuals are not disadvantaged by virtue of adventitious collective identities like race, color, creed, gender, or sexual orientation.

The question is whether such a world is psychologically plausible. Is a world of pure individuals possible? Or do all individuals need collective identities, and because they need them, must they construct invidious collective comparisons on them? In other words, is some element of collective intolerance the inevitable price we have to pay for having the collective boundaries necessary to human identity itself? This question arises because the liberal goal of a tolerant society is constantly accused of psychological implausibility, of demanding of old Adam and Eve a redemption beyond their powers.

The question is not whether individuals need collective identities: history shows they self-evidently do. The issue is whether they need to use collective identities to make invidious comparisons; whether such negative comparisons are essential to identity formation itself. A potential contradiction thus opens up between liberal individualism as utopia, and to some degree as a juridical practice, and psychic reality. Freud's theory about the narcissism of minor differences, however, does suggest that while some measure of collective antagonism is inevitable in human relations, this antagonism is not fixed or immutable. It changes its objects. In the British class system, for example, groups that once loathed each other because of the vast gulf between their economic fortunes now merely make fun of each other because they dress or speak differently. Freud suggests that hostility and antagonism are built into the human negotiation of difference. That's the pessimistic message. The hopeful message, and the one to conclude with, is that these differences can become less murderous with time. To the degree that individuals can ever learn to think for themselves—that is, to become true individuals—they can free themselves, one by one, from the deadly dynamic of the narcissism of minor differences.

Notes

1. Sigmund Freud, "The Taboo of Virginity," in *On Sexuality*, Pelican Freud Library, Vol. 7 (Harmondsworth: Penguin, 1977), pp. 271–272.

2. Ibid., p. 272.

3. Sigmund Freud, "Group Psychology and the Analysis of the Ego," in *Civilization, Society and Religion*, Pelican Freud Library, Vol. 12 (Harmondsworth: Penguin, 1985), pp. 130–131.

4. Ibid., p. 131.

5. John Locke, *A Letter Concerning Toleration*, (Indianapolis, IN: Bobbs Merrill, 1990), p. 21.

6. For a fuller discussion of civic and ethnic nationalism in relation to tolerance and intolerance, see my *Blood and Belonging: Journeys into the New Nationalism* (London: BBC: Chatto and Windus, 1993).

7. It is worth enlarging on the narcissistic role of the concept of "Europe" in nationalist consciousness. The slogan that all the societies of Eastern Europe took to using as they exited from the communist era was that they were "returning to Europe." By this they meant a return to the European values of toleration, freedom, and democracy, abandoned or betrayed by the communist experiment; a return to the European capitalist market; and, prospectively at least, insertion in the "European" community. Because these societies had always been European, the return to Europe meant integration in Western Europe. This "return" has proved difficult, not least because Western Europe, for all its high-flown talk about a continent stretching from Liverpool to Vladivostok, in its heart of hearts believes that Europe actually ends at the Oder-Neisse line.

8. Samuel P. Huntington, "The Clash of Civilizations?" *Foreign Affairs*, Vol. 72, No. 3 (Summer 1993).

9. Ernest Gellner, *Nations and Nationalism* (London: Basil Blackwell, 1983).

10. David McCrone, *Understanding Scotland: The Sociology of a Stateless Nation* (London: Routledge, 1992), p. 211.

Index